JOHNSON ON SHAKESPEARE

Johnson on Shakespeare

SECOND EDITION

Selected and Introduced by
R.W. DESAI, *Ph.D., Northwestern University, Illinois*
Professor
Department of English
Delhi University

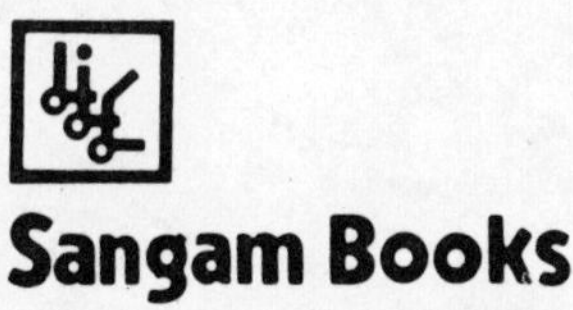

SANGAM BOOKS LIMITED
57 London Fruit Exchange
Brushfield Street, London E1 6EP, U.K.

By arrangement with
Orient Longman Limited
3-6-272 Himayatnagar, Hyderabad 500 029 (A.P.), India

Published by
Sangam Books Limited, 1997
Reprinted 1998

ISBN 0 86131 584 7

Printed in India at
Baba Barkha Nath Printers
Delhi 110 015

Publisher's Note

Several important Shakespearean critics have maintained that Johnson's *Preface* is still the best estimate of Shakespeare ever written. Because of the continuing worth of the *Preface*, it is important that the reader of Johnson understands the nature of his approach to Shakespeare's plays and the critical climate of the times.

This selection has been made to meet this need. Johnson's *Preface* has been introduced at considerable length so that the reader becomes familiar with the general features of Johnson's thought and critical work, and is adequately prepared for an intensive study of Johnson's writings on Shakespeare. The annotations at the end of this volume supplements the Introduction by explicating and commenting on the finer and more specific aspects of Johnson's criticism.

The selection naturally highlights Johnson's *Preface* to his edition of Shakespeare's plays and his Notes to the texts of the plays (of which a very generous sample has been included here). The Drury Lane *Prologue*, an essay from the *Rambler* and the text of the *Proposals* for Johnson's edition of Shakespeare provide a framework for the entire study. The volume has been carefully designed for detailed study as well as rapid reference.

Contents

INTRODUCTION

Introduction

SHAKESPEARE'S POWER TO STIR THE READER

In Boswell's *Life of Johnson* there is a record of Johnson having quoted Shakespeare a few days before his death. The lines Johnson quotes are uttered by Macbeth when he hears from the doctor of the illness that afflicts his wife. Johnson himself, tormented by the fear of death all his life and now in his old age suffering from dropsy, appropriately enough found a powerful correspondence between his own disquiet and the state of perturbation described by Macbeth. Boswell's account is as follows:

> About eight or ten days before his death, when Dr. Brocklesby paid him his morning visit, he seemed very low and desponding, and said, 'I have been as a dying man all night.' He then emphatically broke out, in the words of Shakespeare:—
>
> 'Can'st thou not minister to a mind diseas'd;
> Pluck from the memory a rooted sorrow;
> Raze out the written troubles of the brain;
> And, with some sweet oblivious antidote,
> Cleanse the stuff'd bosom of that perilous stuff,
> Which weighs upon the heart?'

To which Dr. Brocklesby readily answered, from the same great poet:—

'——————therein the patient
Must minister to himself.'

Johnson expressed himself much satisfied with the application.

(*Life*, p. 1379 [Dec. 1784])

That Johnson was "much satisfied" with Dr. Brocklesby's

ability to complete the quotation is an indication of the value he attached to poetry that could capture his own experience of life even though that experience was one of illness inevitably leading on to death. Perhaps it is safe for us to speculate that very few men could, like Johnson, derive satisfaction from an aesthetic parallel when lying at death's door.

It is this kind of a close connection between lived experience and its artistic representation that Johnson finds in the greatest literature, above all, in Shakespeare. Time and again in his *Preface* we find Johnson responding to scenes in Shakespeare's plays that are able to grip the reader and intensify his understanding of life. "We are agitated in reading the history of *Henry the Fifth*" (57), he declares; Constance's grief over her son Arthur is "very affecting" (Note on *King John*); of *King Lear* Johnson is convinced that "there is perhaps no play which keeps the attention so strongly fixed; which so much agitates our passions and interests our curiosity" (Note on *King Lear*); and concerning the distress of Ophelia Johnson says that it "fills the heart with tenderness" (Note on *Hamlet*). Johnson is deeply moved by *Othello*, and though he politely grants that Addison's *Cato* possesses "innumerable beauties of sentiment and diction," he goes on to say that it falls short of *Othello* in that "its hopes and fears communicate no vibration to the heart" (73). But even Shakespeare has his weak spots. *Julius Caesar*, though "universally celebrated," Johnson grants, fails to move him: "I have never been strongly agitated in perusing it and think it somewhat cold and unaffecting compared with some other of Shakespeare's plays" (Note on *Julius Caesar*). Thus does Johnson make the reader's response to Shakespeare the ultimate test for the success or the failure of the play. Its power to move him is the deciding factor, and it is on this intensely personal foundation that the reader must build his estimate of Shakespeare.

At the same time, while it is for the reader to discover Shakespeare's power upon his own pulses, it is Shakespeare who wields this power over the minds of his readers. Shakespeare "never fails to attain his purpose; as he commands us, we laugh or mourn, or sit silent with quiet expectation, in tranquillity without indifference" (26). Thus Johnson sees Shakespeare and the reader as collaborators in the creation of the aesthetic experience. What, then, according to Johnson, is the role of the critic? In his *Proposals for Printing by Subscription the Dramatic Works of William Shakespeare* that Johnson published in 1756, he tells us that "the business of him that republishes an ancient book is to correct what is corrupt and to explain what is obscure." We may well ask what original contribution Johnson makes in his *Preface* to our understanding of Shakespeare, and what is his contribution as editor to the production of a text of Shakespeare which is as close to the original as could be achieved in Johnson's time. In the ensuing paragraphs we shall consider these matters in some detail.

THE STRUCTURE OF THE PREFACE: A GENERAL SURVEY

The four opening paragraphs of Johnson's *Preface* constitute, in some ways, an interesting epitome of Johnson's entire approach to Shakespeare. On analysing these four paragraphs, we will note that he advances to his final position in the fourth paragraph through a series of movements in the three previous paragraphs that seem to lead in different directions, but that in reality point towards his final position. The opening sentence of the first paragraph, with its stately inversion, tells us of persons, who are incapable of advancing the frontiers of truth because of their mediocrity, but who nevertheless consider themselves to be eminent. These persons are painfully conscious of the fact that their self-designated eminence is not recognized by their contemporaries, and they attribute this to envy. They complain that only those authors who are dead are venerated. Obviously these persons should scorn such praise for themselves. But they don't. Paradoxically, and this is one of "the heresies of paradox," they hope that after they are dead they too will win praise from posterity. They hope that 'time' will grant them what envy denies them, namely, fame.

In the second paragraph Johnson partly agrees with them, for, he says, it is no doubt true that antiquity is often honoured for no other reason than that it is ancient. It is not 'reason' that dictates this reverence but prejudice, that is, a favourable bias (see *OED*) for what is ancient. Thus, in this paragraph Johnson moves further towards what might seem to us is a position in which he ridicules those who worship the ancients simply because they are ancient.

But with the third paragraph he slightly shifts the emphasis by arguing that in the humanities (as distinct from the sciences) if an author is venerated by posterity, this is a proof of his excellence, of his timelessness, and he cites Homer as an example.

In the fourth paragraph Johnson moves away from the position he seemed to favour in the second by declaring that those who venerate the ancients do so not just because they are ancient, but because the truths that they hold forth are well grounded in human consideration and understanding spread over a long period of time. Having drawn his conclusion, he applies it to Shakespeare in the succeeding paragraphs of the essay. Shakespeare "may now begin to assume the dignity of an ancient and claim the privilege of established fame and prescriptive veneration" for "he has long outlived his century, the term commonly fixed as the test of literary merit" (5). Shakespeare is inherently great, but the proof of his greatness rests with the collective recognition of his readers in terms of their numerical might spread over a hundred years.

While tracing the lines of Johnson's thought through these four paragraphs, the impression we form is that of a man scrutinizing an object from various angles, turning it around and holding it up to the light in order to observe its characteristics clearly, and accompanying the examination with a mind constantly at work, picking out its salient features and reflecting upon them. This opening demonstration is in fact a paradigm of Dr. Johnson's entire approach to Shakespeare. In the *Preface* Johnson convinces us of the validity of what we may call his multidimensional —as opposed to a unidimensional—approach to Shakespeare. He considers Shakespeare from several angles and presents to his readers a Shakespeare who is timeless, but also a product of his age and his country, a Shakespeare who has many "graces," but who also suffers from serious "deformities" (95).

The *Preface* falls into two main divisions, each division being further subdivided into two parts, so that there are four parts, these being followed by a final section dealing with Shakespeare's text and the editions that preceded Johnson's. The *Preface* can be represented schematically thus:

Shakespeare, timeless and universal (1–9) *a historical*		Shakespeare, a 16-17th century dramatist (64-98) *historical*		
Praise (10–31) *The First Part*	Blame (32–48) *The Second Part*	Praise (65–94) *The Third Part*	Blame (95–101) *The Fourth Part*	(102–156) *Section on the text of Shakespeare*

Praise and blame structurally balance each other, an eighteenth-century patterning of human endeavour that conforms to the age's predilection for arriving at an assessment of things in terms of opposites.

The two main divisions under which Johnson views Shakespeare may be designated as *a historical* and *historical*. Under the first division Shakespeare is considered as an author who has become timeless because "he has long outlived his century." Time has sifted Shakespeare's works of "personal allusions, local customs, or temporary opinions" and what survives is universal. His plays are now "read without any other reason than the desire of pleasure and are therefore praised only as pleasure is obtained" (5). Elizabethan manners and customs are no longer familiar to us, so that the appeal that Shakespeare's plays had for his contemporaries in terms of representing to them their own world can have no relevance for succeeding ages. "Particular manners can be known to few, and therefore few only can judge how nearly they are copied" (7). Apart from those scholars who have specialized in the manners and customs of the Elizabethan age, the rest of mankind continue to admire Shakespeare for reasons other than the correctness with which he depicts his own society. "The mind can only repose on the stability of truth" (7), Johnson asserts, and it is this quality of Shakespeare, transcending local and topical details, that ensures him permanence of esteem.

How, according to Johnson, are we to determine what is truly great in literature? Earlier he has carefully differentiated between scientific truth which is absolute, and the excellence or otherwise of works that are "not absolute and definite, but gradual and comparative" (3). Johnson's distinction is sound.

He explains "absolute" by pointing out that "of the first building that was raised, it might be with certainty determined that it was round or square" (3). Scientific truth is something indisputable. Works of art, however, cannot be judged thus. There are two tests that Johnson considers valid for such works: a comparison "with other works of the same kind" (3), and whether a high value is placed on such works by succeeding generations of readers (4). Thus it is the collective response of Shakespeare's readers over a long period of time that establishes the greatness of Shakespeare. "No other test can be applied than length of duration and continuance of esteem" (3), Johnson declares. Further, the greatness of a writer is established only when it is recognised by the general public which consists of readers who are not specialists or scholars. "Nothing can please many, and please long, but just representations of general nature" (7), Johnson maintains, thus placing upon common humanity the responsibility of determining whether a writer has achieved greatness or not.

Likewise in *Rasselas*, when the prince scoffs at the idea of there being ghosts, Imlac the philosopher gravely corrects the young man with these words: "That the dead are seen no more I will not undertake to maintain against the concurrent and unvaried testimony of all ages and of all nations. There is no people, rude or learned, among whom apparitions of the dead are not related and believed." Widespread belief, or, in Johnson's language, "the general evidence," is not to be lightly dismissed, for the belief in apparitions "could become universal only by its truth," and Johnson then goes on to say that "experience" alone has made it "credible."[1] "Truth" in these terms is, for Johnson, something that man creates collectively.

It is in this sense that Johnson sees the achievement of a writer as a joint product of both writer and audience. The audience's recognition of the greatness of a work of art is an essential part of the status it enjoys, and, this being so, even Shakespeare's greatness is partly created by us, his admirers. "Yet it must be at last confessed that as we owe everything to him, he owes something to us; that, if much of his praise is paid by perception and judgement, much is likewise given by custom and veneration" (95). Nearly two centuries later, W.H. Auden was to say something similar to this with reference to Yeats:

> The words of a dead man
> Are modified in the guts of the living.
> ("In Memory of W.B. Yeats")

Other examples of Johnson's respect for the collective opinion of mankind that we should note occur in his *Lives of the English Poets*. In the "Life of Savage" he points out that Savage's poem "The Wanderer" lacks art, and goes on to add, "this criticism is universal, and therefore it is reasonable to believe it at least in a great degree just." Again, Johnson records that even though Addison gave the accolade to Tickell's *Homer* rather than to Pope's, "the voice of the public were not long divided, and the preference was universally given to Pope's performance" (*Lives*, II, pp. 124, 256). Thus, though it is the critic's business to guide public opinion, in the ultimate analysis the critic must himself bow before the numerical superiority of the readers, for it is by their appraisal and not his that a work of art will either survive or perish.

The First Part of the Preface

In the first part of the first main division of the *Preface*, Johnson emphasizes Shakespeare's genius as "the poet of nature" whose characters "speak by the influence of those general passions and principles by which all minds are agitated and the whole system of life is continued in motion" (8). Within this main theme Johnson finds much to praise in Shakespeare. Shakespearean drama is "the mirror of life" and even though Shakespeare has Romans, Danes, senators, and kings thronging his plays, essentially they are men exhibiting qualities that are found in all parts of the world and among all strata of society: drunkards, buffoons, usurpers, and murderers (13–15). It is in keeping with Johnson's insistence on Shakespeare's universality that he sees his plays as being "not in the rigorous and critical sense either tragedies or comedies," but rather, as representations of "the real state of sublunary nature" (17) in which, to quote Blake, "joy and woe are woven fine."

Shakespeare's plays yield instruction and pleasure, and they have "the power to move" (21). They retain these qualities from generation to generation, not only because they come so close "to the appearance of life" (20), but also because the characters exhibit "genuine passion" (29). Here Johnson employs a telling metaphor to bring his point home to us. The make-up used by those who wish to beautify themselves, being artificial, soon fades "to a dim tinct, without any remains of former lustre," but "the discriminations of true passion are the colours of nature; they pervade the whole mass and can only perish with the body that exhibits them" (29). Johnson is identifying Shakespeare's plays with one whose face reflects "true passion," whose emotions are visible in her countenance and complexion, and since this perfect correspondence between feeling and expression is an organic one, it can only cease when the person dies. It is through metaphors such as these that Johnson convinces us of the power that he feels animates Shakespeare's works. As Hamlet had upbraided Ophelia for painting her face (III, i, 148-50), so does Johnson turn away from "superficial dyes" to "the colours of nature" which he finds in such abundance in Shakespeare.

It is perhaps on account of Johnson's desire that art be a true representation of human feelings that he launches his famous attack on Milton's "Lycidas," regarding the poem as artificial and therefore false. "Where there is leisure for fiction there is little grief," is Johnson's devastating criticism, for, had Milton genuinely grieved over the death of Edward King, he would not have written so fanciful a poem. "It is not to be considered as the effusion of real passion; for passion runs not after remote allusions and obscure opinions," is Johnson's scathing condemnation of the poem. And when he goes on to declare, "In this poem there is no nature, for there is no truth," we recognize that for Johnson it is Shakespeare, the poet of the pathetic, who shows us "the real state of sublunary nature" (17). Likewise, despite Johnson's genuine admiration for *Paradise Lost*, he criticizes it in "that it comprises neither human actions nor human manners" (*Lives*, I, pp. 112, 126). It is worth recalling that Wordsworth, just twenty years later, was to say that his own poetry would seek to represent "the essential passions of the heart." It might be instructive to place alongside "Lycidas" the last three stanzas of Johnson's moving poem "On the Death of Dr. Robert Levet."[2] Unlike Milton in "Lycidas," Johnson fixes his attention on Levet and introduces nothing that is not immediately concerned with his dead friend. Even though we do not have in Johnson's poem the anguish present in Wordsworth's lines "But she is in her grave, and, oh,/ The difference to me!" the sense of loss that Johnson feels is unmistakable. In the magnificent last stanza of the poem, Johnson succeeds in transcending this feeling through imagery that embodies the Biblical utterance, "Death is swallowed up in victory":

> His virtues walk'd their narrow round,
> Nor made a pause, nor left a void;
> And sure th'Eternal Master found
> The single talent well employed.
>
> The busy day, the peaceful night,
> Unfelt, uncounted, glided by;
> His frame was firm, his powers were bright,
> Tho' now his eightieth year was nigh.
>
> Then with no throbbing fiery pain,
> No cold gradations of decay,
> Death broke at once the vital chain,
> And free'd his soul the nearest way.[3]

In his criticism of "Lycidas" Johnson is raising the important question of sincerity in literature. When Macbeth, after murdering Duncan, describes the body thus:

> Here lay Duncan,
> His silver skin laced with his golden blood,
> And his gashed stabs looked like a breach in nature
> For ruin's wasteful entrance. . . .
>
> (II, iii, 117–20)

Johnson's note on the lines is a shrewd, psychologically acceptable explanation that does not, however, rule out other equally acceptable explanations. Johnson argues that Macbeth is acting a part, is pretending horror, hence the artificiality of the lines: "It is not improbable, that Shakespeare put these forced and unnatural metaphors into the mouth of Macbeth as a mark of artifice and dissimulation, to show the studied language of hypocrisy and the natural outcries of sudden passion. This whole speech so considered is a remarkable instance of judgement, as it consists entirely of antithesis and metaphor"

(Note on *Macbeth*). On the other hand, we may argue that the speech reflects Macbeth's sense of the enormity of the crime he is guilty of. Further, this elevation of sensibility is not peculiar to Macbeth: if Macbeth can speak of his hand that will "the multitudinous seas incarnadine," Macduff can declare that "most sacrilegious murder hath broke ope/The Lord's anointed temple." In short, it may well be that the lines illustrate the difference between poetry and prose. Johnson's interpretation—which he only suggests, does not categorically state—however, is a good illustration of the suspicion with which he views any expression that is "forced and unnatural."

It is not surprising, then, that Johnson should repeatedly in his *Preface* emphasize the humanity that displays itself time and again in Shakespeare's plays. Far from portraying flights of fancy that have little or no relationship with human feelings, Shakespeare's "scenes are occupied only by men, who act and speak as the reader thinks that he should himself have spoken or acted on the same occasion" (13). Appropriately, this part of the essay concludes with one of those unforgettable pictures that Johnson can create so effectively through an admirable deployment of metaphors: "The stream of time, which is continually washing the dissoluble fabrics of other poets, passes without injury by the adamant of Shakespeare" (29). Time is, for Johnson, both foe as well as friend. To lesser poets it is a foe, for it deals in summary fashion with them, and their works are soon forgotten; but to Shakespeare it is a friend for it has no effect on him other than to enhance his reputation by its continual passage. Stream, fabric, and adamant have been brought together with marvellous restraint.

The Second Part of the Preface

Even Shakespeare has faults, and in keeping with the *a historical* half of the main division under which they are listed, Johnson points out that these faults are not peculiar to the Elizabethan age but are of a universal nature: "His first defect is that to which may be imputed most of the evil in books or in men. He sacrifices virtue to convenience and seems to write without any moral purpose" (33). But Johnson's criticism is tempered by a concession: "From his writings indeed a system of social duty may be selected, for he that thinks reasonably must think morally" (33). Later we shall examine in some detail Johnson's attitude towards morality and art; here all that needs to be said is that Johnson finds Shakespeare's presentation of morality not overt enough. He grants that it is present, but he wishes that it had been more pronounced. We have of course every right to disagree with Johnson here, though, as we shall see later, perhaps Johnson is not as wrong as we might at first glance consider him to be.

Other objections that Johnson raises against Shakespeare may be reduced to three main points: (1) carelessness in plot construction and a failure to adhere to historical accuracy; (2) difficult and tedious language; and (3) an irresistible weakness for conceits and quibbles. As Johnson had concluded his praise of Shakespeare with a metaphor that summed up his excellences, so does he conclude his blame of Shakespeare with a striking metaphor that displays something of Johnson's humour, an ingredient that must make us view all that he has said in criticism of Shakespeare as being slightly tongue in cheek: "A quibble was to him the fatal Cleopatra for which he lost the world and was content to lose it" (44).

Johnson's defence of Shakespeare against the common charge of his having violated the unities now follows. We shall consider this defence later in the Introduction; for the time being it is sufficient for us to note that Johnson is not an admirer of a scrupulous "observation of critical rules" when, in the process, qualities that contribute "to the nobler beauties of variety and instruction" (60) have to be sacrificed. In short, for Johnson, a play is an organic growth and, as such, should be insubordinate to mechanical rules. That Johnson was acutely conscious of the unprecedented stand he was taking in thus exalting Shakespeare's genius above "the joint authority of poets and of critics" (45) is evident from the comparison he draws between himself and Aeneas: "I am almost frightened at my own temerity and, when I estimate the fame and the strength of those that maintain the contrary opinion, am ready to sink down in reverential silence; as Aeneas withdrew from the defence of Troy when he saw Neptune shaking the wall and Juno heading the besiegers" (62).

The Third Part of the Preface

With the third part of the *Preface* we come to the second main division under which Johnson views Shakespeare, namely, the historical division (see diagram on page 5). Here Johnson presents us with a Shakespeare who is not timeless and universal, but rather, who is an Elizabethan, a product of his age. The opening sentence of this section sets the tone of what is to follow: "Every man's performance, to be rightly estimated, must be compared with the state of the age in which he lived and with his own particular opportunities" (64). Johnson begins this section by demarcating the human limits within which Shakespeare produced his plays. Whereas in the first part of the essay Johnson had granted Shakespeare absolute greatness, here he finds Shakespeare conditioned by the times in which he lived. "The English nation, in the time of Shakespeare, was yet struggling to emerge from barbarity," and a little later, "Nations, like individuals, have their infancy" (65 and 66). We may well ask whether Johnson is here inclined to over simplify, to view the Elizabethans in a patronizing manner. Does he regard them as "being yet unacquainted with the true state of things," as being "a rude people" (66 and 71) because his own age, the eighteenth century, prided itself on its reason and enlightenment?

Nevertheless, even though Johnson considers the Elizabethan taste naive and unrefined, he goes on to see Shakespeare's achievement in terms of a transcendence of what would otherwise have remained low and inferior. Out of the crude source material that gratified the fancy of the Elizabethans, that of "adventurers, giants, dragons, and enchantments," Shakespeare has written plays that excite "restless and unquenchable curiosity" (66 and 71) in the mind of the spectator or the reader. Again, perhaps Johnson is too condescending when he argues that the Elizabethans were more interested "in pomps or processions than in poetical language," and therefore Shakespeare, in order to please them, filled his plays with "shows and bustle" (72). Thus Johnson recoils from the blinding of Gloucester's eyes in *King Lear* with the following statement: "But I am not able to apologize with equal plausibility for the extrusion of Gloucoster's eyes, which seems an act too horrid to be endured in dramatic exhibition, and such as must always compel the mind to relieve its distress by incredulity. Yet let it be remembered that our author well knew what would please the audience for which he wrote" (Note on *Lear*). It is worth noting that about a century and a half later,

Yeats was to contrast the unity and the restraint of Greek drama "with the troubled life of Shakespearian drama" and point to "the blinding of Gloucester" as an example of this.[4]

Not only does Johnson consider Shakespeare as a part of his age, but he also attempts an estimate of the debt, if any, that Shakespeare owed to his literary ancestors. "It has been much disputed whether Shakespeare owed his excellence to his own native forces, or whether he had the common helps of scholastic education, the precepts of critical science, and the examples of ancient authors" (75). In discussing this question, Johnson's attitude is scrupulously just. On the one hand he seems to subscribe to the popular notion of Shakespeare having "wanted learning, that he had no regular education, nor much skill in the dead languages" (76). On the other hand, Johnson is convinced that though Shakespeare was probably not very well conversant with the classical and the modern European languages, "there is, however, proof enough that he was a very diligent reader, nor was our language [*i.e.*, English] then so indigent of books but that he might very liberally indulge his curiosity without excursion into foreign literature" (84). As earlier Johnson had seen Shakespeare's plays as a total transformation of his crude source material, so does he now brush aside the question as to whether Shakespeare was learned or not with the declaration, "But the greater part of his excellence was the product of his own genius" (85).

Johnson, it is true, subscribes to the Lockean idea of the mind as a *tabula rasa*, or a blank slate, on which sensations and impressions are progressively recorded. This is clear from his statement, "Nature gives no man knowledge, and when images are collected by study and experience, can only assist in combining or applying them" (86). But Johnson does not stop short here. In continuation of his earlier statement concerning Shakespeare's "excellence" being "the product of his own genius," Johnson now seems to verge on the Coleridgean brink of the imagination being a creative power when he pays to Shakespeare a tribute that leaves the Lockean way of looking at things far behind: "There is a vigilance of observation and accuracy of distinction which books and precepts cannot confer; from this almost all original and native excellence proceeds. Shakespeare must have looked upon mankind with perspicacity, in the highest degree curious and attentive" (87), and a few paragraphs later, "Perhaps it would not be easy to find any author, except Homer, who invented so much as Shakespeare" (92). Nearly twenty years earlier in his "Prologue" for the opening of the Theatre in Drury Lane, Johnson praised Shakespeare thus:

> Each Change of many-colour'd Life he drew,
> Exhausted Worlds, and then imagin'd new.[5]

Coming to Shakespeare's biography, Johnson, like all biographers before him and after him, is handicapped by the paucity of reliable material on the life of Shakespeare. Consequently Johnson deals with this aspect of Shakespeare in very general terms, yet it is difficult not to believe that when Johnson sees Shakespeare coming to London "a needy adventurer" and goes on to assert, "The genius of Shakespeare was not to be depressed by the weight of poverty nor limited by the narrow conversation to which men in want are inevitably condemned" (89), Johnson, who himself came to London in 1737, a needy adventurer with an unfinished tragedy entitled *Irene*, is identifying himself with Shakespeare. Some years after his *Preface*, Johnson was to publish his *Lives of the English Poets* in which biographical criticism, perhaps for the first time in English letters, becomes a critical tool with which the critic seeks to understand the writer's works. Since with Shakespeare the lack of biographical detail prevents Johnson from wielding this tool, he has to content himself with an insight that convinces us of its truth, even though unsubstantiated by factual evidence: "Many works of genius and learning have been performed in states of life that appear very little favourable to thought or to inquiry; so many that he who considers them is inclined to think that he sees enterprise and perseverance predominating over all external agency and bidding help and hindrance vanish before them" (89). And when Johnson marvels at Shakespeare's achievement despite his having "had so many difficulties to encounter and so little assistance to surmount them" (90), we can catch certain unmistakable echoes from Johnson's letter to Lord Chesterfield written when the *Dictionary* was about to be published: "Seven years, my Lord, have now past, since I waited in your outward rooms, or was repulsed from your door; during which time I have been pushing on my work through difficulties, of which it is useless to complain, and have brought it, at last, to the verge of publication, without one act of assistance, one world of encouragement, or one smile of favour" (*Life*, p. 185 [1784]). Boswell records that "Johnson and Savage were sometimes in such extreme indigence, that they could not pay for a lodging; so that they have wandered together whole nights in the streets". (*Life*, p. 119 [1744]), and in his poem "London" Johnson has this couplet:

> This mournful truth is every where confess'd,
> SLOW RISES WORTH, BY POVERTY DEPRESS'D!

Boswell's comment on this is worth quoting: "We may easily conceive with what feeling a great mind like his, cramped and galled by narrow circumstances, uttered this last line, which he marked by capitals" (*Life*, p. 94, [May, 1738]). It need not surprise us that Johnson, who during the first twenty-five years of his career in London struggled against poverty and could yet produce his *Dictionary*, should say in admiration of Shakespeare that "the incumbrances of his fortune were shaken from his mind, *as dewdrops from a lion's mane*" (89).

Johnson sees the Elizabethan age as being extrovertist; self-searching, the mind turning inward upon itself had not as yet commenced. "Speculation had not yet attempted to analyse the mind, to trace the passions to their sources, to unfold the seminal principles of vice and virtue, or sound the depths of the heart for the motives of action" (88). Though in this section of Johnson's *Preface*, as we have noted, Shakespeare is being viewed as a child of his age, Johnson is not prepared to limit Shakespeare by the boundaries of extrovertism. Shakespeare crosses these, for, though in his times "neither character nor dialogue were yet understood," "Shakespeare may be truly said to have introduced them both amongst us and in some of his happier scenes to have carried them both to the utmost height" (85). Johnson's splendid analysis of Hamlet's "To be, or not to be" soliloquy is an example of his recognition that with Shakespeare "the superficial appearances of action" (Note on *Hamlet*) are things of the past, for the complexities of the mind are now being opened up.

As in the first part of the essay Johnson had given us a powerful pictorial impression of the enduring quality of Shakespeare's genius which defies the stream of time, so in this section Johnson represents Shakespeare as a product of his age, untamed and barbaric, yet possessing a unique grandeur. He employs a double metaphor: the garden contrasted with the forest, and a piece of jewellery contrasted with a mine that contains untold riches.

> The work of a correct and regular writer is a garden accurately formed and diligently planted, varied with shades, and scented with flowers: the composition of Shakespeare is a forest, in which oaks extend their branches, and pines tower in the air, interspersed sometimes with weeds and brambles, and sometimes giving shelter to myrtles and to roses; filling the eye with awful pomp and gratifying the mind with endless diversity. Other poets display cabinets of precious rarities, minutely finished, wrought into shape, and polished unto brightness. Shakespeare opens a mine which contains gold and diamonds in unexhaustible plenty, though clouded by incrustations, debased by impurities, and mingled with a mass of meaner minerals (74).

Though the eighteenth century had a penchant for art that was neat and presentable, for which the garden, or "nature methodiz'd," is the best metaphor, it is clear from the above passage that Johnson's unhesitating preference was for Shakespeare's forest. If a writer's choice of metaphors is indicative of the way in which he interprets his subject, then Johnson's identification of Shakespeare with adamant that suffers no injury from the passage of time, with a forest, and with a mine are eloquent pointers towards the manner in which he comprehends Shakespeare. All three metaphors are anchored to a nature untouched by the hand of man. Shakespeare's genius is, for Johnson, as mysterious and overpowering as life itself.

The Fourth Part of the Preface

Balancing Johnson's praise of Shakespeare is the last part of the quartet in which he blames Shakespeare for "his deformities" (95). Shakespeare made no effort to publish his plays; he was content to be a popular writer with his contemporaries and had no thought for posterity. Anxious only to cater to the taste of his ill-educated and unrefined audience, "he has corrupted language by every mode of depravation" (95), having no care for later readers who would have endless difficulty in disentangling his thoughts from the convolutions of his language. "The style of Shakespeare was in itself ungrammatical, perplexed, and obscure" (101), and this, allied with his failure to publish his plays, the negligence of those who copied his plays, and the carelessness of the printers, has resulted in a text that is corrupt.

Today, when Shakespeare's greatness is universally recognized by not only the general public but by the educated classes of society which includes the academicians, Johnson's listing of Shakespeare's faults might seem curious and even amusing. But it must be remembered that in Johnson's age, though Shakespeare's plays were immensely popular on the stage as far as the general public was concerned, they were not regarded with much respect by the intellectually elite. They felt that Shakespeare provided good entertainment for the masses, but was hardly a writer to be taken very seriously. While Johnson's attitude to Shakespeare does at times coincide with that of his age, his admiration for Shakespeare overwhelms any reservations that he might have about his greatness. He admits that Shakespeare's work is "debased by impurities" (74), but at the same time points out that the classical restraint of Addison's *Cato*, admired by Voltaire, is correct but cold. "Let him [Voltaire] be answered," Johnson states in measured tones, "that Addison speaks the language of poets; and Shakespeare, of men" (73). The alternate praise and blame that Johnson bestows upon Shakespeare is, in one sense, a new critical stance that he introduces, for it combines the attitudes of both the general public and the elite of Johnson's times.

Boswell in his *Life of Johnson* takes note of Johnson's dualistic position thus:

> A blind indiscriminate admiration of Shakespeare had exposed the British nation to the ridicule of foreigners. Johnson, by candidly admitting the faults of his poet, had the more credit in bestowing on him deserved and indisputable praise; and doubtless none of all his panegyrists have done him half so much honour (p. 350, [1765]).

And Johnson himself, in a letter that he wrote to Charles

Burney shortly after the appearance of the *Preface*, explained that his dualistic approach would only serve to enhance Shakespeare's reputation: "We must confess the faults of our favourite to gain credit to our praise of his excellencies. He that claims, either in himself or for another, the honours of perfection, will surely injure the reputation which he designs to assist" (*Life*, p. 352, [Oct., 1765]). We may detect in Johnson's stand the truth of Hamlet's observation concerning "the censure of the which one must in your allowance o'erweigh a whole theater of others" (III, ii, 30–31).

The Fifth Part of the Preface

The fifth and final section of Johnson's *Preface* (102–156), which concerns itself with Shakespeare's text, is both descriptive and historical. Here Johnson describes the state of Shakespeare's text and gives a brief history of the editions through which it passed, concluding with his own edition, its aims and objectives. What follows in this introduction is a survey of the various stages through which Shakespeare's text passed upto Johnson's edition that appeared in 1765.

THE TRANSMISSION OF SHAKESPEARE'S TEXT

Unlike Ben Jonson who published his plays under the title *Works*, Shakespeare did not publish his plays. When an author brings out his own works in printed form, we can reasonably expect that, barring printers' errors, the text comes close to the original manuscript that was prepared by the author. Presumably the author has read the proofs, and generally insisted on the finished product conforming to his wishes. However, since Shakespeare wrote his plays to be acted and made no attempt to have them printed, this expectation is not valid. By what means, then, do we now have printed texts of Shakepeare's plays? Let us reconstruct some of the more important stages in the process that a play of Shakespeare must have gone through before being acted, and later printed.

Foul Copy

The playwright handed over the manuscript of his play, known as the 'holograph' because it was in his own handwriting, to the manager of the acting company. The holograph has come to be called the 'foul copy' because in most cases the author had made deletions and insertions in the margins and between the lines so that, in general, the manuscript presented an untidy appearance. The manager, therefore, gave the foul copy to a scribe who copied out the play on fresh sheets of paper and prepared a 'fair copy' for production. Any mistakes made by the scribe thus became a part of the text. Next, the fair copy went to the 'prompter' who revised the play, striking out any objectionable matter (e.g., swear words, or bawdy language) and inserting detailed stage directions. This was known as the 'prompt copy'. Sometimes these stage directions were confused with the text of the play by those who later had the play printed. At this point the play was ready to be licensed. The prompt copy was submitted to an official appointed by the Crown, known as the Master of the Revels, who went through the play and censored it. Politically offensive references, profanity, and anti-religious sentiments were excised, and a license was then issued to the manager of the acting company permitting him to present the play on the stage.

Fair Copy

Prompt Copy

The prompt copy then went to the copyist who copied out the parts of the different characters in the play separately. These parts were distributed to the actors, and the play was now ready to be rehearsed, the prompt copy being used by the prompter who was an important official backstage, controlling the entrances and exits of the actors, signalling to the musicians and those responsible for the sound-effects to perform their tasks at the right time, and generally directing the action. After the play was performed, the prompt copy was kept by the acting company, and, if the play had proved popular, the author's foul copy, or the fair copy, might be sold to a printer who, after printing the play, hoped to make good profits by selling copies of a play that had become famous and was being much talked about. Such a transaction was of course perfectly straightforward since the printer was now the legal owner of the copyright which he secured by having the play registered in the Stationers' Register on payment of a fee. This registration gave him the sole right to publish the play. The printer generally printed the play in the form known as 'Quarto' because the sheets of paper used for the printing were folded twice so as to comprise four sheets or eight pages. The word 'quarto' means

Good Quartos

that the pages are a quarter of the size of the original sheet, each page being about 7 inches wide and 9 inches high, that is, slightly larger than the pages on which this book is printed. The sheets were then stitched together and sold. It is obvious that despite the usual carelessness of the Elizabethan printer, such a quarto would be tolerably reliable, being based on the original manuscript, or the holograph, of the playwright. Such a quarto is therefore known as a 'good quarto'. The second quarto of *Hamlet* (Q2) is an instance of such a printing.

Bad Quartos

Not all quartos, however, were derived from this source. An unscrupulous printer who was not prepared to pay the price for the play to the acting company, or who found the play already sold to another printer, could try to pirate the play by approaching some of the actors and buying from them their-parts, and then filling up the gaps by asking the actors to reproduce as much as they could of the original play from memory. These 'bad quartos', as they are called, create all kinds of complications for the editor of Shakespeare because many lines are spurious. At the same time, some passages may well be genuine and therefore extremely valuable.. The first quarto of *Hamlet* (Q1) is possibly an instance of such a pirated version. Apparently a considerable portion of the text was obtained from the actor who played the part of Marcellus, and one (or more) of the other actors was bribed to reproduce as much of the original play as he could. Since during rehearsals he had heard the play time and again, he must have been fairly conversant with the other parts, but certainly not to the extent of being able to correctly reproduce the entire play. Obviously, where memory failed, inventiveness must have come to his rescue. The product is a garbled version of the original. Compare, for example, Hamlet's famous "To be, or not to be" soliloquy with the version that features in Q1:

To be, or not to be, I there's the point,
To Die, to sleepe, is that all? I all;
No, to sleepe, to dreame, I mary there it goes,
For in that dreame of death, when wee awake,
And borne before an euerlasting Judge,
From whence no passenger euer retur'nd,
The vndiscouered country, at whose sight

The happy smile, and the accursed damn'd.
But for this, the joyfull hope of this,
Whol'd beare the scornes and flattery of the world,
Scorned by the right rich, the rich curssed of the poore?
The widow being oppressed, the orphan wrong'd,
The taste of hunger, or a tirants raigne,
And thousand more calamities besides,
To grunt and sweate under this weary life,
When that he may his *Quietus* make,
With a bare bodkin, who would this indure,
But for a hope of something after death?
Which pusles the braine, and doth confound the sence.
Which makes us rather beare those euilles we haue.
Than flie to others that we know not of.
I that, O this conscience makes cowardes of us all,
Lady in thy orizons, be all my sinnes remembred.

Clearly, this version is full of echoes from the soliloquy as we know it, and it retains much of its power as well, but it is thoroughly unreliable. To sum up, then: Q1 of *Hamlet* is a pirated version of the original play; Q2, on the other hand, being based on the original manuscript, is as authentic as we could wish for in the given circumstances. In other words, it is an authorized text of the play.

By the time Shakespeare died in 1616, fourteen of his plays had appeared as authorized quartos. In addition, there were numerous bad quartos of these and his other plays floating about. What further complicates matters is that some of the quartos are perhaps based on Shakespeare's foul papers. Thus it is evident that the editor of Shakespeare has to take into account all the different versions of the plays and choose those which seem, in his judgement, to furnish the most authentic readings. This process is known as 'collation'.

Collation

Three years after the death of Shakespeare, in 1619, two printers brought out a volume of ten plays, ostensibly by Shakespeare, but in reality these were almost entirely based on the bad quartos. It was to remedy this deplorable state of affairs that in 1623, seven years after Shakespeare's death, two admirers of his and fellow actors, Heminge and Condell, published the First Folio, so called because, unlike the sheets of paper used for

The First Folio

the quartos which were folded twice, the sheets of paper used for the printing of the Folio were folded only once so as to comprise two sheets, or four pages. The pages of the Folio are larger than those of a quarto; they are about 10 inches wide and 16 inches high. The First Folio was therefore a large and handsome volume, prefaced by eulogies on Shakespeare, among which was one by Ben Jonson.

The First Folio (F1) was a collection of Shakespeare's plays under the headings Comedies, Histories, and Tragedies. Unfortunately, in spite of the genuine esteem in which these two editors held Shakespeare, their editorial methods leave much to be desired. The correct editorial procedure for them to adopt in preparing the text would have been to try to lay hands, in descending order of importance, on the foul copies or the holographs, the fair copies, the prompt copies, the good quartos, and finally the bad quartos. Instead, Heminge and Condell indiscriminately used both good and bad quartos, perhaps not realising that by so doing they, as the first real editors of Shakespeare, were conferring upon the bad quartos an authenticity that they did not deserve. Subsequent editors of Shakespeare in the seventeenth and eighteenth centuries, including Dr. Johnson, attached more importance to the First Folio than to the good quartos, thus perpetuating Heminge and Condell's error of judgement.

Later Folios

After the First Folio (1623), three more Folios appeared—the Second Folio (1632), the Third Folio (1663), and the Fourth Folio (1685). F2, F3, and F4 were merely reprints of F1, having no reference to the quartos, the fair copies, or the foul copies. From the editor's point of view, therefore, they are valueless and need not detain us here.

Elizabethan Printing

Something needs to be said on the standard of printing during the Elizabethan age and later. There is no evidence that Shakespeare ever involved himself with the printing of his plays, even though, as we have seen, during his lifetime several of his plays did appear in print as quartos. At the same time it is very likely that Shakespeare did, at some period in his career, consider bringing out a collected edition of his plays. Ben Jonson published a collected edition of his own works in 1616, the year of Shakespeare's death, and it is reasonable to suppose that

Shakespeare knew of this enterprise while it was being got ready for publication. Since Shakespeare and Johnson were friends as well as rivals, it is quite likely that Shakespeare too had considered embarking on a similar project. This is implied in the Preface that Heminge and Condell wrote to the First Folio where they regret Shakespeare's not having "liu'd to have set forth, and ouerseen his owne writings." Again, we can be almost certain that Shakespeare was directly concerned with the printing of his poems *Venus and Adonis* (1593) and *The Rape of Lucrece* (1594), most probably in the reading of the proofs and in the supervising of the printing. Richard Field, printer and publisher of these poems, was, like Shakespeare, a native of Stratford. He set up shop in London and by 1600 had a flourishing business. Undoubtedly he and the poet were friends, and the excellence of the texts of these two poems is an indication of their close cooperation in their preparation.

It is unfortunate that Shakespeare did not supervise an edition of his plays. Elizabethan printing was erratic: 'u' and 'v' were often confused as can be seen in the quotation from the Preface to the First Folio given twelve lines above; spellings were arbitrary and varied over a wide range of diversity; and compositors were far from accurate. One example of the variations in the spellings of the words from several different printings of the same play, *Hamlet*, I, i, will illustrate how capricious English spellings were in the Elizabethan period and even later:

the sleaded pollax (Q1, Q2, Q3)
the sleaded Pollax (Q4, Q5)
the sledded Pollax (F1, F2)
the sledded Pollax (F3)
the sleded Poleaxe (F4)

From the above example some idea can be formed of the problems that face the editor of Shakespeare. Which reading is the correct one? Which text is he to use? Should he not collate all the different versions and evolve what seems to him to be the most authentic one? Here he must allow himself to be guided by objective considerations; he should choose a particular reading, not because it appeals to him, but because he is convinced that this comes closest to what Shakespeare wrote. Even a bad quarto may be helpful in that it may provide the editor with a correct reading. Besides these problems, there is the further one of additions to the original text of the play being made by writers other than the author. These interpolations create all kinds of difficulties, the chief of these being the grounds on which to decide whether a passage is an interpolation or not. To determine this by stylistic characteristics alone is often not reliable. The Hecate scenes in *Macbeth* (III, v and IV, i) are examples of interpolations; these are almost certainly not by Shakespeare but by Middleton. The editor's task is indeed hard.

Having looked at some of the problems facing the editor of Shakespeare, it now remains for us to consider the contribution that Dr. Johnson makes to the editing of the plays.

JOHNSON'S EDITION OF SHAKESPEARE

Johnson's edition of Shakespeare was twenty years in gestation before finally appearing in 1765. In 1745 he had published a pamphlet entitled *Miscellaneous Observations on the Tragedy of Macbeth* along with a single sheet, in the form of an advertisement, setting forth *Proposals for a New Edition of Shakespeare* and examples of the kinds of type to be used. But Johnson was unable to follow up the *Proposals* with an edition of Shakespeare because a local bookseller claimed possession of the copyright on Shakespeare's works and threatened to file a suit if he went ahead with his plans. The following year Johnson began work on his *Dictionary of the English Language*. Though this necessitated shelving his project on Shakespeare, his interest in the plays remained strong. Shakespeare is the most frequently quoted author in the *Dictionary*, there being over 80,000 quotations from the plays.

In 1756 Johnson returned to Shakespeare with the publication of his *Proposals for Printing by Subscription, the Dramatic Works of William Shakespeare, corrected and illustrated by Samuel Johnson*. Though he promised, with reckless confidence, to bring out the work the following year, it was after nine years that the set of eight volumes finally appeared.

Boswell felt it was Johnson's "indolence [that] prevented him from pursuing [this project] with that diligence which alone can collect those scattered facts that genius, however acute, penetrating, and luminous, cannot discover by its own force" (*Life*, p. 226, [1756]). But Boswell is only speculating. He first met Johnson in 1763, seven years after Johnson had published his *Proposals*, and so can hardly be considered qualified to say why it took Johnson nine years to bring out his edition. Besides, when we reflect upon the dimensions of the undertaking, on the fact that Johnson was working singlehanded, that his eyesight was weak, that he was simultaneously writing essays for *The Idler* and published *Rasselas* in 1759, and that only two years before issuing his *Proposals* he had completed the stupendous task of bringing out his *Dictionary*, a project lasting seven years, then a period of nine years for the editing of Shakespeare does not seem at all disproportionate to the nature of the work he was performing. That Boswell is not sure of his ground is clear from his remarks. With reference to the year 1760, he says, "Johnson was now either very idle, or very busy with his edition of *Shakespeare*" (*Life*, p. 250), a statement that means very little. Then with reference to the year 1761 he makes an equally unhelpful statement: "In 1761 Johnson appears to have done little. He was still, no doubt, proceeding in his edition of *Shakespeare*, but what advances he made in it cannot be assertained" (*Life*, p. 253). The charge of indolence that Boswell levels at Johnson seems very tenuous indeed.

The humorous account that Boswell gives of Churchill's satire on Johnson's procrastination being instrumental in forcing him to bestir himself and publish his edition in 1765, enjoyable though it be, is probably an oversimplification. No doubt the subscribers who had contributed payment in advance towards the edition were growing impatient, and Churchill's lines must have been expressive to some extent of their growing misgivings, but it is difficult for us to conclude with Boswell "that the Caesarian operation was performed by the knife of Churchill, whose upbraiding satire, I dare say, made Johnson's friends urge him to dispatch.

> He for subscribers bates his hook,
> And takes your cash; but where's the book?
> No matter where; wise fear, you know,
> Forbids the robbing of a foe;

But what, to serve our private ends,
Forbids the cheating of our friends?"

(*Life*, pp. 226-7, [1756])

In any event, these lines of Churchill appeared in 1762, and it still took Johnson three years to complete his edition, so that Churchill's "Caesarian operation" was obviously ineffectual.

Johnson's Predecessors

In what form were Shakespeare's works available to the non-specialist reader in the period between the Fourth Folio (1685) and Johnson's edition (1765)? It was generally recognized that the later Folios, being simply reprints of the First Folio, were inadequate and that the greatness of Shakespeare deserved a better textual presentation of his plays. Even though in the early part of the eighteenth century the intricacies of editorial work were not properly comprehended, it was felt that a text more readable than the Folios was necessary. The first 'edition' of Shakespeare, in this limited sense of the word, was that by

Rowe

Nicholas Rowe which appeared in 1709, the year of Johnson's birth. Rowe knew next to nothing of correct editorial procedure; he used the Fourth Folio as his basic text which, as we have noted, was thoroughly unreliable, and he did not think it necessary to consult the First Folio or any of the quartos.

Despite these shortcomings, Rowe did make some contribution to an understanding and enjoyment of Shakespeare. He corrected some of the more obviously corrupt passages, relying upon his own intelligence in so doing. While it is true that Rowe has hit upon the right word in several instances, his method is far from being the right one, for, as Dr. Johnson points out towards the close of his *Preface*, if the editor's "ejection of a word for one that appeared to him more elegant or more intelligible" (140) is permitted, then the text as Shakespeare wrote it will be at the mercy of each editor's whim, and the reader will not know whether he is reading Shakespeare or his editors.

Rowe divided the plays into acts and scenes, modernized the spellings, marked the entrances and exits of characters, and prefixed a list of *dramatis personae* to each play; in short, he made the text of Shakespeare more intelligible and attractive to eighteenth-century readers than it was before. Besides, his edition contained the first formal biography of Shakespeare, a contribution to Shakespearean scholarship that Johnson regarded with conditional approval for, as he says in his *Preface*, he included it in his edition even though it was "not written with much elegance or spirit" (103). That Johnson should thus animadvert on Rowe's Life of Shakespeare is understandable, for Johnson was himself a master of the art of biography as any one who has read *The Lives of the English Poets* knows well; as early as 1744 he had written his *Life of Richard Savage*, a book running into about 180 pages and one of the most vivid and compelling of Johnson's works.

The next edition of Shakespeare, that by Alexander Pope, came out in 1725. Far from being an improvement on Rowe's edition, it represented a further debasement of the text. Pope made Rowe's edition his base text which, as we have seen, was in turn based on the defective Fourth Folio. Surprisingly, though Pope had stated in his Preface that the Quartos were more reliable than the Folios, he did not put into practice this fundamental knowledge that he possessed. Having begun with this grave error, Pope went further in the same direction by making copious emendations according to his own taste and fancy, and by omitting many words and even whole lines when he thought that by so doing he was improving the rhythm. Being a poet himself, Pope perhaps felt that he enjoyed the right to teach Shakespeare a thing or two. In addition to this audacity of Pope, his Preface is dull and uninspired; it fails to compensate for the grave inadequacies that are so pronounced a feature of his edition. Pope

Johnson, who admired Pope as a poet, is polite to him as an editor, but only to the extent that Pope's edition seemed to promise much though it fulfilled little. Johnson is mistaken when he credits Pope with having "collated the old copies" (104), though he is quite right in censuring Pope—perhaps a little too mildly—because "he rejected whatever he disliked and thought more of amputation than of cure" (104). Johnson is understandably annoyed with Pope for speaking contemptuously of "the dull duty of an editor" (106) and for not realising that in actuality it posed an intellectual challenge of the highest order. Though properly severe on Pope for his poor editorship, Johnson is generous in his praise of Pope's Preface and his notes, even though to us Pope's Preface might seem commonplace.

heobald

Pope's edition was followed by that of Lewis Theobald (pronounced Tib'bald) in 1734. Theobald was the first editor of Shakespeare in the proper sense of the word. He brought genuine scholarship to bear on the work, located many of the quartos, and used the First Folio as his base text. Johnson recognizes Theobald's valuable contribution when he says that "he collated the ancient copies and rectified many errors" (109). At the same time Johnson also notes that Theobald's commendation of the Second Folio is misplaced for "the truth is that the first is equivalent to all others, and that the rest only deviate from it by the printer's negligence" (110).

In 1726 Theobald had published his *Shakespeare Restored*, a work in which he criticized Pope's edition of Shakespeare for the many errors it contained. Pope, stung into retaliation, made Theobald the original hero of *The Dunciad* (1728). Johnson, an admirer of Pope as a poet, is less than fair to Theobald when he calls him "weak and ignorant, thus mean and faithless, thus petulant and ostentatious" (112) for having crossed swords with Pope. The truth of the matter is that Theobald had rightly pinpointed Pope's incompetence as a scholar, and Johnson, though he was fully aware of the deficiencies in Pope's edition of Shakespeare, nevertheless denigrates Theobald because he had dared to point out Pope's faults. In fact, it is to Theobald that we owe the famous emendation of Mistress Quickly's account of the death of Falstaff. Whereas both the quarto and the Folio readings are "His nose was as sharp as a pen and a Table of greene fields" (*Henry V*, II, iii, 17-18), a reading that is perhaps corrupt, it must, however, be pointed out that the original reading has strong defenders: see, e.g., R.F. Fleissner, "Putting Falstaff to Rest: 'Tabulating' the Facts," *Shakespeare Studies*, 16 (1984) 57-74. Theobald emended the latter part of the statement to read "and a' babbled of green fields," a reading that has since been accepted by most editors. However, it should be noted that other emendations too have been suggested that might seem equally plausible, for example, "His nose was as sharp as a pen and a talk'd of greene fields," and "His nose was as sharp as a pen on a Table of greene fields," the latter emendation carrying several sexual innuendoes that the Elizabethan audience would not have missed.

Something needs to be said here on the dangers attendant on emendation. W.W. Greg (1875-1959), one of the most important names in modern bibliographical scholarship in Shakespeare and Elizabethan drama, defines an acceptable emendation as "one that strikes a trained intelligence as supplying exactly the sense required by the context, and which at the same time reveals to the critic the manner in which the corruption arose." Errors that are obvious misprints pose no real problem but there are other kinds of errors that call for an intimate knowledge of Elizabethan printing techniques and Renaissance handwriting, among other things. Lacking these qualifications, the editor who goes in for reckless emendation may well appear ridiculous to discerning readers. One of the most fantastic emendations was that by Pope who conjectured that "and a Table of greene fields" was not part of the text but a stage direction to the effect that a table was to be brought on stage at this point.

Another famous disputed passage occurs in Hamlet's first soliloquy (I, ii, 129) which in the First Folio reads "O that this too too solid flesh would melt," whereas Q1 and Q2 read "sallied flesh." Editors generally accepted the Folio reading, until J. Dover Wilson argued that the "sallied" of the quartos is a misprint for "sullied," the 'a' and the 'u' being easily confused in Renaissance handwriting. What further seems to strengthen Dover Wilson's point is that "sullied" fits in well with the sense of pollution that Hamlet feels he suffers from as a result of his being the son of a mother who has established an incestuous relationship with his uncle. Here is an example of scholarship and a fine insight into the play's meaning having joined together to produce a happy result.

Hanmer

And so, the next edition of Shakespeare to be published after Theobald's is a failure precisely because the editor indulges in emendation without the slightest realisation of the scandalous liberties he is taking with the text. Sir Thomas Hanmer's edition (1744) has negligible editorial value for, as Dr. Johnson notes, "by inserting his emendations, whether invented or borrowed, into the page without any notice of varying copies, he has appropriated the labour of his predecessor, and made his own edition of little authority" (115). Hanmer, in fact, consulted no edition older than that by Pope, and, like Pope, lopped off whole passages that he disliked and made changes in others with amazing temerity. Johnson has considerable respect for Hanmer's wide reading and knowledge of the Elizabethan age. Also, Johnson tells us that "he had, what is the first requisite to emendatory criticism, that intuition by which the poet's intention is immediately discovered" (113), but Johnson also observes that he was too anxious to impose eighteenth-century ideas of grammatical order and logic upon Shakespeare's style: "He is solicitous to reduce to grammer what he could not be sure that his author intended to be grammatical. Shakespeare regarded more the series of ideas than of words: and his language, not being designed for the reader's desk, was all that he desired it to be if it conveyed his meaning to the audience" (113). We come across some of Johnson's profoundest utterances on Shakespeare in his distaste for the way in which so many of his contemporaries sought to remake Shakespeare in the image of their own age and times. And though Johnson is appreciative of Hanmer's powers of intuition, Johnson is too experienced an editor not to know that such a gift can be dangerous when indulged to excess. As we shall see, in his notes on Warburton, the next editor of Shakespeare, Johnson balances intuition with the need for sound scholarship.

Warburton

As with Pope, Johnson's attitude to Warburton is one of deference mingled with some censure. There were reasons for this. In 1745, as we have seen, Johnson had published a pamphlet *Miscellaneous Observations on the Tragedy of Macbeth*. William Warburton's edition of Shakespeare came out two years later, and Warburton, in his Preface, while scoffing at other editors of Shakespeare, pays a handsome compliment to Johnson for his pamphlet. Warburton writes, "As to all those things which have been published under the titles of *Essays*, *Remarks*, *Observations*, *&C*. on Shakespeare, if you except some critical notes on *Macbeth*, given as a specimen of a projected edition, and written, as appears, by a man of parts and genius, the rest are absolutely below a serious notice" (*Life*, pp. 127–28 [1745-1746]). Johnson, who was at this time an unknown and struggling writer, never forgot the encouragement that this afforded him. "He praised me at a time when praise was of value to me," he said to Boswell many years later (*Life*, p. 128 [1746]). Understandably, Johnson always retained a soft corner for Warburton, and, when he came to write his *Preface* twenty years later, could not bring himself to be as severely critical of Warburton as he might have been otherwise.

In actuality, as Johnson knew very well, Warburton's edition was no better than Hanmer's. Warburton's text was based on Pope's edition which, as we have seen, was inferior to Rowe's. Discreetly, Johnson avoids any reference to Warburton's text and confines himself to some general praise of his notes and commentary. He recognizes Warburton's "quick discernment," or intuition, but goes on to say that this by itself is not enough, for it can give rise to "that confidence which presumes to do, by surveying the surface, what labour only can perform, by penetrating the bottom" (118). There is no substitute for "labour" or scholarship. Johnson confers upon him "genius and learning," and then diplomatically speaks of his notes "which he ought never to have considered as part of his serious employments, and which, I suppose, since the ardour of composition is remitted, he no longer numbers among his happy effusions" (117). Thus, courteously, does Johnson spare Warburton the condign indictment that his edition deserves, while, at the same time, making us aware of the limitations from which it suffers. Johnson's *Preface*, while telling us a great deal about Johnson's attitude to Shakespeare, also tells us something about the human relationships that Johnson had with his fellow writers.

Johnson has the rare ability to stand back and look at the entire project, on which he and his predecessors have spent so much time and labour, with ironic and humorous detachment. The dignity of Johnson the man asserts itself when he gently reprimands those engaged in literary enterprises for their vanity and acrimony, for the "invective and contempt" (127) that they discharge against each other. With his keen sense of time passing and the insignificance of human endeavour when viewed against the backdrop of the numerous others who had gone before him in editing Shakespeare, Johnson surveys the scene with trepidation, and presents us once again with a metaphoric picture of his situation: "To dread the shore which he sees spread with wrecks is natural to the sailor. I had before my eye so many critical adventures ended in miscarriage that caution was forced upon me" (152). And even while pointing out the defects in the work of his predecessors, Johnson knows that as scholarship advances his own work will in due course of time be overtaken and outdistanced: "I was forced to censure those whom I admired and could not but reflect, while I was dispossessing their emendations, how soon the same fate might happen to my own, and how many of the readings which I have corrected may be by some other editor defended and established" (152). It is touches such as these that impress us with Johnson's profound sense of the insignificance of the scholar and the abiding magnificence of Shakespeare which the stream of time passes by without injury.

Upton and Grey

Having considered all the editions of Shakespeare that appeared prior to his own edition, Johnson then glances at two commentators on Shakespeare, John Upton and Zachary Grey. For the first he has scant respect, since, like most editors, he "is unable to restrain the rage of emendation." Johnson's disgust with those who thus recklessly practise conjecture stirs him into the utterance of some of his most eloquent condemnations: "Every cold empiric, when his heart is expanded by a successful experiment, swells into a theorist, and the laborious collator at some unlucky moment frolics in conjecture" (124). Johnson knows that sound editorial procedure requires that the editor first of all evolve a theory of the text, based on as much factual evidence as he can gather, and that then only he permit himself to cautiously suggest changes in the text, consistent with the theory. The empiric, on the other hand, rushes into the fray relying on his native intelligence, his enthusiasm unrestrained by a theory, and tampers with the text confident of success. Johnson's excellent grasp of correct editorial practice is evident in the warning he utters near the end of his *Preface*: "That a conjectural critic should often be mistaken, cannot be wonderful, either to others or himself, if it be considered that in his art there is no system, no principal and axiomatical truth that regulates subordinate positions. His chance of error is renewed at every attempt; an oblique view of the passage, a slight misapprehension of a phrase, a casual inattention to the parts connected, is sufficient to make him not only fail, but fail ridiculously; and when he succeeds best, he produces perhaps but one reading of many probable, and he that suggests another will always be able to dispute his claims" (153).

For the second commentator, Zachary Grey, Johnson has nothing but respect. Grey "neither attempts judicial nor emendatory criticism" (125), Johnson declares. "It were to be wished that all would endeavour to imitate his modesty," Johnson drily adds. Of course, Grey's work was not an edition of Shakespeare and, as such, did not provide much scope for emendation; nevertheless Johnson praises his restraint.

From the foregoing survey it is clear that Johnson brought to his task as editor an abhorrence of the urge to amend the early texts of Shakespeare, defective though they might be on account of the vagaries of transmission occasioned by the carelessness of actors and printers. Further, Johnson was fully aware of the unreliability of the Folio, and so of the need to supplement it with the quartos.

Since Johnson could declare of Shakespeare that "with his excellencies [he] has likewise faults" (32), we are entitled to investigate the excellencies and the faults of Johnson's edition of Shakespeare. First it must be said that Johnson's theory is better than his practice. "Sir," Johnson once said humorously to Sir Joshua Reynolds the painter, "there are two things which I am confident I can do very well: one is an introduction to any literary work, stating what it is to contain, and how it should be executed in the most perfect manner; the other is a conclusion, shewing from various causes why the execution has not been equal to what the author promised to himself and to the public."[6] This is perhaps the best comment on Johnson's edition, for, textually, it does not match the theoretical knowledge that Johnson possessed of sound editorial procedure.

Johnson, as we have seen, knew very well that the good quartos were more reliable than the folios, yet his efforts to lay hands on the quartos were perfunctory. "I collated such copies as I could procure and wished for more, but have not found the collectors of these rarities very communicative" (139). Thus does Johnson exonerate himself of the responsibility of scrutinizing the quartos. The insinuation here, as Boswell points out, is that Garrick who had a large collection of quartos was uncooperative. Boswell's account is worth quoting in full:

> I regretted the reflection in his Preface to Shakespeare against Garrick, to whom we cannot but apply the following passage: 'I collated such copies as I could procure, and wished for more, but have not found the collectors of these

> rarities very communicative.' I told him, that Garrick had complained to me of it, and had vindicated himself by assuring me, that Johnson was made welcome to the full use of his collection, and that he left the key of it with a servant, with orders to have a fire and every convenience for him. I found Johnson's notion was, that Garrick wanted to be courted for them, and that, on the contrary, Garrick should have courted him, and sent him the plays of his own accord. But, indeed, considering the slovenly and careless manner in which books were treated by Johnson, it could not be expected that scarce and valuable editions should have been lent to him.
>
> (*Life*, p. 493, [Spring, 1772])

Was it Johnson's indolence that stood in the way of his trying to locate the quartos as assiduously as he should have? Perhaps this is a question to which no definite answer can be given. The textual scholar's task is a strenuous one requiring much zeal, patience, tact, and a thorough knowledge of the manner in which Shakespeare's text was prepared by the copyists, the printers, the actors, and the many others who may have had a hand in the process. Such knowledge is cumulative. In the twentieth century there has been an increased awareness of the need to study the transmission of Shakespeare's texts in their earliest extant form—that is, the quartos—and to determine exactly what were the conditions—that is, the printing techniques—under which these texts were produced. The entire aim of textual criticism of Shakespeare is to try to recover as much, and as accurately as is humanly possible, of the exact words, which includes spelling, punctuation, capitalization etc., that Shakespeare wrote. Since no handwritten manuscript of Shakespeare's is extant, the textual critic has to fall back upon the quartos and the Folio. His endeavour should be to try to identify the kind of manuscript that served as the printer's copy for a Shakespeare first edition. Was it the holograph, the fair copy, or the prompt copy, that the printer used? As we have noted, the second and the third phases through which the text passed represent some distortion of the original text because of the intervention of the scribe or the copyist. Further complications arise when a bad quarto has been used in conjunction with a good quarto to provide the printer of the First Folio with a combined text with which to set up his type. *King Lear* and *Richard II*, it has been shown by twentieth-century textual scholars, were typeset from printed copies of this kind.

Thus it can be seen that textual criticism is a highly complex study, the mastery of which lies outside the life span of a single individual, no matter how zealous he be. Recent researches have been in the direction of employing computers and collating machines in order to determine on scientific and not on impressionistic evidence the words of the manuscript as they may have been written by Shakespeare. Fredson Bowers, whose *On Editing Shakespeare and the Elizabethan Dramatists* (1955) presents an admirable picture of the entire scene, has this to say: "The end in view is a bold one: to discover from the maximum penetration of the physical facts the new evidence that can be applied to the textual criticism of Shakespeare. It is such evidence alone that can lead to an authoritative, modern reevaluation of the results of the great critical effort of a hundred years ago that produced the standard Globe text. On the basis of this new technical knowledge that has been accumulating since World War II, the definitive text designed to replace the Globe will be constructed from the combined application of bibliographical, linguistic, and critical scholarship of a kind that could not have been envisaged by an earlier generation." That Johnson's editorial contribution was but a link in a chain was fully recognized by Johnson himself, a recognition concerning their own contributions that Johnson's predecessors, and many of his successors, sadly lack. "Every work of this kind is by its nature deficient, and I should feel little solicitude about the sentence were it to be pronounced only by the skilful and the learned," are Johnson's concluding words to his *Preface*.

Johnson was in several ways a great pioneer. He was the first editor to provide his readers with a variorum edition of Shakespeare, by which is meant that in addition to the actual text, the editor gives a list of all variant readings of particular passages. An example of this may be seen on page 23 above where we have variant readings of Horatio's line "He smote the sledded Polacks on the ice." In addition Johnson furnishes a collection of annotation and commentary by earlier editors and critics. In his *Proposals* (1756) Johnson had described his projected edition thus: "The edition now proposed will at least have this advantage over others. It will exhibit all the observable varieties of all the copies that can be found; that, if the reader is not satisfied with the editor's determination, he may have the means of choostter being for himself." Johnson's conception of a variorum edition has fructified in the form of the New Variorum edition which was begun in 1871. So far over twenty-seven plays have appeared in this series, forthcoming titles being *Titus Andronicus* and *The Comedy of Errors*.

Perhaps the most significant contribution that Johnson made to Shakespearean textual scholarship was to emphasize the importance of the quartos (what Johnson calls "the oldest copies" and "the old copies" see paras 104 on p. 122 and 140 on p. 131), and closely connected with this, to refuse to "improve" the text of Shakespeare by making changes, emendations and corrections. Johnson devotes several pages of his *Preface* to showing how dangerous it is for the editor of Shakespeare to tamper with the texts of the plays (see 136-156). "To alter is more easy than to explain" (100), Johnson ironically says, and goes on to insist that it is the editor's duty to explain a difficult passage, rather than to emend it so as to simplify its meaning: "Had the author published his own works, we should have sat quietly down to disentangle his intricacies and clear his obscurities; but now we tear what we cannot loose and eject what we happen not to understand" (100). Not only did Johnson eschew the general craze for emendation that all his predecessors seem to have displayed, but he tried to undo in his edition the damage that they had done. "By examining the old copies [i.e. the quartos], I soon found that the later publishers, with all their boasts of diligence, suffered many passages to stand unauthorized, and contented themselves with Rowe's regulation of the text even where they knew it to be arbitrary and with a little consideration might have found it to be wrong. Some of these alterations are only the ejection of a word for one that appeared to him more elegant or more intelligible. These corruptions I have often silently rectified; for the history of our language and the true force of our words can only be preserved by keeping the text of authors free from adulteration" (140).

The following three statements by Johnson define precisely the wariness with which he approached emendation, and the scholar's respect that he had for Shakespeare's text:

(1) Conjecture, though it be sometimes unavoidable, I have not wantonly nor licentiously indulged. It has been my settled principle that the reading of the ancient books is probably true and therefore is not to be disturbed for the sake of elegance, perspicuity, or mere improvement of the sense (142).

(2) But my first labour is always to turn the old text on every side and try if there be any interstice through which light can find its way.... I have rescued many lines from the violations of temerity and secured many scenes from the inroads of correction (143).

(3) As I practised conjecture more, I learned to trust it less; and after I had printed a few plays, resolved to insert none of my own readings in the text. Upon this caution I now congratulate myself, for every day increases my doubt of my emendations (148).

But this does not mean that Johnson refrains altogether from emendation; at times he does proffer an alternative reading, as he admits: "...where any passage appeared inextricably perplexed, [I] have endeavoured to discover how it may be recalled to sense with least violence" (143). However, Johnson always remains a purist; whenever he suggests an emendation, it is confined to the margin and the text is left unchanged. Johnson expressly mentions this in the *Preface*: "Since I have confined my imagination to the margin, it must not be considered as very reprehensible if I have suffered it to play some freaks in its own dominion. There is no danger in conjecture if it be proposed as conjecture; and while the text remains uninjured those changes may be safely offered which are considered even by him that offers them as necessary or safe" (149). Constantly Johnson makes us aware of the speculative nature of the editor's contribution, of the precariousness and impermanence of his work. "And indeed, where mere conjecture is to be used, the emendations of Scaliger and Lipsius, notwithstanding their wonderful sagacity and erudition, are often vague and disputable, like mine or Theobald's" (155). Thus does Johnson remind us that the scholar's quest is an endless one, and that in scholarship there is no finality.

Whereas editors prior to Johnson had regarded Shakespeare

as an inspired barbarian who needed their intervention in order to be intelligible and enjoyable to readers, Johnson's approach is different. For him, Shakespeare's work is its own greatest recommedation; the editor's duty is slight. Once he has performed it, he had best retire from the scene and leave the reader to establish his own personal relationship with Shakespeare. "I have always suspected that the reading is right which requires many words to prove it wrong; and the emendation wrong that cannot without so much labour appear to be right" (151). All the editors before Johnson had emended Claudius's line in *Hamlet* "In hugger-mugger to inter him" (IV, v, 81) to "In private to inter him." Johnson restored the original, and his comment is worth quoting: "That the words now replaced are better, I do not undertake to prove; it is sufficient that they are Shakespeare's. If phraseology is to be changed as words grow uncouth by disuse or gross by vulgarity, the history of every language will be lost; we shall no longer have any words of any author; and, as these alterations will be often unskilfully made, we shall in time have very little of his meaning" (Note on *Hamlet*). Johnson's sensibility is that of the scholar who seeks to preserve the original against the inroads of pseudo-scholars who seek to popularize Shakespeare.

In his note on the Duke's lines announcing his decision to relinquish his authority, "We have with a leaven'd and prepared choice/Proceeded to you" (*Measure for Measure*,, I, i, 52), Johnson has this stern comment on Warburton's having changed "leaven'd" to "level'd": "No emendation is necessary. *Leaven'd choice* is one of Shakespeare's harsh metaphors. His train of ideas seems to be this. *I have proceeded to you with choice* mature, concocted, fermented, *leavened*. When Bread is *leavened*, it is left to ferment: a *leavened* choice is therefore a choice not hasty, but considerate." Of Bolingbroke's line "England shall double gild his treble guilt" (*2H4*, IV, v, 129), Warburton had pronounced with absolute self-assurance, "Evidently the nonsense of some foolish Player," to which Johnson gives an admirable reply: "I know that why this commentator should speak with so much confidence what he cannot know, or determine so positively what so capricious a writer as our poet might either deliberately or wantonly produce. This line is indeed such as disgraces a few that precede and follow it, but it suits well enough with the *daggers hid in thought, and whetted on the flinty hearts*; and the answer which the prince makes, and which is applauded for wisdom, is not of a strain much higher than this ejected line." Concerning Capulet's line to Paris "Earth-treading stars that make dark HEAVEN'S light" (*Romeo & Juliet*, I, ii, 25) Warburton had declared, "This nonsense should be reformed thus, 'Earth-treading stars that make dark EVEN light.'" Johnson's reply: "But why nonsense? Is anything more commonly said, than that beauties eclipse the sun?" Not only does Johnson refuse to alter, but he explains with perspicacity.

Not that Johnson always approves of Shakespeare's language—Johnson is vexed by Shakespeare's lack of clarity in Camillo's statement "Where of the execution did cry out/Against the non-performance" (*The Winter's Tale*, I, ii, 260): "This is one of the expressions by which Shakespeare too frequently clouds his meaning. This sounding phrase means, I think, no more than *a thing necessary to be done*." And when Johnson is baffled by Shakespeare's lines, he frankly admits defeat: of Falstaff's retort to the Chief Justice "The young Prince hath misled me. I am the fellow with the great belly, and he my dog" (*2H4*, I, ii, 166), Johnson is disarmingly honest, "I do not understand this joke. Dogs lead the blind, but why does a dog lead the fat?" Nevertheless, Johnson will not change the lines in order to make them comprehensible, and it is in his refusal to do what others before him had freely done that his superiority over them, as editor, lies.

It was Johnson who by insisting on the supremacy of the earliest texts over the meddling distortions of later editors, paved the way for three outstanding textual scholars, contemporaries of Johnson who greatly admired his work, and who, on publishing their own editions of Shakespeare, separately and individually established Shakespeare's text on a firm basis of sound scholarship. Edward Capell was the first editor to study minutely the quartos and collate them with scrupulous care; Edmond Malone did original research on Shakespeare's stage, tried to establish the order of composition of the plays, and wrote a 500-page life of Shakespeare which became the basis of all later biographies of the dramatist; and George Steevens, like Capell, made a close study of the quartos and was the first editor to include *Pericles* in the Shakespearean canon.

The degree of enlightenment that Johnson reveals in his *Preface* was something he arrived at after long years of labour during which his edition was in preparation. The early Johnson, the Johnson of the *Miscellaneous Observations on the Tragedy of Macbeth* (1745), was, like his predecessors, quite prepared to substitute a word from the original text for one that he felt made more sense. Of Malcolm's report on the diginity with which Cawdor died ("As one that had been studied in his death/To throw away the dearest thing he owed/As 'twere a careless trifle" —*Macbeth*, I, iv, 9–11) Johnson had no hesitation in declaring, "As the word *owed* affords here no sense, but such as is forced and unnatural, it can not be doubted that it was originally written, the dearest thing he *owned*; a reading which needs neither defence nor explication."[7] As we have seen, the later Johnson repudiated the taking of liberties with the text, insisting upon its sacrosanctity and the critic's duty to explicate it rather than conveniently change it.

If Johnson became increasingly suspicious of emendation, he likewise turned away from other forms of modernising the plays of Shakespeare. Reluctantly, he continues the practice that Rowe had initiated of breaking up the plays into acts, a practice that has now become an integral part of the way in which we visualize the text of a Shakespeare play. Evidently Johnson continues the practice for the convenience of the reader, but from the tone of the following passage it is clear that he disapproves of this imposition of a later age's idea of order and pattern upon the Shakespearean vision: "I have preserved the common distribution of the play into acts, though I believe it to be in almost all the plays void of authority. Some of those which are divided in the later editions have no division in the first Folio, and some that are divided in the Folio have no division in the preceding copies. The settled mode of the theatre requires four intervals in the play; but few, if any, of our author's compositions can be properly distributed in that manner." Johnson points out that "the restriction of five acts" is "accidental and arbitrary"; it breaks up the continuity of the play and destroys our sense of its being an organic whole. Shakespeare, Johnson suggests, conceived the play as a total expression, and the pauses could be either more or less than five, depending upon the exigencies of Shakespeare's artistic purpose; not upon a rigid formula that a less creative age was to inflict upon his creations. "This Shakespeare knew," Johnson affirms, "and this he practised; his plays were written and at first printed in one unbroken continuity and ought now to be exhibited with short pauses interposed as often as the scene is changed or any considerable time is required to pass. This method would at once quell a thousand absurdities" (144). That Johnson should anticipate Granville-Barker, who revolutionised Shakespearean production by accelerating the pace with a continuous flow of action, need not surprise us, for Johnson was, in many ways, ahead of his age.

Not only does Johnson anticipate Granville-Barker, but more important, Yeats as well who recoiled from the elaborate stage versions of the nineteenth century which called for long pauses between acts in order that scene changes might be effected. Yeats's distaste for the way in which *The Merchant of Venice* was staged in a London production comes close to Johnson's unhappiness over the "unbroken continuity" of Shakespeare being parcelled out by later editors. In a letter of 1905 to Frank Fay Yeats writes, "The Trial scene was moving, but owing to the stage management the rest was broken up. Shakespeare had certainly intended those short scenes of his to be played one after the other as quickly as possible and there is no reason that they should not, if played in this way, keep the sense of crisis almost as living as in the long scenes." Johnson and Yeats are separated by a span of a hundred and fifty years; Johnson belongs to the age of reason, Yeats to an age that produced *The Symbolist Movement in Literature*,[8] yet both men share a community of taste when they speak of Shakespeare.

Johnson's reluctance to intrude between Shakespeare's text and the reader manifests itself in the writing of his notes and observations on the plays. True, in certain difficult passages explanatory notes may help the reader, Johnson concedes, "but the general effect of the work is weakened. The mind is refrigerated by interruption; the thoughts are diverted from the principal subject; the reader is weary, he suspects not why, and at last throws away the book which he has too diligently studied" (158). Excessive scholarship destroys the pleasure that literature should yield, and for Johnson "the desire of pleasure" (5) is the primary object of the reader when faced with works that appeal "to observation and experience" (3). Besides, the writer of explanatory notes can never hope to exhaust all that needs to be clarified. Johnson points out that a dramatist with the range and variety of Shakespeare has numerous references to "customs too minute to attract the notice of the law, such as modes of dress, formalities of conversation, rules of visits, disposition of furniture, and practices of ceremony" (132). All these will naturally be unfamiliar to later ages, and no "single scholiast" can hope to know them fully. Johnson implies that such historical research is endless and cumulative, and, in a sense, futile. The intrinsic Shakespeare is beyond all this. Always, for Johnson, it is the reader who must make direct contact with the writings of Shakespeare; the critic is an interloper. "The poetical beauties or defects I have not been very diligent to observe," Johnson informs us, and goes on to say, "the reader, I believe, is seldom pleased to find his opinion anticipated; it is natural to delight more in what we find or make than in what we receive" (134). Thus the reader, for Johnson, is a maker like the dramatist, and the play is a product of the collaborative efforts of both dramatist and reader.

In perhaps one of the most eloquent disclaimers of the validity of his own profession as critic, Johnson exhorts the reader to discover Shakespeare for himself without being distracted by the voices of the commentators: "Notes are often necessary, but they are necessary evils. Let him that is yet unacquained with the powers of Shakespeare and who desires to feel the highest pleasure that the drama can give, read every play, from the first scene to the last, with utter negligence of all his commentators. When his fancy is once on the wing, let it not stoop at correction or explanation. When his attention is strongly engaged, let it disdain alike to turn aside to the name of Theobald and of Pope. Let him read on through brightness and obscurity, through integrity and corruption; let him preserve his comprehension of the dialogue and his interest in the fable. And when the pleasures of novelty have ceased, let him attempt exactness and read the commentators" (157). Shakespeare's plays provide for Johnson "the highest pleasure that the drama can give," and his image of the reader's fancy soaring aloft through the realm of Shakespeare's imagination, disdaining the mundane earth below peopled by dull editors and commentators, shows a remarkable appreciation of that aspect of Shakespeare that we usually consider to have been opened up by the Coleridgean sensibility.

Johnson is perhaps one of the earliest of the great subjective critics of Shakespeare who brings to bear on the plays a sustained investigation. For Johnson, the critic performs a necessary function, but his role becomes meaningful only after the reader has fallen under the spell of Shakespeare, and in this enchantment the critic has no part. Johnson's definition of a critic in his *Dictionary* is "a man skilled in the art of judging of literature; a man able to distinguish the faults and beauties of writing." The critic, then, in Johnson's view, is not to be a mere explicator; he must also be a judge. And yet, as we have seen time and again, even as an explicator Johnson is strikingly effective. His experience as a lexicographer had given him an extraordinary skill in precise, brief explication.

Johnson's Response to Shakespeare's Poetry

One of the most serious charges levelled against Johnson the critic of Shakespeare is that he was deaf to the overtones of Shakespeare's poetry at its most sublime (e.g., William Kenrick, *A Review of Dr. Johnson's New Edition of Shakespeare*, 1765; William Hazlitt, "Preface," *The Characters of Shakespeare's Plays*, 1817). According to Hazlitt, Johnson's putative failure as a Shakespearean critic springs from his inability to appreciate the poetic elements in Shakespeare, and this, in turn, is the direct outcome of the limited sensibility of his age. Hazlitt, of course, is using Johnson as a straw man in order to establish the validity of his own approach to Shakespeare, and we can condone his attack on Johnson for being a tactical device often employed by a critic of a later period seeking to distinguish his identity from those of his predecessors. On actually examining Johnson's response to Shakespeare's poetry, however, we may well conclude that Hazlitt's criticism is unfounded, if not perverse. Johnson, we have already noted, deliberately refrains from informing his reader that a particular passage is poetically superb; he leaves the reader to discover this for himself. It is therefore less than fair to Johnson to attribute his reticence in this direction to a lack of appreciation of Shakespeare's poetry at its best.

The Johnson who could say of Lady Macbeth's lines, "Come, thick night,/ And pall thee in the dunnest smoke of hell" (I, v, 48–52), "In this passage is exerted all the force of poetry, that force which calls new powers into being, which embodies sentiment and animates matter"; of the Duke's lines in *Measure for Measure*, "Thou hast nor youth nor age;/ But, as it were an after-dinner's sleep,/Dreaming on both" (III, i, 32), "This is exquisitely imagined"; and of Macbeth's "Now o'er the one half-world/Nature seems dead" (II, i, 49), "This image, which is perhaps the most striking that poetry can produce. . ." was certainly not a Johnson devoid of a keen sensitivity to Shakespeare's poetry.

When Johnson and Boswell visited Scotalnd in 1773, they passed through the places associated with *Macbeth*. Both have described the experience. Johnson's account is as follows: "We went forwards the same day to Fores, the town to which Macbeth was travelling, when he met the weird sisters in his way. This to an Englishman is classic ground. Our imaginations were heated, and our thoughts recalled to their old amusements." Boswell's account of the same experience is thus: "In the afternoon, we drove over the very heath where Macbeth met the witches, according to tradition. Dr. Johnson again solemnly repeated—

How far is't called to Fores? What are these
So wither'd, and so wild in their attire?
They look not like the inhabitants o' the earth,
And yet are on't."[9]

A comparison of the two accounts might yield some slight points of interest: in Johnson's account the dramatic truth that Shakespeare creates impresses itself upon his mind so that Macbeth is for him not just a historical character but an imaginative reality; this is borne out by his statement "our imaginations were heated." In Boswell's account the phrase "according to tradition" lessens Shakespeare's achievement by making him share it with the historical source from which the details of the play are derived. Again, Johnson's account lays emphasis on the power of Shakespear'es art to stir our imaginations; "classic ground," "our imaginations," "our thoughts," and "old amusements" all seem to stress the presence of an interaction between the work of art and the reader. Boswell's account, by contrast, contains none of the overtones that Johnson's does.

Johnson has been criticized for his supposed failure to respond to Lady Macbeth's lines "That my keen knife see not the wound it makes, / Nor heaven peep through the blanket of the dark, / To cry Hold, hold' " (I, v, 48-52) (see, e.g., J.W.H. Atkins, *English Literary Criticism, 17th and 18th Centuries*, London Methuen, 1966, p. 240). But far from deriding Shakespeare's use of 'low' terms like "knife" and "blanket," what Johnson is doing is to illustrate the way in which words that in one age are respectable, in a succeeding age may become debased. Earlier he has said, "Words which convey ideas of dignity in one age are banished from elegant writing or conversation in another, because they are in time debased by vulgar mouths and can be no longer heard without the involuntary recollection of unpleasing images." Thus Johnson finds Lady Macbeth's use of the word "knife" responsible for a lowering of the imaginative temperature, because "this sentiment is weakened by the name of an instrument used by butchers and cooks in the meanest employments." Since Shakespeare uses words, and words are subject to "corruption and decay," as Johnson tells us in his *Preface to the English Dictionary*, Shakespeare too comes under the eroding power of time and a changing society. Johnson concludes his *Preface* with the following moving statement: "It is to be lamented that such a writer should want a commentary; that his language should become obsolete or his sentiments obscure" (161). If we are inclined to feel that the eighteenth century was unnecessarily fastidious in taking umbrage at the word "knife" on account of its association with the kitchen, we should remember that a word like "naughty," which today is used to describe badly behaved children, had quite a different connotation in Shakespeare's time; whereas Portia's use of the word when she says

> How far that little candle throws his beams:
> So shines a good deed in a naughty world

was quite appropriate for Shakespeare's audience, it never fails to amuse children in the twentieth century.

Johnson and the Acting of Shakespeare's Plays

Johnson's refusal to entertain the presence of a mediator between the reader and Shakespeare is not confined to the editor but extends to the actor as well. He had scant regard for the actor's profession, and justified the exclusion of the name of Garrick from his *Preface* on the ground that the stage presentation often distorted the play. Boswell's record of his conversation with Johnson on this subject is worth noting: "I complained that he had not mentioned Garrick in his Preface to Shakespeare; and asked him if he did not admire him. JOHNSON. Yes, as 'a poor player, who frets and struts his hour upon the stage;—as a shadow. BOSWELL. But has he not brought Shakespeare into notice?' JOHNSON. Sir, to allow that, would be to lampoon the age. Many of Shakespeare's plays are the worse for being acted: *Macbeth* for instance. BOSWELL. What, Sir, is nothing gained by decoration and action? Indeed, I do wish that you had mentioned Garrick. JOHNSON. My dear Sir, had I mentioned him, I must have mentioned many more: Mrs. Pritchard, Mrs. Cibber,—nay, and Mr. Cibber too; he too altered Shakespeare" (*Life*, p. 416, [19 Oct, 1769]). Unable to tolerate the emendation of Shakespeare's text by officious critics and editors, Johnson found the adaptations of Shakespeare's plays—some of them immensely popular in the eighteenth century—equally intolerable. Colley Cibber, whom Johnson mentions with such distaste, produced his own version of *Richard III* (1700) in which he cut Shakespeare's play in half and interpolated sections from 3 *Henry VI*, *Richard II*, *2 Henry IV*, *Henry V*, and some lines of his own composition. Two years later Garrick acted the part of Richard III in Cibber's monstrosity, and thereafter, for over thirty years, this adaptation was staged almost every year at the Drury Lane Theatre. We must applaud Johnson's refusal to honour Garrick by excluding him from his *Preface*.

Besides, when we remember that Garrick wrote a dying speech for Macbeth, combined *A Midsummer Night's Dream* and *The Tempest* into an opera called *The Fairies*, adapted *The Taming of the Shrew* as *Catharine and Petruchio*, and *The Winter's Tale* as *Florizel and Perdita*, and that he had the audacity to produce his own version of *Hamlet*—of which more a little later—we can well sympathize with Johnson's disgust for the acting profession, of which Garrick was the age's greatest exponent. As examples of the extent to which Garrick could go in deforming Shakespeare, we will look at two of his adaptations: in his *Florizel and Perdita* he condensed the first three acts of *The*

Winter's Tale into a dialogue between Camillo and a Gentleman written in his own language, and yet had the effrontery to claim that it was his "plan/To spill no drop of that immortal man." Again, in his *Hamlet*, he omitted the grave-diggers and Ophelia's funeral, did not show the queen being poisoned on stage but let her off, only to later inform the audience that her sense of guilt had driven her insane, and showed the king defending himself vigorously against an incensed Hamlet, and finally being killed by Hamlet. Impressed and influenced by Voltaire's assessment of Shakespeare's achievement as consisting of "a few pearls" in an "enormous dunghill," Garrick could declare with comparable smugness, "I had sworn I would not leave the stage till I had rescued that noble play [*Hamlet*] from all the rubbish of the fifth act. I have brought it forth without the grave-digger's trick and the fencing match. The alteration was received with general approbation." In passing, we should note here Garrick's self-portrayal as one who "rescues" the play from Shakespeare's clumsiness, and yet more audacious, as one who gives the play a new birth by having "brought it forth."

Dr. Johnson's contempt for the stage was well founded, and in his emphatic statement, "A play read affects the mind like a play acted" (58), we can see his refusal to concede that it is only through the stage that the full content of a Shakespearean play can be assimilated. Here he anticipates Charles Lamb's argument that *King Lear* is too vast a play to be encompassed by a mere stage, and the part of King Lear too titanic to be impersonated by a mere actor tottering about with a walking stick in a simulated storm. Johnson had said much the same thing to Boswell, which Boswell recorded in shorthand form thus: "No tragedy is so strong on stage as alone. The effect all imagi[nation], and when alone, nothing to counteract it; whereas in playhouse, see 'tis stage, not wild heath; Garrick, not Macbeth."[10]

Mingled with Johnson's dislike of the actor and distaste for the stage was the uncomfortable awareness that Shakespeare himself was both actor and playwright, inextricably involved with the stage. How to reconcile Shakespeare's genius with this undesirable occupation was a problem that Johnson solved in the *Preface* by suggesting repeatedly that Shakespeare despised his own profession. Johnson sees Shakespeare as one who disdains his own work, meant for the stage and therefore ephemeral, and prefers to allow it to lapse into obscurity rather than to seek fame through its instrumentality. Johnson implies that this was the reason for Shakespeare not having published his works, and for the contempt—which to us must appear amazing—with which he regarded them, for it was only Heminge and Condell's regard for the plays that rescued them from oblivion. Was it indifference to fame, or was it something even finer than this that made Shakespeare so careless of the fate of his writings? Johnson would have us believe the latter: "... that which must happen to all, has happened to Shakespeare, by accident and time; and more than has been suffered by any other writer since the use of types has been suffered by him through his own negligence of fame or perhaps by that superiority of mind which despised its own performances when it compared them with its powers, and judged those works unworthy to be preserved which the critics of following ages were to contend for the fame of restoring and explaining" (161). Shakespeare despised the actor's profession and the stage; he wrote his plays to earn a living, and having achieved success in this direction, had no desire to pass on his works to posterity.

Johnson's Shakespeare is a man who wears his greatness lightly, who attaches little importance to his works: "It does not appear that Shakespeare thought his works worthy of posterity, that he levied any ideal tribute upon future times, or had any future prospect than of present popularity and present profit. When his plays had been acted, his hope was at an end; he solicited no addition of honour from the reader" (97). In thus creating Shakespeare's personality, Johnson is of course overstepping the limits of historical accuracy, but as an imaginative biographer Johnson has every right to thus decipher Shakespeare the man, not only from his plays and what he did, but also from what he did not do. Thus Johnson places before us a Shakespeare who has a grandeur of personality that cannot be engaged by the usual measures that other men take to perpetuate their names, nor does his Shakespeare care to remain in harness beyond the period of time absolutely necessary for his welfare, but retires from his profession while still at the height of his mental powers. "So careless was this great poet of future fame that, though he retired to ease and plenty while he was yet little *declined into the vale of years*, before he could be disgusted with fatigue or disabled by infirmity, he made no collection of his works . . ." (98). In suggesting that Shakespeare did not think his works worthy of posterity, Johnson sees Shakespeare as the most exacting critic of his plays; what will pass as a play to the spectator will not stand up to the scrutiny of the reader, and so Shakespeare neglects to publish them, not because of indolence, but by design.

Johnson attributes the occasional lack of artistry in the plays to Shakespeare's own disregard for the stage and his audience. Of the ending to *All's Well That Ends Well* Johnson seems to feel that the very title establishes Shakespeare's indifference to artistic necessity—the slapdash manner in which events are manipulated testifies to this: "Shakespeare is now hastening to the end of the play, finds his matter sufficient to fill up his remaining scenes, and therefore, as on other such occasions, contracts his dialogue and precipitates his action." Bertram could surely have been given a form of punishment in proportion to his perfidy, but Shakespeare could not care less. "Of all this Shakespeare could not be ignorant, but Shakespeare wanted to conclude his play." Johnson's Shakespeare is deficient neither in morality nor in art; it is his scant respect for his profession that makes him conclude the play so hastily.

The blinding of Gloucester on stage that Johnson finds grossly inartistic, is not, according to Johnson, to be blamed entirely on Shakespeare—"yet let it be remembered that our author well knew what would please the audience for which he wrote" (see note on *Lear*). The Elizabethan audience, accustomed to public hangings followed by disembowellings and quarterings, could hardly have recoiled from the blinding of Gloucester as later audiences were to do, and Johnson is right in making Shakespeare's audience partly responsible for scenes offensive to later, and less robust, sensibilities. Johnson is convinced that the artist in Shakespeare must have rebelled against the making of such compromises, but other considerations prevailed and Shakespeare wrote to please the masses: "I am indeed far from thinking that his works were wrought to his own ideas of perfection; when they were such as would satisfy the audience, they satisfied the writer" (96). Time and again does Johnson see Shakespeare's excesses and carelessness in plot construction as an unavoidable part of his profession. A dramatist writing for the popular stage, Shakespeare on this account cannot exercise the critical restraint that would otherwise have prevented him from committing such lapses in good taste and in artistry, and his works, despite all their greatness, fall short of his full capacity.

The Universality of Shakespeare's Characters

As opposed to the view that Shakespeare's characters are highly individualised, Johnson maintains that "they act and speak by the influence of those general passions and principles by which all minds are agitated," and then makes the startling assertion, "In the writings of other poets a character is too often an individual; in those of Shakespeare it is commonly a species" (8). This fits in with Imlac's famous observation in *Rasselas*: "The business of a poet is to examine not the individual but the species; to remark general properties and large appearances: he does not number the streaks of the tulip, or describe the different shades in the verdure of the forest. He is to exhibit in his portraits of nature such prominent and striking features, as recall the original to every mind; and must neglect the minuter discriminations . . . ."[11] How tenable is Imlac's argument? Johnson himself tells us next to nothing about Rasselas or Imlac's appearance, their height, build, or the clothes they wore, quite unlike, for example, Dickens's minute description of Mr. Micawber or of Mr. Pickwick. What details does Shakespeare give us of, say, Hamlet, or of Macbeth? We know that Hamlet has been a student, that he reads omnivorously, that he knows a great deal about acting that he has been practising his fencing and is an expert in the game. All these are, as Imlac puts it, "prominent and striking features," they are not "the minuter discriminations." The same might be said of Macbeth. Undoubtedly, when Shakespeare's plays were first acted, the dramatist himself must have been interested in seeing that the actor playing the role of Hamlet conformed, more than less, to his physical impression of the prince of Denmark, and the play, being a visual presentation, depicted much detail that is absent in its reading, nevertheless Johnson's reflection on Shakespeare's characters acting and speaking "by the influence of those general passions and principles by which all minds are agitated" holds good.

Johnson's point is well illustrated in his justification of Shakespeare's depiction of Claudius—though a king—as a drunkard, and of Menenius—though a Roman senator—as a buffoon. "Shakespeare always makes nature predominate over accident," and "His story requires Romans or kings, but he thinks only on men" (15), Johnson tells us. Claudius is a king, true, but along with his royalty goes a weakness for wine, something that he shares with the rest of mankind. Shakespeare's characters are typical; they are reflections of the human condition that obtains in all parts of the earth and in all periods of history. Each reader finds in them an echo of feelings that he would himself have experienced, given a similar situation.

It is by this measure that Johnson, despite his finding little to praise in the poetry of Gray, confers upon the *Elegy* the highest tribute that one poet can give to another: "The *Churchyard* abounds with images which find a mirror in every mind, and with sentiments to which every bosom returns an echo. The four stanzas beginning *Yet even these bones*, are to me original: I have never seen the notions in any other place; yet he that reads them here, persuades himself that he has always felt them" (*Lives*, II, p. 464). Even originality, for Johnson, exists only when the reader apprehends its truth as a personally felt experience.

And yet, Johnson can also simultaneously insist that "no poet ever kept his personages more distinct from each other" (12). This in no way negates his earlier statement that Shakespeare's characters reflect the human condition. They remain "ample and general" insofar as they are embodiments of human feelings and human passions; at the same time they remain "discriminated" (12) from each other in that they are representative of the walks of life from which they spring. Thus, since Macbeth is a soldier, he is particularly sensitive to "the reproach of cowardice," and more so when urged by a woman (Note on *Macbeth*).

Shakespeare's Heroes

"Shakespeare has no heroes" (13), Johnson declares, an astounding statement for generations of readers brought up on Bradley, yet Johnson intends it as the highest compliment he can pay Shakespeare. Johnson is here contrasting Shakespeare's plays with heroic tragedy, a descendant of the romantic play that came into vogue with Beaumont and Fletcher. Love and Honour were the twin forces that propelled the heroic play to its grand finale, the heroic couplet instead of blank verse being the vehicle used for the propagation of these two sentiments. The distinction of the heroic lover from all others "is that he is a lover of extraordinary emotional capacity. His love is so sudden and intense that it surprises everybody including himself.... The audience is amazed at such superhuman devotion and loyalty.... But love in the heroic play does not arouse only admiration; it also arouses compassion. It involves so much of pining and whining on the part of the lover, that, in the true romantic tradition, he is always on the verge of dying." His dedication to Honour, or Valour, is equally astonishing: "Valour is of course the most outstanding trait of this Hero. He is a great warrior and conqueror sweeping across the world in quest of glory and honour. He performs incredible feats. As we learn from Settle's *Conquest of China* (I, i), conquering a 'few million soldiers' is a mere trifle for him."[12] Exaggerated sentiments, ranting, crude psychology or none at all, these were the stock in trade of heroic tragedy, all admirably summed up and dismissed by Johnson in the same breath: "The theatre, when it is under any other direction, is peopled by such characters as were never seen, conversing in a language which was never heard, upon topics which will never arise in the commerce of mankind" (10). It is Shakespeare's truth to nature that exposes the absurdity of heroic tragedy.

Perhaps Dryden's plays afford the best examples of heroic drama. They are superior to other plays of this genre because Dryden had genuine regard for Shakespeare's genius, but they lack passion, a quality incommensurate with the restraints of common sense and reason that the age espoused. Johnson's remarks on Dryden's play *The Conquest of Granada* are indicative of the mixed feelings heroic drama could elicit from him—a preponderance of amusement at the inflated notions of love and honour, mingled with an element of genuine admiration for the play's energy and drive:

> The two parts of the *Conquest of Granada* are written with a seeming determination to glut the publick with dramatick wonders; to exhibit in its highest elevation a theatrical

> meteor of incredible love and impossible valour, and to leave no room for a wilder flight to the extravagance of posterity. All the rays of romantick heat, whether amorous or warlike, grow in Almanzor by a kind of concentration. He is above all laws; he is exempt from all restraints; he ranges the world at will, and governs wherever he appears. He fights without enquiring the cause, and loves in spite of the obligations of justice, of rejection by his mistress, and of prohibition from the dead. Yet the scenes are, for the most part, delightful; they exhibit a kind of illustrious depravity, and majestick madness: such as, if it is sometimes despised, is often reverenced, and in which the ridiculous is mingled with the astonishing. (*Lives*, I, pp. 247-8).

It is against this kind of a fantastic background that Johnson sees in the plays of Shakespeare "human sentiments in human language" (14).

In *The Conquest of Granada*, just before the ghost of Almanzor's mother appears to Almanzor, he utters the following lines:

> A hollow Wind comes whistling through that Door;
> And a cold Shiv'ring seizes me all o'er:
> My Teeth, too, chatter with a sudden Fright;
> These are the Raptures of too fierce Delight!

We have only to compare this passage with that in *Hamlet* when the Ghost makes its first appearance to see how Shakespeare succeeds where Dryden fails:

> MARCELLUS. Peace, break thee off. Look where it comes again!
> BERNARDO. In the same figure, like the King that's dead.
> MARCELLUS. Thou art a scholar. Speak to it, Horatio.
> BERNARDO. Looks it not like the King? Mark it, Horatio.
> HORATIO. Most like. It harrows me with fear and wonder
> (I, i. 40-44)

The tense, whispered ejaculations of Shakespeare's characters convey terror, whereas the rhyming couplets of Dryden's Almanzor are comical. Dryden's ghost is a children's bogey man; Shakespeare's is a visitant from the regions of the dead. Whether we believe in ghosts or not has no relevance to the situation with which Shakespeare confronts us. Art, Johnson suggests, is not life, yet it must have the ring of psychological truth if it is to convince and move the audience. In Shakespeare he finds that "even where the agency is supernatural, the dialogue is level with life" (13). The emphasis is not on the ghost, but on the reaction of the human beings to the ghost's appearance. It is through their reaction that we apprehend the ghost.

As with heroic tragedy, so with heroic comedy. With its firm belief in the inherent goodness of the human soul, the age produced comedies in which the humane qualities of mankind were painted in glowing colours. The stage was now peopled, not by men and women of whose constitutions it might be said, "The web of our life is of a mingled yarn, good and ill together" (*All's Well*, IV, iii, 83), but by ideal types, by abstractions that existed only in the minds of the dramatists. It was in keeping with this trend that the drama of the time carefully excluded characters from the lower strata of society as being incapable of exhibiting the ideals that were cherished. Whereas Shakespeare brings a Dogberry, or a drunken porter, on stage, the drama of this period was the preserve of middle and upper class society.

In contrast to such a preoccupation, Johnson holds up Shakespeare as the poet whose "characters are not modified by the customs of particular places, unpractised by the rest of the world; by the peculiarities of studies or professions which can operate but upon small numbers; or by the accidents of transient fashions or temporary opinions" (8). Johnson's brilliant analysis of the character of Polonius, as opposed to Warburton's is a good example of Johnson's awareness of Shakespeare's ability to create complex characters that refuse to be pigeonholed as 'types'. Warburton had interpreted Polonius as a "weak, pedant, minister of state," as a satire on Elizabethan courtly moralizing and sermonizing. But Johnson is not satisfied with this limited view of Polonius. "The commentator," he says, "makes the character of Polonius a character only of manners, discriminated by properties superficial, accidental, and acquired. The poet intended a nobler delineation of a mixed character of manners and of nature" (Note on *Hamlet*). What follows is Johnson's detailed interpretation of Polonius's character, a marvellous exposé that leaves Warbarton's Polonius far behind. Johnson sees Polonius as a man who once possessed a vigorous and discerning mind, and who even now, though old, can draw upon the wealth of his experience, but with diminishing effectiveness. Thus for Johnson Shakespeare's Polonius is not a type of a superannuated politician, but a character drawn from "the genuine progeny of common humanity, such as the world will always supply, and observation will always find" (8). The emphasis here is on "always"; Shakespeare's characters are neither dated nor topical because they have their roots in common humanity."

Such characters, as Johnson sees them, are true to life, for they are the products of Shakespeare's observation and not of an idealised concept that can have no corresponding human expression. Thus the dialogue in his plays is directly related to the situation being shown, not to some abstract idea that exists in a never never land. "But the dialogue of this author is often so evidently determined by the incident which produces it, and is pursued with so much ease and simplicity, that it seems scarcely to claim the merit of fiction, but to have been gleaned by diligent selection out of common conversation and comman occurrences" (10). Jean H. Hagstrum in his chapter entitled "Nature"[13] discusses perceptively Johnson's view of nature, of truth to life, as distinct from romanticism and religion. When Johnson praises Shakespeare's plays for scarcely claiming the merit of fiction, what does he mean by "fiction"? In his *Dictionary* he defines *fiction* as "The act of feigning or inventing," and "A falsehood, a lye." A *lye* he defines as "A vitious falsehood." When Johnson says that Shakespeare's plays can scarcely be regarded as fiction, because they are so true to life, he is complimenting Shakespeare in the highest terms of his critical vocabulary.

Repeatedly Johnson salutes Shakespeare for having alighted upon some subtle aspect of human nature: "There is much of nature in this petty perverseness of Rosalind," Johnson says of her changeable moods when with Celia (Note on *As You Like It*); "There are many touches of nature in this conference of John with Hubert," is Johnson's observation on King John's putting the blame for Arthur's murder on Hubert (Note on *King John*); Johnson is deeply moved by the plight of Queen Katharine and has eloquent praise for Shakespeare's handling of the scene: "This scene is above any other part of Shakespeare's tragedies, and perhaps above any scene of any other poet, tender and pathetic, without gods, or furies, or poisons, or precipices, without the help of romantic circumstances, without improbable sallies of poetical lamentation, and without any throes of tumultuous misery." Without using any of the claptrap of heroic drama, Shakespeare is able to express the pathetic in a scene "which may be justly numbered among the greatest efforts of tragedy" (Note on *Henry VIII*).

Shakespeare, the Poet of Nature

The first great quality of Shakespeare in winning Johnson's admiration is his being "above all writers, at least above all modern writers, the poet of nature, the poet that holds up to his readers a faithful mirror of manners and of life" (8). Here of course Johnson is deliberately echoing Hamlet's advice to the players: "For anything so overdone is from the purpose of playing, whose end, both at the first and now, was and is to hold as 'twere the mirror up to Nature—to show virtue her own feature, scorn her own image, and the very age and body of the time his form and pressure" (III, ii, 22–27). Hamlet's actors, under his direction, are about to present a play that holds the mirror up to Claudius's crime, for what they enact comes close to being an exact reproduction of the poisoning of Hamlet's father by Claudius. Hamlet expects Claudius, watching the play, a work of art, to blench, not only on realising that his secret is known, that the truth has become public, but also on recognizing the enormity of his crime —which Claudius does when he struggles to pray immediately after Hamlet's staging of the play. It is in this sense that Dr. Johnson accords to Shakespeare the skill of showing us in his plays the truth of our own natures. We look into Shakespeare's art, and see ourselves.

Repeatedly does Johnson discover in Shakespeare a dramatic rendering of the experience of life, its human complexities and situations that we realize through art more fully than while experiencing them in the process of living. "This, therefore, is the praise of Shakespeare, that his drama is the mirror of life; that he who has mazed his imagination in following the phantoms which other writers raise up before him, may here be cured of his delirious ecstasies by reading human sentiments in human language, by scenes from which a hermit may estimate the transactions of the world and a confessor predict the progress of the passions" (14). The hermit and the priest are themselves detached from, and perhaps ignorant of, life, yet by looking into the imaginative world that Shakespeare creates, they come face to face with the life they have renounced.

Johnson admires Shakespeare's genius time and again for having brought to light some little explored tract of human nature, and it is with delighted recognition that Johnson the critic, drawing upon his own experience of life, confirms the truth of what Shakespeare represents. "The arguments by which Lady Macbeth persuades her husband to commit the murder afford a proof of Shakespeare's knowledge of human nature," Johnson declares, and then goes on to analyse the tension between Macbeth and his wife that she exploits with such astuteness (Note on *Macbeth*). Numerous other instances can be cited. Posthumus's speech in *Cymbeline* "seems to issue warm from the heart," and "the play has many just sentiments" (Note on *Cymbeline*). Praising Shakespeare's depiction of the way in which Desdemona is drawn to Othello, Johnson categorically states, "Whoever ridicules this account of the progress of love shows his ignorance, not only of history, but of nature and manners"; going on to examine the subtlety with which Iago poisons Othello's mind against Desdemona, Johnson notes that these scenes are "proofs of Shakespeare's skill in human nature as, I suppose, it is vain to seek in any modern writer" (Note on *Othello*). When considering Leontes's repentance in *The Winter's Tale* after the Oracle has vindicated Hermione, Johnson observes, "This vehement retractation of Leontes, accompanied with the confession of more crimes than he was suspected of, is agreeable to our daily experience of the vicissitudes of violent tempers and the eruptions of minds oppressed with guilt" (Note on *The Winter's Tale*). Warburton, and successive critics after him, have meticulously pointed out the inconsistencies in the play: that Bohemia has no sea coast; that the presence of the Oracle, a Greek device, is not consistent with a sheep-shearing festival, something typically English; that it is incredible Paulina should have been able to keep Hermione concealed for sixteen years. But Johnson brushes all those objections aside. "These are the petty cavils of petty minds" (15) as he says elsewhere concerning objections of a similar kind. For Johnson *The Winter's Tale* is satisfying because the human psychology portrayed "is agreeable to our daily experience," and the play "is, with all its absurdities, very entertaining. The character of Autolycus is very naturally conceived and strongly represented" (Note on the *Winter's Tale*).

As we shall see in the following section of this Introduction ("Art and Life" pp. 58–62), truth to nature is not all. "The character of Autolycus is very naturally conceived and strongly represented." In this comment Johnson accords to nature the distinction of being the starting point for the dramatist's creation of the character, but what follows immediately is its being "strongly represented," that is, the artistic achievement of the dramatist is more than his having given us an accurate reflection of nature. Thus, even though Shakespeare is "the poet of nature, the poet that holds up to his readers a faithful mirror of manners and of life" (8), this by itself is not enough. Elsewhere Johnson has argued that if a writer merely describes the corrupt state of the world, why should we read him? We may as well look directly at the world: "If the world be promiscuously described, I cannot see of what use it can be to read the account; or why it may not be as safe to turn the eye immediately upon mankind as upon a mirror which shows all that presents itself without discrimination" (*Rambler* No. 4). But this and other related matters must be reserved for "Art and Life."

After the symbolistic approach of Wilson Knight and L.C. Knights, the historical approach of E.E. Stoll, the anthropological approach of Northrop Frye, the sociological approach of Alfred Harbage, the biographical approach of Frank Harris, the psychoanalytical approach of Ernest Jones, and the "image cluster" approach of Caroline Spurgeon, it is refreshing to turn to Johnson who sees Shakespeare as the poet of human emotions. In replying to Voltaire's praise of Addison and criticism of Shakespeare, Johnson says with marvellous economy of words, "Let him be answered that Addison speaks the language of poets; and Shakespeare, of men" (73).

Art and Life

For Johnson, as we have noted, drama is to be judged by its "power to move" men's minds (21). In keeping with his being the poet of nature, Shakespeare breaks away from the classical tradition of separating tragedy and comedy, and creates a new kind of drama which comes close to what we actually encounter in life. Shakespeare's plays are not in the rigorous and critical sense either tragedies or comedies, but compositions of a distinct kind; exhibiting the real state of sublunary nature, which partakes of good and evil . . . in which, at the same time, the reveller is hasting to his wine, and the mourner burying his friend . . ." (17). It is important for us to particularly note Johnson's rejection of the notion that Shakespeare's plays are exclusively either tragedies or comedies, and his introduction of a new set of values by which his plays are to be judged. (In the section entitled "Tragedy," pp. 71–78 below, we shall see how this approach of Johnson's governs his strictures on Shakespeare as a writer of tragedy.) Shakespeare excites "laughter and sorrow not only in one mind but in one composition" (19), something that later critics were to applaud, calling the technique "comic relief," the most celebrated example of this being the appearance of the drunken porter immediately after the murder of Duncan. But to Johnson must go the credit of recognizing that though such a combination of the serious and the ludicrous "is a practice contrary to the rules of criticism"—and Johnson now comes to Shakespeare's defence—there is always an appeal open from "criticism to nature" (20). The French neo-classicists had systematically rejected a mingling of the tragic and the comic, and though in England during the early part of the Restoration comic elements did invade heroic tragedy, this was not generally viewed with favour. Thus Dryden's Lisideius in the *Essay of Dramatic Poesy* (1668) condemns tragi-comedy because it results in confused emotions on the part of the audience. Here the term 'tragi-comedy' does not mean 'a serious play with a happy ending' but, as we have seen, a mingling of the serious and the comic.[14]

When Johnson praises Shakespeare for having successfully combined these contrary elements in the same play on the grounds that the play comes close to "the appearance of life" (20), he is not suggesting that the sorrow we experience while watching tragedy on the stage is the same as the sorrow that might assail us in life. Later he asserts, "The delight of tragedy proceeds from our conciousness of fiction; if we thought murders and treasons real, they would please no more" (65). Johnson is here making a careful distinction between art and life in terms of the experience undergone by the reader, or the spectator, of the play. The pleasure we derive from art is an aesthetic pleasure in that it stands by itself though it is at the same time related to our knowledge and understanding of what goes on in life. "Imitations" produce pain or pleasure, not because they are mistalken for realities, but because they bring realities to mind. When the imagination is recreated by a painted landscape, the trees are not supposed capable to give us shade, or the fountains coolness; but we consider how we should be pleased with such fountains playing beside us and such woods waving over us" (57). We enter the world of art imaginatively; we identify ourselves with its representation, but only up to a point, not entirely. When talking of the actor identifying himself so wholly with his role that he considered himself to be the character he was representing, Johnson declared, "And if Garrick really believed himself to be that monster, Richard the Third, he deserved to be hanged every time he performed it" (*Life*, p. 1252, [Oct, 1783]). Total identification for Johnson is not only undesirable but ridiculous.

In Johnson's view we derive a special kind of pleasure from art because it is an improvement upon life. "The greatest graces of a play are to copy nature and instruct life" (61). Here Johnson uses the word 'instruct' not in the narrow, didactic sense of 'to teach', but rather, to recreate the experience of life in terms of the dramatist's own vision, "for it is always a writer's duty to make the world better" (33), Johnson has said earlier. Nature is the base, but the dramatist's art improves upon it; the finished product is a remoulding of life near to the heart's desire. Yeats expresses the same idea differently:

All those things whereof
Man makes a superhuman
Mirror-resembling dream.

('The Tower')

The work of art resembles, because it mirrors, life; yet it also embodies the dream of the artist that made him want to reshape his experience of life into something rich and strange. Life is often untidy, ugly, unjust; the dramatist in his art does not show us what life is, but what it should be.

How, then, according to Johnson, is the dramatist to bring about 'pleasure' in the reader? Unrelieved suffering and grief may well be true to life, but as we have seen, for Johnson, art is not to be a tame copy of nature. Suffering must be relieved by laughter, and vice versa, in the play, for "all pleasure consists in variety" (21), he tells us. The first great quality in *Hamlet* that wins Johnson's approval is "the praise of variety" (Note on *Hamlet*); in *Antony and Cleopatra* "the variety of incidents, and the quick succession of one personage to another, call the mind forward without intermission from the first act to the last" (Note on *Antony and Cleopatra*); and *Macbeth* is "deservedly celebrated for the ... variety of its action" (Note on *Macbeth*). "Through all these denominations of the drama, Shakespeare's mode of composition is the same: an interchange of seriousness and merriment, by which the mind is softened at one time and exhilirated at another" (26). We must pause here so as to consider the sense in which Johnson employs the word 'composition'—the action of combining, a conscious and deliberate process aimed at achieving a certain end. Thus when Johnson says that Shakespeare's plays are "compositions" of a distinct kind; exhibiting the real state of sublunary nature, which partakes of good and evil, joy and sorrow" (17), he sees the dramatist as one who rearranges life so as to form a combination that can yield aesthetic pleasure. Johnson's approval of the "mingled drama" of Shakespeare is based on two counts: first, that it comes near "to the appearance of life," to nature, and second, that "the high and the low," or the serious and the comic, "cooperate in the general system by unavoidable concatenation." Shakespeare juxtaposes these varied elements so as to promote the overall design, "the general system," and it is in the creation of this design that the dramatist's artistic triumph lies (20).

At the same time, for Johnson, the act of creation is not mechanical. There is no formula for success that the dramatist can follow. A play may fulfil all the demands of the exacting critic and yet fail to move the reader. Johnson finds that *Troilus and Cressida* "is more correctly written than most of Shakespeare's compositions but it is not one of those in which either the extent of his views or elevation of his fancy is fully displayed" (Note on *Troilus and Cressida*). Though technically sound, it fails to grip the reader and so fails to earn full marks from Johnson. On the other hand, Johnson observes that *The Merry Wives of Windsor* suffers from many weaknesses, chief of which is that "Falstaff could not love but by ceasing to be Falstaff." In addition, "the conduct of the drama is deficient; the action begins and ends often before the conclusion," yet Johnson goes on to recognize the dramatic power the play possesses, "that power by which all works of genius shall finally be tried," for the play "never yet had reader or spectator who did not think it too soon at an end" (Note on *The Merry Wives*). Shakespeare is, for Johnson, the author who can flout all the rules of dramatic construction with impunity, and yet triumph.

Johnson's defence of Shakespeare against the charge of violating the unities might seem to us today like a soldier shooting at a straw man, but in Johnson's time the issue was very much alive. Shakespeare was often faulted for having disregarded the unities. Dryden, among others, had criticised Shakespeare for writing history plays that "are rather so many chronicles of kings, or the business many times of 30 or 40 years, cramped into a representation of two hours and a half." And, as is well known, Ben Jonson had long before, in his prologue to *Every Man In His Humour*, laughed at Shakespeare's failure to observe the unities. From the time of Corneille onwards, eighteenth-century dramatists in England had drawn their inspiration from the ancients through the medium of the French classical dramatists. Johnson's vindication of Shakespeare is on the grounds that drama is an imaginative experience, not a slice of life. As we have seen, Johnson insists on "our consciousness of fiction" being an essential ingredient in our enjoyment of drama. As such, the unities of time and place are not essential in order that drama might create its effects. Johnson explains our flexibility of approach when dealing with them to the fact that "in contemplation we easily contract the time of real actions and therefore willingly permit it to be contracted when we only see their imitation" (55). By making such a comparison Johnson is lifting drama out of the world of the actual and placing it in the realm of the imagination. As in real life, when we look back at past events that have taken place over a span of many years and compress them into a few moments, our minds dominating time and distance, so does the dramatist through his art bend and shape the stuff of life to suit his requirements.

For Johnson, the play takes place in the mind of the spectator and what passes on the stage is only a pointer towards this inner reality. Johnson ironically tells us that no sane spectator "really imagines himself at Alexandria and believes that his walk to the theatre has been a voyage to Egypt" (53). Such a literal acceptance of drama would deny to the spectator's imagination the power of appreciating "the comprehensive genius of Shakespeare" (59). Johnson concludes his argument by placing firmly within their own respective spheres the reality of life and the imaginative reality of art: ". . . the action is not supposed to be real" (58)—a statement so obvious that it reduces to absurdity the strenuous attempts of those who would seek to govern drama by the laws of life. It is in Johnson that we can detect some of the great liberating influences that later found their fullest expression in romantic critical theory, particularly that of Coleridge, which emphasized the autonomy of the work of art. It was Coleridge who maintained that the writer must not try to make a surface reproduction of nature's details, but "must imitate that which is within the thing for so only can he hope to produce any work truly natural in the object and truly human in the effect."

A play, then, is, for Johnson, an artifice, an arrangement of life, a pattern, and the behaviour of the characters is in conformity with its demands, or what he calls "unavoidable concatenation" (20). Accompanying this, their behaviour is to be psychologically consistent with the situations in which they find themselves placed. In the greatest art the two coincide exactly. Johnson finds this psychological truth in Shakespeare: "Shakespeare approximates the remote and familiarizes the wonderful; the event which he represents will not happen, but, if it were possible, its effects would probably be such as he has assigned" (13). The psychological plausibility of the character's behaviour is a stroke of realism even though the situation might be one that is never encountered in life. Thus Johnson objects neither to the Ghost in *Hamlet* nor to the Ghost in *Julius Caesar*. Eighteenth-century rationalism and twentieth-century scepticism may, along with Horatio in *Hamlet*, dismiss ghosts as being improbable, but to Johnson this objection is irrelevant, for "Shakespeare . . . has not only shown human nature as it acts in real exigences, but as it would be found in trials to which it cannot be exposed" (13). Art exists on the frontier that separates the real from the unreal, and it exploits this strategic location by raiding both territories.

Dr. Johnson's insistence on the artist being an artificer, a maker, finds perhaps its most powerful expression in his objection to the death of Cordelia, a passage that has become famous: "And if my sensations could add anything to the general suffrage, I might relate that I was many years ago so shocked by Cordelia's death that I know not whether I ever endured to read again the last scenes of the play till I undertook to revise them as an editor" (Note on *Lear*). Though Johnson insists that drama is not life, that "the spectators are always in their senses and know, from the first act to the last, that the stage is only a stage, and that the players are only players" (54), he feels that Cordelia's death oversteps the limits of artistic decorum, and here we should note that Johnson grants that in real life the death of Cordelia would be permissible because not improbable, but not in art. "A play in which the wicked prosper and the virtuous miscarry may doubtless be good, because it is a just representation of the common events of human life; but since all reasonable beings naturally love justice, I cannot easily be persuaded that the observation of justice makes a play worse" (Note on *Lear*).

As is well known, to Johnson death and damnation were very terrible and very real. Throughout his *Life*, Boswell tells us time and again of his "aweful dread of death, or rather, 'of something after death" (p. 579, [Friday, 20 January, 1775]), of "the horror of death which I had always observed in Dr. Johnson" (p. 839, [Wednesday, 17 September, 1777]), of Johnson's own statements while in conversation with Boswell and Mrs. Knowles:

> MRS. KNOWLES. The Scriptures tell us, 'The righteous shall have *hope* in his death'. JOHNSON. Yes, Madam; that is, he shall not have despair. But consider, his hope of salvation must be founded on the terms on which it is promised that the mediation of our SAVIOUR shall be applied to us,—namely, obedience; and where obedience has failed, then, as suppletory to it, repentance. But what man can say that his obedience has been such, as he would approve of in another, or even in himself upon close examination . . .. MRS. KNOWLES. But divine intimation of acceptance may be made to the soul. JOHNSON. Madam, it may; but I should

not think the better of a man who should tell me on his death-bed he was sure of salvation . . . . BOSWELL. Then, Sir, we must be contented to acknowledge that death is a terrible thing. JOHNSON. Yes, Sir. I have made no approaches to a state which can look on it as not terrible (pp 949-50, [Wednesday, 15 April, 1778]).

If the prospect of natural death was so dreadful to Johnson, it need not surprise us that a death like that of Cordelia, undeserved and unjustified in his eyes, should have been unbearably horrifying. Likewise it makes little difference to him that *Hamlet* is a play and not historical truth. The horror of damnation is so overwhelming that its impact on him, though this be but in the context of a play, causes him to declare that the following passage, in which Hamlet "contrives damnation for the man that he would punish, is too horrible to be read or to be uttered" (Note on *Hamlet*):

Up, sword, and know thou a more horrid hent.
When he is drunk asleep, or in his rage,
Or in the incestuous pleasure of his bed—
At gaming, swearing, or about some act
That has no relish of salvation in't—
Then trip him, that his heels may kick at Heaven
And that his soul may be as damned and black
As Hell, whereto it goes (III, iii, 88-95).

Is Johnson confusing life with art? In a sense, yes; but in another sense, no. Johnson is granting to Shakespeare's art the highest honour that he can confer upon it, namely, that of recognising its power to be more disturbing than even life itself.

We should recall that the murder of Duncan does not shock him, nor is he particularly disturbed by the rejection of Falstaff (Notes on *Macbeth* & *2H4*). It has been suggested that the sturdy unsentimentality of Johnson prevents him from voicing the kind of indignation against Hal that the nineteenth-century felt so abundantly, perhaps most representatively displayed in A.C. Bradley's sensitive essay "The Rejection of Falstaff."[15] But Johnson, as we have seen, is not invariably unsentimental; often it is his feelings that determine his response to Shakespeare: he laments "the untimely death of Ophelia, the young, the beautiful, the harmless, and the pious" (Note on *Hamlet*). Perhaps there is another reason for Johnson resenting so strongly the death of Cordelia, but not those of many other characters in Shakespeare who perish. Thus; in *Romeo and Juliet*, Johnson is captivated by "Mercutio's wit, gaiety, and courage," adding that he will always have "friends that wish him a longer life," yet, at the same time, Johnson is not unduly distressed by his premature death because "his death is not precipitated, he has lived out the time allotted him in the construction of the play" (Note on *Romeo and Juliet*). Perhaps it is in this remark that we must find the answer to our question.

Johnson's remark indicates that for him a character in a play is not simply a human being lifted from life and transplanted into a different environment, but rather, he now lives a new kind of life "in the construction of the play." Artistic necessity determines the slaying of Mercutio; he has fulfilled his function in the requirements that the play posits and may now be disposed of without loss to the artistic beauty of the whole.

On the other hand, for Johnson, the slaying of Cordelia and "the extrusion of Gloucester's eyes" are acts that are not dictated by artistic necessity but are gratuitous and do not arise inevitably from the events preceding them. Cordelia's death goes "contrary to the natural ideas of justice, to the hope of the reader." In contrast to this, Johnson approves on aesthetic grounds of Edmund's role in the play, for here Shakespeare has made him "cooperate with the chief design" (Note on *Lear*), or, in other words, Edmund's villainy has its larger counterpart in that of Lear's two elder daughters, and it is this that constitutes the chief design of the play. Again, in contrast to the death of Cordelia, Johnson found Desdemona's murder painful, but not inartistic. His comment on this scene, "I am glad that I have ended my revisal of this dreadful scene. It is not to be endured" (Note on *Othello*), is the highest compliment that Johnson can pay Shakespeare. Here is, for Johnson, an instance of Shakespeare's supreme power to command our emotions at his will, to agitate our minds. "Every man finds his mind more strongly seized by the tragedies of Shakespeare than of any other writer" (71). Johnson is shaken by Desdemona's death even as when reading *Macbeth* he "looks round alarmed and starts to find himself alone" (Note on *Macbeth*).

If we consider Johnson's reactions to Shakespeare's four greatest tragedies under his 'General Observations," we find him detecting some faults in each of them, the only exception being *Othello*. The faults in *King Lear* we have already looked at; *Macbeth* has "solemnity, grandeur, and variety . . . but it has no nice discriminations of character" (Note on *Macbeth*); *Hamlet* has "the praise of variety," yet "the conduct is perhaps not wholly secure against objections." There is no "adequate cause" for the feigned madness of Hamlet. "The catastrophe is not very happily produced." The Ghost appears "to little purpose" for Hamlet dies while in the act of carrying out his behest (Note on *Hamlet*). But for *Othello* Johnson's admiration is unalloyed. "The beauties of this play impress themselves so strongly upon the attention of the reader that they can draw no aid from critical illustration." Johnson has unreserved praise for the character delineation in *Othello* which displays "Shakespeare's skill in human nature." So impressed is he by the artistic perfection of this play that he concludes with the observation, "Had the scene opened in Cyprus, and the preceding incidents been occasionally related, there had been little wanting to a drama of the most exact and scrupulous regularity" (Note on *Othello*).

Why is it that Johnson considers Desdemona's end, though painful, not objectionable—unlike that of Cordelia? Perhaps the answer lies in his note on the play in which, analysing the Othello-Desdemona relationship, he finds it based on "deceit and falsehood," and eyes askance "the imprudent generosity of disproportionate marriages" which, "when the first heat of passion is over," are easily succeeded by suspicion." Also we should recall Boswell's record of Johnson having insisted that "*Othello* has more moral than almost any play." Desdemona's death is not gratuitous for she and Othello have wilfully entered into "an unequal match" which is instrumental in causing Othello to yield so "readily to suspicion" (*Life*, p. 745, [Friday, 12 April, 1776]). Johnson views Cordelia, on the other hand, as an innocent victim. We may disagree with Johnson's reasons for accepting Desdemona's death as artistic, and for taking umbrage at Cordelia's death for having gone "contrary to the natural ideas of justice, to the hope of the reader" (Note on *Lear*), but we cannot maintain that Johnson's objections are groundless. Granting him the consistency of his normal sensibilities, we must conclude that for him art and morality go hand in hand, that the latter validates and reinforces the former. A play in which these important moral considerations are flouted cannot but be inartistic.

Till recently, critics have tended to be indignant with Johnson for reducing the romantic relationship between Othello and Desdemona to one of deception and disproportion,[16] but of late a few voices have been raised that would seem to vindicate Johnson's position. Desdemona is now not always regarded as being totally innocent and uncalculating, and Iago has come to be viewed by some as not so much the cause of the rift between Othello and Desdemona, as the catalyst that precipitates the rift.[17] Thus what might have seemed to be an excessively moralistic and heavy handed stricture by Johnson on the Othello/Desdemona relationship, may now be seen as a profound insight into the psychological truth that lies behind the play.

Johnson's disagreement with Rymer for having suggested that the handkerchief was responsible for the tragedy (Thomas Rymer, *Short View of Tragedy*: " . . . a warning to all good Wives, that they look well to their Linnen") derives from his approach to the play as being a psychological drama in which the situations are subordinate to a deeper truth inherent in the characters and their relationships with one another. "The handkerchief," Johnson said, in conversation with Boswell, "is merely a trick, though a very pretty trick. . . . No, Sir, I think *Othello* has more moral than almost any play" (*Life*, p. 745, [Friday, 12 April, 1776]). Johnson dismisses the handkerchief as being something ancillary to what is basic, namely, the inequality of the match and Othello's credulity.

Art and Morality

Aesthetic pleasure for Johnson is closely related to morality. Whereas in Johnson's age the tendency was to believe that the pleasure principle was subordinate to a moral purpose, Johnson holds that only that art can yield true pleasure which is undergirded by a serious moral framework. With Johnson, then, pleasure is not secondary to morality, but the two coexist; they are not separate ingredients, but rather, together they form a compound, a new product, an organic whole. It is in these terms that Johnson regrets Shakespeare s failing to give us, in the last act of *As You Like It*, the scene between Duke Frederick and the hermit that brought about the former's repentance and transformation from sinner to saint. While it is possible for us to regard Johnson's complaint against Shakespeare as being excessively conditioned by his moral preoccupations, on the other hand it is equally possible to argue that artistically Johnson is right. We are naturally anxious to know what marvellous advice the "old religious man" gave to Duke Frederick that converted him in a few brief moments from sinner to saint. Duke Frederick's transformation is an integral part of the play for Johnson, not merely the convenient "happy ending" that Shakespeare has turned it into.

It is also possible to argue that Johnson here expects from Shakespeare something more substantial than what the sentimental drama of the eighteenth century could offer. Colley Cibber, Johnson's contemporary and a popular dramatist whom Johnson heartily despised (see *Life*, pp. 416, 1252, [Thursday, 19 October, 1769, and October 1783]), had set the fashion for the sentimental comedy that flourished at the time. In Cibber's play *Love's Last Shift* (1696) the usual licentious characters and themes of the period are to be found, but in the last act of the play a 'moral' ending is superimposed—all the sinners repent and turn into saints. Perhaps it is on account of Johnson's distaste for this kind of an artificial and hypocritical morality that he resents Shakespeare having taken the same kind of a short cut in concluding *As You Like It* with Duke Frederick's astonishing conversion. Still, Johnson will not condemn Shakespeare for this. Because Shakespeare is "hastening to the end of his work," he "suppressed the dialogue between the usurper and the hermit and lost an opportunity of exhibiting a moral lesson in which he might have found matter worthy of his highest powers" (Note on *As You Like It*). Himself only too well aware of the pressures under which an author often writes, Johnson is ready to excuse Shakespeare for his lapses because occasioned by similar pressures.

It is as the result of such pressures giving rise to haste and carelessness that Johnson complains about Shakespeare having sacrificed, "virtue to convenience" (33). In Act V of *All's Well* "Shakespeare is now hastening to the end of the play" and so is not particularly concerned about retribution being meted out to the villain, Bertram. Despite his despicable behaviour, he is "dismissed to happiness" (Note on *All's Well*), and Johnson finds it impossible to reconcile himself to the manner in which Shakespeare concludes the play. Likewise Johnson notes of Angelo in *Measure for Measure* that "every reader feels some indignation when he finds him spared." Before objecting to Dr. Johnson's charge against Shakespeare for making "no just distribution of good or evil" (33), we should ask ourselves whether *Othello* would have been aesthetically satisfying without Emilia's denunciation of Othello, and his subsequent death, and likewise *Macbeth*, without our witnessing Macbeth's receiving due retribution in the form of his head being brought on stage by a victorious Macduff. Clearly, in these cases moral judgement is an integral part of the aesthetic experience, and Johnson's unhappiness at this fundamental truth being at times ignored by Shakespeare is consistent with the approval with which we regard the endings of *Othello* and *Macbeth*.

To Johnson, Shakespeare often "makes no just distribution of good or evil" because he "is so much more careful to please than to instruct" (33). Thus the marriage of Olivia to Sebastian in *Twelfth Night* fails to satisfy Johnson because it is simply a marriage of convenience. Shakespeare wanted to send his audience home happy, and since Olivia cannot marry Viola, her twin brother will do equally well. Johnson concedes that such an ending is "well enough contrived to divert on the stage," but it "wants credibility and fails to produce the proper instruction required in the drama" (Note on *Twelfth Night*). Is Johnson bringing to Shakespeare's comedies too literal a mind to catch the strains that poetic drama emits? Is his critical sensibility too sturdily commonsensical to truly appreciate the subtleties of Shakespearean comedy? It would be easy to reply in the affirmative and dismiss Johnson for his apparent insistence on comedy being as consistent as life itself. But, perhaps, by so doing, we would overlook Johnson's warm approval of Shakespeare's comic scenes: ". . . in comedy he seems to repose, or to luxuriate, as in a mode of thinking congenial to his nature"; ". . . his comedy often surpasses expectation or desire"; ". . . his comedy pleases by the thoughts and the language"; and "his comedy seems [to be] instinct" (28). For this side of Shakespeare Johnson's appreciation knows no dilution, but when Shakespeare hurries towards his endings with little regard for plausibility or propriety, Johnson states his disapproval. He wishes that Shakespeare had brought to the writing of his plays, from start to finish, the same high seriousness that manifests itself so impressively in his best scenes.

Tragedy

To what extent does Johnson's psychology colour his attitude to tragedy, particularly Shakespearean tragedy? Johnson was subject to frequent fits of melancholy which he considered closely allied to madness. "He laboured under a severe depression of spirits" is Boswell's observation on Johnson during 1765, the year in which his edition of Shakespeare appeared (*Life*, p. 345). A devotional record of Johnson, dated 1767, reads thus, "I have been disturbed and unsettled for a long time" (*Ibid*, p. 386); and a year later we find Boswell observing, "It appears from his notes of the state of his mind, that he suffered great perturbation and distraction in 1768" (*Ibid*, p. 387). Boswell goes on to point out that the opening lines of the prologue, written by Johnson, to Goldsmith's play *The Good-natured Man*, a comedy, are paradoxically full of pessimism and reflect "the dismal gloom of his mind":

> Press'd with the load of life, the weary mind
> Surveys the general toil of human kind
>
> (*Ibid*, p. 387).

It is not difficult for us to see why Johnson should have felt that Shakespeare's plays, which exhibit "good and evil, joy and sorrow, mingled with endless variety of proportion and innumerable modes of combination" (17), by coming so close to his own experience of life enriched his "consciousness of being" (*Life*, p. 363 [Saturday, 10 May, 1766]), a striking description of himself that Johnson made in a letter written a year after his *Shakespeare* was published.[18]

Oppressed as Johnson was by melancholia, it is not surprising that Boswell should record an after-breakfast conversation with Johnson, that took place eleven years later, in the following gloomy terms: "On Saturday, September 20, after breakfast, when Taylor was gone out to his farm, Dr. Johnson and I had a serious conversation by ourselves on melancholy and madness" (*Life*, p. 856 [Saturday, 20 September, 1777]). We recall that the learned astronomer in *Rasselas*, who labours under various fantastic delusions, confesses to fears that haunted Johnson all his life—the fear of loneliness and the dark: " 'If I am accidentally left alone for a few hours', said he, 'my inveterate persuasion rushes upon my soul, and my thoughts are chained down by some irresistible violence . . . I am like a man habitually afraid of spectres, who is set at ease by a lamp and wonders at the dread which harassed him in the dark, yet, if his lamp be extinguished, feels again the terrors which he knows that when it is light he shall feel no more.' "[19] Good sense and reason must acknowledge defeat when confronted by a primeval terror that brings into existence a plane of consciousness long submerged. "He that peruses Shakespeare looks round alarmed and starts to find himself alone" is one of Johnson's observations on the scene preceeding the murder of Duncan, a scene of darkness in which "nothing but sorcery, lust, and murder is awake" (Note on *Macbeth*).

The astronomer's unhappy experience resembles that of Johnson as may be seen in Johnson's prescription for melancholia, reported by Boswell: "We put up at the Angel inn, and passed the evening by ourselves in easy and familiar conversation. Talking of constitutional melancholy, he observed, 'A man so afflicted, Sir, must divert distressing thoughts, and not combat with them.' BOSWELL. 'May not he think them down, Sir? JOHNSON. 'No Sir. To attempt to *think them down* is madness. He should have a lamp constantly burning in his bed-chamber during the night, and if wakefully disturbed, take a book, and read, and compose himself to rest" (*Life*, p. 690 [Wednesday, 20 March, 1776]). According to Johnson, the remedy for melancholia is diversion. Understandably, the power of Shakespearean tragedy was too painful for him, unless relieved by comedy, and this, as we have seen, explains his appreciation for plays characterized by "variety."

Johnson, shaken by the deaths of Desdemona and Cordelia, is in the same frame of mind as Keats was in when he sat down to read *King Lear* once again.

> . . . once again, the fierce dispute
> Betwixt damnation and impassion'd clay
> Must I burn through; once more humbly assay
> The bitter-sweet of this Shakespearean fruit.

Does Johnson bring to Shakespearean tragedy a sensibility acuter than what the age of reason would readily allow? Is it possible that Johnson's deep sympathy for the weak and the helpless nourished his response to Shakespearean tragedy? The Johnson who, while himself almost destitute, "was accustomed to slip pennies into the fists of sleeping urchins,"[20] who "frequently gave all the silver in his pocket to the poor" (*Life*, p. 437 [1770]), who for many years maintained in his own house a group of penniless dependents, otherwise virtual outcasts from society, and who carried home and gave shelter to a poor and diseased woman till she was fully recovered (*Ibid*, p. 1313 [June, 1784]) was a man particularly sensitive to the painful in Shakespeare's plays. Though Johnson can comfortably assure us that "the delight of tragedy proceeds from our consciousness of fiction; if we thought murders and treasons real, they would please no more" (56), there are moments when Johnson the man comes closer to the truth than Johnson the critic.

We have already considered Johnson's vindication of Shakespeare against the criticism that he mingled his tragic and comic scenes to the detriment of both. Perhaps erroneously, Johnson goes on to deny to Shakespeare and his age the sense of an organic tragic—or comic—unity in any particular play. Whereas much twentieth-century criticism has come to regard Shakespeare's tragedies and comedies as distinct genres, creations produced out of a distinct mode of apprehending reality and having an intrinsic controlling artistic consistency, Johnson, along with his age, would tend to regard Shakespeare and the Elizabethans as devoid of this heightened artistic sensibility. Yet Johnson is not pejorative here. He simply points it out as a trait indicative of the naivete that marked the Elizabethans. Heminge and Condell, Johnson points out, "who in their edition divided our author's works into comedies, histories, and tragedies, seem not to have distinguished the three kinds by any very exact or definite ideas" (22). It was the ending that determined whether a play was a tragedy or a comedy, and even the history plays were "not always very nicely distiguished from tragedy," Johnson tells us (25). Johnson sees Shakespeare's plays as being neither tragedies nor comedies, but rather, "an interchange of seriousness and merriment, by which the mind is softened at one time and exhilirated at another" (26).

It is important to recognize that though we in the twentieth century might resent Johnson's declining to grant Shakespeare a controlling vision—whether tragic or comic—that informs his plays, Johnson, far from censuring Shakespeare for his eclectic and all-comprehensive survey of life, praises him for the range and variety of emotions that he can elicit from his audience: "As he commands us, we laugh or mourn" (26).

With this background we now come to Johnson's famous attack on Shakespeare's tragedies: "In tragedy he often writes, with great appearance of toil and study, what is written at last with little felicity; but, in his comic scenes, he seems to produce without labour, what no labour can improve. In tragedy he is always struggling after some occasion to be comic; but in comedy he seems to repose, or to luxuriate, as in a mode of thinking congenial to his nature. In his tragic scenes there is always something wanting, but his comedy often surpasses expectation or desire. His comedy pleases by thoughts and the language, and his tragedy for the greater part by incident and action. His tragedy seems to be skill, his comedy to be instinct" (28). A severe indictment, but what exactly does Johnson mean?

As we have seen, when Johnson uses the term 'tragedy' he is not using it as Bradley does in his book *Shakespearean Tragedy.* Whereas Bradley applies the term to the four great tragedies of Shakespeare, Johnson is thinking of individual scenes that have a tragic complexion, what Johnson calls "serious or distressful" (23). That Johnson is thinking only of scenes and not of entire plays is suggested in his statement quoted above, "In tragedy . . . but in his comic scenes. . . ." Nor is he thinking of the action or the psychology in the plays, but essentially of the language, the verbal aspects of such scenes. This may seem inconsistent to us who have been led to believe by modern critical theory that language and content are inseparable, that content is realised and expressed only through language. But it must be remembered that the eighteenth-century view of this matter was different. A thought, or an idea, was one thing; its expression something else. An idea could be good, but its expression poor. Pope's well known line, "What oft was thought, but ne'er so well expressed," sums up this attitude best. Perhaps the most cogent argument that can be advanced in favour of this attitude is the fact that poets revise their early drafts time and again until they are satisfied that the finished product is a poem. The revisions of a Keats, a Yeats, or an Eliot are all endeavours to suit the word to the thought, and even the thought to the word. Yeat's lines from "Adam's Curse" come to mind:

> I said, "A line will take us hours maybe;
> Yet if it does not seem a moment's thought,
> Our stitching and unstitching has been naught."

And Johnson, who raised conversation to a fine art, confessed to Boswell "that he always laboured when he said a good thing," and that "it delighted him, on a review, to find that his conversation teemed with point. and imagery" (*Life*, p. 923 [Friday, 10 April, 1778]). Imagery enhances the idea which might otherwise have remained bare and unadorned.

Johnson's displeasure with Shakespeare for writing his tragic scenes "with great appearance of toil and study, what is written at last with little felicity" arises from what he considers is Shakespeare's failure—on account of carelessness—to polish his language to perfection. Johnson faults Shakespeare's obscurity of language, a propensity that manifests itself more readily in his tragic than in his comic scenes. As examples, Johnson draws, not upon the four greatest tragedies, but upon the other plays. In *Richard II* (III, iii, 155) he feels that the lines "Or I'll be buried in the King's high way,/Some way of common Trade, where Subject's feet/May hourly trample on their Sovereign's head" are pathetic and therefore moving, but when Richard goes on to dilate on his predicament in the light of this metaphor, "For on my heart they tread now whilst I live,/And buried once, why not upon my head," Johnson finds his sentiments excessive: "Shakespeare is very apt to deviate from the pathetick to the ridiculous" (Note on *Richard II*). Here is an example of Johnson's complaint against Shakespeare that "in tragedy he is always struggling after some occasion to be comic."

Again, in *Antony and Cleopatra* (IV, ix, 15, Johnson is unhappy with Shakespeare for giving Enobarbus lines that sink him into bathos. Johnson's comment on the lines "Throw my heart/Against the flint and hardness of my fault" is uttered more in sorrow than in anger: "The pathetick of Shakespeare too often ends in the ridiculous. It is painful to find the gloomy dignity of this noble scene destroyed by the intrusion of a conceit so far-fetched and unaffecting" (Note on *Antony & Cleopatra*). Johnson's impatience with Shakespeare evidently arises from his sense of being let down after having been raised to a high pitch of expectation. Had Shakespeare been a lesser poet, Johnson's expectations would have been proportionately modest. But with Shakespeare the potential is always so great; the fulfilment sometimes inadequate. In short, Johnson's criticism of Shakespeare's tragic scenes is born out of his admiration for him. Of the last act of *Henry V* Johnson has this to say: "The truth is, that the poet's matter failed him in the fifth act, and he was glad to fill it up with whatever he could get; and not even Shakespeare can write well without a proper subject. It is a vain endeavour for the most skilful hand to cultivate barrenness, or to paint upon vacuity" (Note on *Henry V*). Johnson would regard the last act of the play as essentially serious, and as such, necessitating a treatment that would do justice to it; but on the other hand, here is an instance of Johnson's complaint, "In his tragic scenes there is always something wanting."

Repeatedly Johnson finds Shakespeare's tragic scenes marred by a sudden drop in the emotional temperature caused by some infelicity of language—a pun, a conceit, a hyperbole. In his general observations on *Romeo and Juliet* Johnson is vexed by Shakespeare's femme fatale, the pun: "His comick scenes are happily wrought, but his pathetick strains are always polluted with some unexpected depravations. His persons, however distressed, *have a conceit left them in their misery, a miserable conceit*" (Note on *Romeo & Juliet*). And for Othello's lines, "This Sorrow's heavenly;/It strikes, where it doth love" (V, ii, 21-22), Johnson's embarrassment springs from an attitude that is clearly possessive: "I wish these two lines could be honestly ejected. It is the fate of Shakespeare to counteract his own pathos" (Note on *Othello*). Such criticism is born of genuine admiration.

When Johnson praises Shakespeare's tragic scenes for their "incident and action," he could well have in mind the scene in which Macbeth gradually yields to the instigation to murder, furnished by Lady Macbeth. Of Macbeth's declaration. "I dare do all that may become a man" (I, vii, 46), Johnson is categoric in his praise: it "ought to bestow immortality on the author, though all his other productions had been lost" (Note on

Macbeth). In the section above entitled "Johnson's Response to Shakespeare's Poetry" (see p. 43) we have noted several other examples of Johnson's deep appreciation for Shakespeare's insight into human nature and for his dramatic craftsmanship. Of Hamlet's "To be, or not to be" soliloquy Johnson has much to say. He sees it as an utterance "bursting from a man distracted with contrariety of desires and overwhelmed with the magnitude of his own purposes." Shakespeare, Johnson remarks, has translated the pressure of Hamlet's thoughts as they pass through his mind into a coherent utterance of the tongue, a magnificent achievement. Johnson adds, "I shall endeavour to discover the train [of ideas], and to show how one sentiment produces another." What follows this is Johnson's masterly paraphrase of Hamlet's soliloquy (Note on *Hamlet*).

However, Johnson does not restrict himself to commenting on the tragic scenes in Shakespeare; he can, like Bradley, view Shakespeare as a writer of plays that are tragedies in their overall design and execution. This he does in his consideration of Shakespeare's handling of his sources with the superb statement, "... every man finds his mind more strongly seized by the tragedies of Shakespeare than of any other writer" (71). Here Johnson views the tragedies as composite and organic works of art that have an overwhelming tragic purpose and meaning. In fact, here Johnson is not concerned with "particular speeches" but rather, with Shakespeare's achievement in having created a work of art that grips us from beginning to ending. Shakespeare "always makes us anxious for the event" and it is this compelling power that he alone shares with Homer. We may well be surprised at Johnson's apparent *volte-face*. Whereas earlier he had criticized Shakespeare for often falling short of perfection in his tragic scenes, here he regards Shakespeare's tragedies as being incomparable.

While, as we have seen, in the former passages Johnson is thinking of individual scenes that have a tragic setting and in the latter passage of the tragedies in their entirety—a significant distinction—it is also true that Johnson's critical approach is one of balance, of praise followed by blame. The *Preface* is built up on this dialectical framework, and George Watson aptly points out that this underlies all Johnson's criticism, "The most rapturous paragraphs, such as those that conclude the critical section of the Life of Pope, are always balanced by a hint of detraction. A eulogy beginning: 'Pope had, in proportions very nicely adjusted to each other, all the qualities that constitute genius . . .' may end: 'The construction of his language is not always strictly grammatical; . . . nor was he very careful to vary his terminations or to refuse admission at a small distance to the same rhymes.' The ferrule is always to Johnson's hand ready for use."[21] It is precisely because Johnson can pass strictures on Shakespeare, that his praise of Shakespeare is so meaningful.

Conclusion

In conclusion, the following aspects of Johnson on Shakespeare may be restated. Johnson defends Shakespeare against the charges of disregarding the unities and combining tragic and comic scenes in the same play, not simply on argumentative grounds but also with the categoric and resounding declaration, "It is time therefore, to tell him by the authority of Shakespeare . . . ." (52) Here we have, perhaps for the first time in the history of Shakespearean criticism, an assertion of the plenary rule that Shakespeare exercises over the minds of men, which is able to silence the fussy objections of critics. Shakespeare is no longer a subject; he becomes a lawgiver. It is with Johnson that we detect in embryonic form—and even more fully developed at times—the emancipation of Shakespeare from rule and precepts that was to reach its finest manifestation in the nineteenth and twentieth centuries.

This exaltation of Shakespeare was to find expression in other directions as well. True, the character criticism of Coleridge and Hazlitt had been anticipated by eighteenth-century critics besides Johnson, most notably by Dryden and Maurice Morgann, the last named having written his celebrated *Essay on the Dramatic Character of Sir John Falstaff* (1777), but it was Johnson who, twelve years earlier, had addressed Falstaff face to face, as one man speaking to another, a remarkable recognition of an imaginative creation, a character in a play, overleaping the time barrier and the limits of art and becoming a contemporary, as real as a person one encounters in life: "But Falstaff, unimitated, unimitable Falstaff, how shall I describe thee?" (Note on *2H4*).

Again, in stressing that Shakespeare's style, language, and

phraseology are predominantly drawn from "the common intercourse of life, among those who speak only to be understood, without ambition of elegance" (30), Johnson anticipates Wordsworth in his *Preface to the Lyrical Ballads* where he states that his poetry is based on "the real language of men in a state of vivid sensation" and on "humble and rustic life . . . because in that condition, the essential passions of the heart find a better soil in which they can attain their maturity." Over thirty years before this had Johnson said much the same thing in praise of Shakespeare who prefers "the vulgar" above "the polite" and "the learned": "The polite are always catching modish innovations, and the learned depart from established forms of speech in hope of finding or making better; those who wish for distinction forsake the vulgar, when the vulgar is right" (30). Both Johnson and Wordsworth insist on the language of the common man being the stuff of enduring poetry. In Johnson we see the dawn of the romantic sensibility.

For Johnson, Shakespeare is a phenomenon appearing on the scene Minerva-like, fully formed. Johnson is not concerned with seeing him as a part of a tradition, as being a link in a chain. Shakespeare inherits nothing from his literary or dramatic forbears because he is the pioneer, the starting point, in the development of dramatic art. Before Shakespeare arrives on the scene, all is rude and desolate.

> When Learning's Triumph o'er her barb'rous Foes
> First rear'd the Stage, immortal Shakespeare rose,

are the opening lines of Johnson's *Prologue* to be spoken at the inauguration of the Drury Lane Theatre in 1747 (See p. 83). Shakespeare's age in Johnson's eyes was naive, gazing with open-eyed wonder at "strange events and fabulous transactions" (67), and Shakespeare transforms these legends and tales of a romantic past, by the power of his art, into plays that hold "up to his readers a faithful mirror of manners and of life" (8). And though Johnson may call in question certain aspects of his art, he maintains that Shakespeare is to be praised for his total achievement, for his ability to capture our minds and hold them enthralled while we read his plays. It is appropriate that we conclude this Introduction with Johnson's splendid tribute to

Shakespeare in his "Life of Dryden" where he speaks of great literature affording "allurement and delight":

> Works of imagination excel by their allurement and delight; by their power of attracting and detaining the attention. That book is good in vain, which the reader throws away. He only is the master, who keeps the mind in pleasing captivity; whose pages are perused with eagerness, and in hope of new pleasure are perused again; and whose conclusion is perceived with an eye of sorrow, such as the traveller casts upon departing day.
>
> By his proportion of this predomination I will consent that Dryden should be tried; of this, which, in opposition to reason, makes Ariosto the darling and the pride of Italy; of this, which, in defiance of criticism, continues Shakespeare the sovereign of the drama.[22]

THE TEXTS

Prologue (1747)

Spoken by Mr Garrick
at the Opening of the Theatre in Drury Lane 1747[1]

When learning's triumph o'er her barbarous foes
First reared the stage, immortal Shakespeare rose;
Each change of many-coloured life he drew,
Exhausted worlds, and then imagined new;
Existence saw him spurn her bounded reign
And panting Time toiled after him in vain;
His powerful strokes presiding truth impressed,
And unresisted passion stormed the breast.

Then Jonson came, instructed from the school,
To please in method and invent by rule;
His studious patience and laborious art
By regular approach essayed the heart;
Cold Approbation gave the lingering bays,
For those who durst not censure scarce could praise,
A mortal born he met the general doom,
But left, like Egypt's kings, a lasting tomb.

The wits of Charles found easier ways to fame
Nor wished for Jonson's art or Shakespeare's flame;
Themselves they studied; as they felt, they writ;
Intrigue was plot, obscenity was wit.
Vice always found a sympathetic friend;

They pleased their age and did not aim to mend.
Yet bards like these aspired to lasting praise
And proudly hoped to pimp in future days.
Their cause was general, their supports were strong,
Their slaves were willing, and their reign was long;
Till Shame regained the post that Sense betrayed
And Virtue called Oblivion to her aid.

Then crushed by rules, and weakened as refined,
For years the power of Tragedy declined;
From bard to bard, the frigid caution crept,
Till Declamation roared, while Passion slept.
Yet still did Virtue deign the stage to tread,
Philosophy remained, though Nature fled.
But forced at length her ancient reign to quit,
She saw great Faustus[2] lay the ghost of wit;
Exulting Folly hailed the joyful day,
And pantomime and song confirmed her sway.

But who the coming changes can presage
And mark the future periods of the stage?
Perhaps if skill could distant times explore,
New Behns,[3] new Durfeys[4] yet remain in store.
Perhaps where Lear has raved and Hamlet died,
On flying cars new sorcerers may ride.
Perhaps, for who can guess the effects of chance?
Here Hunt[5] may box, or Mahomet[6] may dance.

Hard is his lot that here by Fortune placed
Must watch the wild vicissitudes of taste,
With every meteor of caprice must play,
And chase the new-blown bubbles of the day.
Ah! Let not Censure term our fate our choice;
The stage but echoes back the public voice.
The drama's laws the drama's patrons give,
For we that live to please must please to live.

Then prompt no more the follies you decry,
As tyrants doom their tools of guilt to die;
'Tis yours this night to bid the reign commence
Of rescued Nature and reviving Sense;
To chase the charms of sound, the pomp of show,
For useful mirth and salutary woe;
Bid scenic Virtue form the rising age
And Truth diffuse her radiance from the stage.

Rambler (1751)

RAMBLER, NUMBER 168. SATURDAY, 26 OCTOBER 1751

Decipit
Frons prima multos; rara mens intelligit
Quod interiore condidit cura angulo. PHAEDRUS [IV.ii.5-7]

The tinsel glitter and the specious mien
Delude the most; few pry behind the scene. [Johnson's translation]

It has been observed by Boileau that 'a mean or common thought expressed in pompous diction generally pleases more than a new or noble sentiment delivered in low and vulgar language; because the number is greater of those whom custom has enabled to judge of words than whom study has qualified to examine things.'

This solution might satisfy if such only were offended with meanness of expression as are unable to distinguish propriety of thought and to separate propositions or images from the vehicles by which they are conveyed to the understanding. But this kind of disgust is by no means confined to the ignorant or superficial; it operates uniformly and universally upon readers of all classes; every man, however profound or abstracted, perceives himself irresistibly alienated by low terms; they who profess the most zealous adherence to truth are forced to admit that she owes part of her charms to her ornaments and loses much of her power over the soul when she appears disgraced by a dress uncouth or ill-adjusted.

We are all offended by low terms but are not disgusted alike by the same compositions, because we do not all agree to censure the same terms as low. No word is naturally or intrinsically meaner than another; our opinion therefore of words, as of other things arbitrarily and capriciously established, depends wholly upon accident and custom. The cottager thinks those apartments splendid and spacious which an inhabitant of palaces will despise for their inelegance; and to him who has passed most of his hours with the delicate and polite, many expressions will seem sordid which another, equally acute, may hear without offence; but a mean term never fails to displease him to whom it appears mean, as poverty is certainly and invariably despised, though he who is poor in the eyes of some may by others be envied for his wealth.

Words become low by the occasions to which they are applied or the general character of those who use them; and the disgust which they produce arises from the revival of those images with which they are commonly united. Thus if, in the most solemn discourse, a phrase happens to occur which has been successfully employed in some ludicrous narrative, the gravest auditor finds it difficult to refrain from laughter, when they who are not prepossessed by the same accidental association are utterly unable to guess the reason of his merriment. Words which convey ideas of dignity in one age are banished from elegant writing or conversation in another, because they are in time debased by vulgar mouths and can be no longer heard without the involuntary recollection of unpleasing images.

When Macbeth[1] is confirming himself in the horrid purpose of stabbing his king, he breaks out amidst his emotions into a wish natural to a murderer:

Come, thick night,
And pall thee in the dunnest smoke of hell,
That my keen knife see not the wound it makes,
Nor heaven peep through the blanket of the dark,
To cry 'Hold, hold.'

In this passage is exerted all the force of poetry, that force which calls new powers into being which embodies sentiment and animates matter; yet perhaps scarce any man now peruses it without some disturbance of his attention from the counteraction of the words to the ideas. What can be more dreadful than to implore the presence of the night, invested not in common obscurity, but in the smoke of hell? Yet the efficacy of this invocation is destroyed by the insertion of an epithet now seldom heard but in the stable, and *dun* night may come or go without any other notice than contempt.

If we start into raptures when some hero of the *Iliad* tells us that . . . his lance rages with eagerness to destroy; if we are alarmed at the terror of the soldiers commanded by Caesar to hew down the sacred grove, who dreaded, says Lucan, lest the axe aimed at the oak should fly back upon the striker—

Si robora sacra ferirent,
In sua credebant redituras membra secures,

None dares with impious steel the grove to rend
Lest on himself the destined stroke descend—

we cannot surely but sympathize with the horrors of a wretch about to murder his master, his friend, his benefactor, who suspects that the weapon will refuse its office and start back from the breast which he is preparing to violate. Yet this sentiment is weakened by the name of an instrument used by butchers and cooks in the meanest employments; we do not immediately conceive that any crime of importance is to be committed with a *knife*; or who does not, at last, from the long habit of connecting a knife with sordid offices, feel aversion rather than terror?

Macbeth proceeds to wish, in the madness of guilt, that the inspection of heaven may be intercepted, and that he may, in the involutions of infernal darkness, escape the eye of providence. This is the utmost extravagance of determined wickedness; yet this is so debased by two unfortunate words that while I endeavour to impress on my reader the energy of the sentiment, I can scarce check my risibility when the expression forces itself upon my mind; for who, without some relaxation of his gravity, can hear of the avengers of guilt *peeping through a blanket*?

These imperfections of diction are less obvious to the reader as he is less acquainted with common usages; they are therefore wholly imperceptible to a foreigner, who learns our language from books, and will strike a solitary academic less forcibly than a modish lady.

Among the numerous requisites that most concur to complete an author, few are of more importance than an early entrance into the living world. The seeds of knowledge may be planted in solitude but must be cultivated in public. Argumentation may be taught in colleges, and theories formed in retirement, but the artifice of embellishment and the powers of attraction can be gained only by general converse.

An acquaintance with prevailing customs and fashionable elegance is necessary likewise for other purposes. The injury that grand imagery suffers from unsuitable language, personal merit may fear from rudeness and indelicacy. When the success of Aeneas depended on the favour of the queen upon whose coasts he was driven, his celestial protectress thought him not sufficiently secured against rejection by his piety, or bravery, but decorated him for the interview with preternatural beauty. Whoever desires, for his writings or himself, what none can reasonably condemn, the favour of mankind, must add grace to strength and make his thoughts agreeable as well as useful. Many complain of neglect who never tried to attract regard. It cannot be expected that the patrons of science or virtue should be solicitous to discover excellencies which they who possess them shade and disguise. Few have abilities so much needed by the rest of the world as to be caressed on their own terms; and he that will not condescend to recommend himself by external embellishments must submit to the fate of just sentiments meanly expressed and be ridiculed and forgotten before he is understood.

Proposals (1756)

for Printing by Subscription
the Dramatic Works of William Shakespeare,
Corrected and Illustrated
by Samuel Johnson

When the works of Shakespeare are, after so many editions, again offered to the public, it will doubtless be inquired why Shakespeare stands in more need of critical assistance than any other of the English writers, and what are the deficiencies of the late attempts which another editor may hope to supply?

The business of him that republishes an ancient book is to correct what is corrupt and to explain what is obscure. To have a text corrupt in many places, and in many doubtful, is, among the authors that have written since the use of types, almost peculiar to Shakespeare. Most writers, by publishing their own works, prevent all various readings and preclude all conjectural criticism. Books indeed are sometimes published after the death of him who produced them; but they are better secured from corruptions than these unfortunate compositions. They subsist in a single copy, written or revised by the author; and the faults of the printed volume can be only faults of one descent.

But of the works of Shakespeare the condition has been far different. He sold them, not to be printed, but to be played. They were immediately copied for the actors and multiplied by transcript after transcript, vitiated by the blunders of the penman or changed by the affectation of the player; perhaps enlarged to introduce a jest or mutilated to shorten the representation; and printed at last without the concurrence of the author, without the consent of the proprietor, from compilations made by chance or by stealth out of the separate parts written for the theatre; and thus thrust into the world surreptitiously and hastily, they suffered another depravation from the ignorance and negligence of the printers, as every man who knows the state of the press in that age will readily conceive.

It is not easy for invention to bring together so many causes concurring to vitiate a text. No other author ever gave up his works to fortune and time with so little care; no books could be left in hands so likely to injure them as plays frequently acted yet continued in manuscript; no other transcribers were likely to be so little qualified for their task as those who copied for the stage, at a time when the lower ranks of the people were universally illiterate; no other editions were made from fragments so minutely broken and so fortuitously reunited; and in no other age was the art of printing in such unskilful hands.

With the causes of corruption that make the revisal of Shakespeare's dramatic pieces necessary, may be enumerated the causes of obscurity, which may be partly imputed to his age and partly to himself.

When a writer outlives his contemporaries and remains almost the only unforgotten name of a distant time, he is necessarily obscure. Every age has its modes of speech and its cast of thought; which, though easily explained when there are many books to be compared with each other, become sometimes unintelligible and always difficult when there are no parallel passages that may conduce to their illustration. Shakespeare is the first considerable author of sublime or familiar dialogue in our language. Of the books which he read, and from which he formed his style, some perhaps have perished, and the rest are neglected. His imitations are therefore unnoted, his allusions are undiscovered, and many beauties, both of pleasantry and greatness, are lost with the objects to which they were united, as the figures vanish when the canvas has decayed.

It is the great excellence of Shakespeare that he drew his scenes from nature and from life. He copied the manners of the world then passing before him and has more allusions than other poets to the traditions and superstition of the vulgar; which must therefore be traced before he can be understood.

He wrote at a time when our poetical language was yet unformed; when the meaning of our phrases was yet in fluctuation, when words were adopted at pleasure from the neighbouring languages, and while the Saxon was still visibly mingled in our diction. The reader is therefore embarrassed at once with dead and with foreign languages, with obsoleteness and innovation. In that age, as in all others, fashion produced phraseology which succeeding fashion swept away before its meaning was generally known or sufficiently authorized; and in that age, above all others, experiments were made upon our language which distorted its combinations and disturbed its uniformity.

If Shakespeare has difficulties above other writers, it is to be imputed to the nature of his work, which required the use of the common colloquial language and consequently admitted many phrases allusive, elliptical, and proverbial, such as we speak and hear every hour without observing them; and of which, being now familiar, we do not suspect that they can ever grow uncouth, or that, being now obvious, they can ever seem remote.

These are the principal causes of the obscurity of Shakespeare; to which may be added that fullness of idea which might sometimes load his words with more sentiment than they could conveniently convey, and that rapidity of imagination which might hurry him to a second thought before he had fully explained the first. But my opinion is that very few of his lines were difficult to his audience, and that he used such expressions as were then common, though the paucity of contemporary writers makes them now seem peculiar.

Authors are often praised for improvement, or blamed for innovation, with very little justice, by those who read few other books of the same age. Addison himself has been so unsuccessful in enumerating the words with which Milton has enriched our language as perhaps not to have named one of which Milton was the author; and Bentley has yet more unhappily praised him as the introducer of those elisions into English poetry which had been used from the first essays of versification among us, and which Milton was indeed the last that practised.

Another impediment, not the least vexatious to the commentator, is the exactness with which Shakespeare followed his authors. Instead of dilating his thoughts into generalities and expressing incidents with poetical latitude, he often combines circumstances unnecessary to his main design, only because he happened to find them together. Such passages can be illustrated only by him who has read the same story in the very book which Shakespeare consulted.

He that undertakes an edition of Shakespeare has all these difficulties to encounter and all these obstructions to remove.

The corruptions of the text will be corrected by a careful collation of the oldest copies, by which it is hoped that many restorations may yet be made; at least it will be necessary to collect and note the variations as materials for future critics; for it very often happens that a wrong reading has affinity to the right.

In this part all the present editions are apparently and intentionally defective. The critics did not so much as wish to facilitate the labour of those that followed them. The same books are still to be compared; the work that has been done is to be done again; and no single edition will supply the reader with a text on which he can rely as the best copy of the works of Shakespeare.

The edition now proposed will at least have this advantage over others. It will exhibit all the observable varieties of all the copies that can be found: that, if the reader is not satisfied with the editor's determination, he may have the means of choosing better for himself.

Where all the books are evidently vitiated, and collation can give no assistance, then begins the task of critical sagacity; and some changes may well be admitted in a text never settled by the author and so long exposed to caprice and ignorance. But nothing shall be imposed, as in the Oxford edition, without notice of the alteration; nor shall conjecture be wantonly or unnecessarily indulged.

It has been long found that very specious emendations do not equally strike all minds with conviction, nor even the same mind at different times; and therefore, though perhaps many alterations may be proposed as eligible, very few will be obtruded as certain. In a language so ungrammatical as the English and so licentious as that of Shakespeare, emendatory criticism is always hazardous; nor can it be allowed to any man who is not particularly versed in the writings of that age and particularly studious of his author's diction. There is danger lest peculiarities should be mistaken for corruptions, and passages rejected as unintelligible, which a narrow mind happens not to understand.

All the former critics have been so much employed on the correction of the text that they have not sufficiently attended to the elucidation of passages obscured by accident or time. The editor will endeavour to read the books which the author read, to trace his knowledge to its source and compare his copies with their originals. If in this part of his design he hopes to attain any degree of superiority to his predecessors, it must be considered that he has the advantage of their labours; that part of the work being already done, more care is naturally bestowed on the other part; and that, to declare the truth, Mr Rowe and Mr Pope were very ignorant of the ancient English literature; Dr Warburton was detained by more important studies; and Mr Theobald, if fame be just to his memory, considered learning only as an instrument of gain and made no further inquiry after his author's meaning when once he had notes sufficient to embellish his page with the expected decorations.

With regard to obsolete or peculiar diction, the editor may perhaps claim some degree of confidence, having had more motives to consider the whole extent of our language than any other man from its first formation. He hopes that, by comparing the works of Shakespeare with those of writers who lived at the same time, immediately preceded, or immediately followed him, he shall be able to ascertain his ambiguities, disentangle his intricacies, and recover the meaning of words now lost in the darkness of antiquity.

When therefore any obscurity arises from an allusion to some other book, the passage will be quoted. When the diction is entangled, it will be cleared by a paraphrase or interpretation. When the sense is broken by the suppression of part of the sentiment in pleasantry or passion, the connexion will be supplied. When any forgotten custom is hinted, care will be taken to retrieve and explain it. The meaning assigned to doubtful words will be supported by the authorities of other writers or by parallel passages of Shakespeare himself.

The observation of faults and beauties is one of the duties of an annotator which some of Shakespeare's editors have attempted and some have neglected. For this part of his task, and for this only, was Mr Pope eminently and indisputably qualified; nor has Dr Warburton followed him with less diligence or less success. But I have never observed that mankind was much delighted or improved by their asterisks, commas, or double commas; of which the only effect is that they preclude the pleasure of judging for ourselves; teach the young and ignorant to decide without principles; defeat curiosity and discernment, by leaving them less to discover; and at last show the opinion of the critic without the reasons on which it was founded, and without affording any light by which it may be examined.

The editor, though he may less delight his own vanity, will probably please his reader more, by supposing him equally able with himself to judge of beauties and faults which require no previous acquisition of remote knowledge. A description of the obvious scenes of nature, a representation of general life, a sentiment of reflection or experience, a deduction of conclusive argument, a forcible eruption of effervescent passion, are to be considered as proportionate to common apprehension, unassisted by critical officiousness; since, to conceive them, nothing more is requisite than acquaintance with the general state of the world, and those faculties which he must always bring with him who would read Shakespeare.

But when the beauty arises from some adaptation of the sentiment to customs worn out of use, to opinions not universally prevalent, or to any accidental or minute particularity which cannot be supplied by common understanding or common observation, it is the duty of a commentator to lend his assistance.

The notice of beauties and faults thus limited will make no distinct part of the design, being reducible to the explanation of obscure passages.

The editor does not, however, intend to preclude himself from the comparison of Shakespeare's sentiments or expression with those of ancient or modern authors, or from the display of any beauty not obvious to the students of poetry; for as he hopes to leave his author better understood, he wishes likewise to procure him more rational approbation.

The former editors have affected to slight their predecessors; but in this edition all that is valuable will be adopted from every commentator, that posterity may consider it as including all the rest and exhibiting whatever is hitherto known of the great father of the English drama.

A Note on the Text

The text of the *Preface* given here is based on that of the first edition, 1765 (the British Library, shelfmark 11766. bbb. 35), a facsimile of which has been published by The Scolar Press, Menston, England, 1969.

In the present edition the spellings have been changed to conform with present practice since such changes do not affect Johnson's style. The punctuation, however, is Johnson's except for about a dozen instances of what were most probably printer's errors since they were corrected in the second edition.

Johnson's punctuation, particularly his frequent use of commas, may seem strange to our ears, but indiscreet tampering with these weakens the force of his utterances. In the following sentence, for example, the comma after "world" is essential if the full impact of the last qualifying phrase is to be grasped:

> A quibble was to him the fatal Cleopatra for which he lost the world, and was content to lose it.

Johnson's own reluctance to emend Shakespeare's language should be a warning for all editors against meddling with his style.

Preface (1765)

1 That praises are without reason lavished on the dead, and that the honours due only to excellence are paid to antiquity, is a complaint likely to be always continued by those, who, being able to add nothing to truth, hope for eminence from the heresies of paradox; or those, who, being forced by disappointment upon consolatory expedients, are willing to hope from posterity what the present age refuses, and flatter themselves that the regard which is yet denied by envy, will be at last bestowed by time.

2 Antiquity like every other quality that attracts the notice of mankind, has undoubtedly votaries that reverence it, not from reason, but from prejudice. Some seem to admire indiscriminately whatever has been long preserved, without considering that time has sometimes cooperated with chance; all perhaps are more willing to honour past than present excellence; and the mind contemplates genius through the shades of age, as the eye surveys the sun through artificial opacity. The great contention of criticism is to find the faults of the moderns, and the beauties of the ancients. While an author is yet living we estimate his powers by his worst performance, and when he is dead, we rate them by his best.

3 To works, however, of which the excellence is not absolute and definite, but gradual and comparative, to works not raised upon principles demonstrative and scientific, but appealing wholly to observation and experience, no other test can be applied than length of duration and continuance of esteem. What mankind have long possessed they have often examined and compared, and if they persist to value the possession, it is because frequent comparisons have confirmed opinion in is favour. As among the works of nature no man can properly call a river deep or a mountain high, without the knowledge of

many mountains and many rivers; so in the productions of genius, nothing can be styled excellent till it has been compared with other works of the same kind. Demonstration immediately displays its power, and has nothing to hope or fear from the flux of years; but works tentative and experimental must be estimated by their proportion to the general and collective ability of man, as it is discovered in a long succession of endeavours. Of the first building that was raised, it might be with certainty determined that it was round or square, but whether it was spacious or lofty must have been referred to time. The Pythagorean scale of numbers[1] was at once discovered to be perfect; but the poems of Homer we yet know not to transcend the common limits of human intelligence, but by remarking, that nation after nation, and century after century, has been able to do little more than transpose his incidents, new-name his characters, and paraphrase his sentiments.

The reverence due to writings that have long subsisted arises therefore not from any credulous confidence in the superior wisdom of past ages, or gloomy persuasion of the degeneracy of mankind, but is the consequence of acknowledged and indubitable positions, that what has been longest known has been most considered, and what is most considered is best understood. 4

The Poet, of whose works I have undertaken the revision, may now begin to assume the dignity of an ancient, and claim the privilege of established fame and prescriptive veneration. He has long outlived his century, the term commonly fixed as the test of literary merit. Whatever advantages he might once derive from personal allusions, local customs, or temporary opinions, have for many years been lost; and every topic of merriment or motive of sorrow which the modes of artificial life afforded him, now only obscure the scenes which they once illuminated. The effects of favour and competition are at an end; the tradition of his friendships and his enmities has perished; his works support no opinion with arguments, nor supply any faction with invectives; they can neither indulge vanity nor gratify malignity, but are read without any other reason than the desire of pleasure and are therefore praised only as pleasure is obtained; yet, thus unassisted by interest or passion, they have 5 passed through variations of taste and changes of manners, and, as they devolved from one generation to another, have received new honours at every transmission.

6 But because human judgment, though it be gradually gaining upon certainty, never becomes infallible; and approbation, though long continued, may yet be only the approbation of prejudice or fashion; it is proper to inquire, by what peculiarities of excellence Shakespeare has gained and kept the favour of his countrymen.

7 Nothing can please many, and please long, but just representations of general nature. Particular manners can be known to few, and therefore few only can judge how nearly they are copied. The irregular combinations of fanciful invention may delight awhile, by that novelty of which the common satiety of life sends us all in quest; but the pleasures of sudden wonder are soon exhausted, and the mind can only repose on the stability of truth.

8 Shakespeare is above all writers, at least above all modern writers, the poet of nature, the poet that holds up to his readers a faithful mirror of manners and of life. His characters are not modified by the customs of particular places, unpractised by the rest of the world; by the peculiarities of studies or professions, which can operate but upon small numbers; or by the accidents of transient fashions or temporary opinions: they are the genuine progeny of common humanity, such as the world will always supply, and observation will always find. His persons act and speak by the influence of those general passions and principles by which all minds are agitated, and the whole system of life is continued in motion. In the writings of other poets a character is too often an individual; in those of Shakespeare it is commonly a species.

9 It is from this wide extension of design that so much instruction is derived. It is this which fills the plays of Shakespeare with practical axioms and domestic wisdom. It was said of Euripides, that every verse was a precept; and it may be said of Shakespeare, that from his works may be collected a system of civil and economical prudence. Yet his real power is not shown in the splendour of particular passages, but by the progress of his fable, and, the tenor of his dialogue; and he that tries to recommend him by select quotations, will succeed like the pedant in Hierocles,

who, when he offered his house to sale, carried a brick in his pocket as a specimen.

It will not easily be imagined how much Shakespeare excels in accommodating his sentiments to real life, but by comparing him with other authors. It was observed of the ancient schools of declamation, that the more diligently they were frequented, the more was the student disqualified for the world, because he found nothing there which he should ever meet in any other place.[2] The same remark may be applied to every stage but that of Shakespeare. The theatre, when it is under any other direction, is peopled by such characters as were never seen, conversing in a language which was never heard, upon topics which will never arise in the commerce of mankind. But the dialogue of this author is often so evidently determined by the incident which produces it, and is pursued with so much ease and simplicity, that it seems scarcely to claim the merit of fiction, but to have been gleaned by diligent selection out of common conversation, and common occurrences. 10

Upon every other stage the universal agent is love, by whose power all good and evil is distributed, and every action quickened or retarded. To bring a lover, a lady and a rival into the fable; to entangle them in contradictory obligations, perplex them with oppositions of interest, and harass them with violence of desires inconsistent with each other to make them meet in rapture and part in agony; to fill their mouths with hyperbolical joy and outrageous sorrow; to distress them as nothing human ever was distressed; to deliver them as nothing human ever was delivered, is the business of a modern dramatist. For this probability is violated, life is misrepresented, and language is depraved. But love is only one of many passions, and as it has no great influence upon the sum of life, it has little operation in the dramas of a poet, who caught his ideas from the living world, and exhibited only what he saw before him. He knew that any other passion, as it was regular or exorbitant, was a cause of happiness or calamity. 11

Characters thus ample and general were not easily discriminated and preserved, yet perhaps no poet ever kept his personages more distinct from each other. I will not say with Pope, that every speech may be assigned to the proper speaker,[3] because many speeches there are which have nothing characteristical; but, 12 perhaps, though some may be equally adapted to every person, it will be difficult to find any that can be properly transferred from the present possessor to another claimant. The choice is right, when there is reason for choice.

13 Other dramatists can only gain attention by hyperbolical or aggravated characters, by fabulous and unexampled excellence or depravity, as the writers of barbarous romances invigorated the reader by a giant and a dwarf; and he that should form his expectations of human affairs from the play, or from the tale, would be equally deceived. Shakespeare has no heroes; his scenes are occupied only by men, who act and speak as the reader thinks he should himself have spoken or acted on the same occasion: even where the agency is supernatural the dialogue is levelled with life. Other writers disguise the most natural passions and most frequent incidents; so that he who contemplates them in the book will not know them in the world. Shakespeare approximates the remote, and familiarizes the wonderful; the event which he represents will not happen, but if it were possible, its effects would be probably such as he has assigned; and it may be said, that he has not only shown human nature as it acts in real exigences, but as it would be found in trials, to which it cannot be exposed.

14 This therefore is the praise of Shakespeare, that his drama is the mirror of life; that he who has mazed his imagination, in following the phantoms which other writers raise up before him, may here be cured of his delirious ecstasies, by reading human sentiments in human language; by scenes from which a hermit may estimate the transactions of the world, and a confessor predict the progress of the passions.

15 His adherence to general nature has exposed him to the censure of critics who form their judgments upon narrower principles. Dennis and Rymer think his Romans not sufficiently Roman;[4] and Voltaire censures his kings as not completely royal. Dennis is offended, that Menenius, a senator of Rome, should play the buffoon;[5] and Voltaire perhaps thinks decency violated when the Danish usurper is represented as a drunkard.[6] But Shakespeare always makes nature predominate over accident; and, if he preserves the essential character, is not very careful of distinctions superinduced and adventitious. His story requires Romans or kings, but he thinks only on men. He knew that Rome, like

every other city, had men of all dispositions; and wanting a buffoon, he went into the senate house for that which the senate house would certainly have afforded him. He was inclined to show an usurper and a murderer not only odious but despicable; he therefore added drunkenness to his other qualities, knowing that kings love wine like other men, and that wine exerts its natural power upon kings. These are the petty cavils of petty minds;[7] a poet overlooks the casual distinction of country and condition, as a painter, satisfied with the figure, neglects the drapery.

The censure which he has incurred by mixing comic and tragic scenes, as it extends to all his works, deserves more consideration. Let the fact be first stated, and then examined. 16

Shakespeare's plays are not in the rigorous or critical sense either tragedies or comedies, but compositions of a distinct kind; exhibiting the real state of sublunary nature, which partakes of good and evil, joy and sorrow, mingled with endless variety of proportion and innumerable modes of combination; and expressing the course of the world, in which the loss of one is the gain of another; in which, at the same time, the reveller is hasting to his wine, and the mourner burying his friend; in which the malignity of one is sometimes defeated by the frolic of another; and many mischiefs and many benefits are done and hindered without design. 17

Out of this chaos of mingled purposes and casualties the ancient poets, according to the laws which custom had prescribed, selected some the crimes of men, and some their absurdities; some the momentous vicissitudes of life, and some the lighter occurrences; some the terrors of distress, and some the gaieties of prosperity. Thus rose the two modes of imitation, known by the names of *tragedy* and *comedy*, compositions intended to promote different ends by contrary means, and considered as so little allied, that I do not recollect among the Greeks or Romans a single writer who attempted both. 18

Shakespeare has united the powers of exciting laughter and sorrow not only in one mind but in one composition. Almost all his plays are divided between serious and ludicrous characters, and, in the successive evolutions of the design, sometimes produce seriousness and sorrow, and sometimes levity and laughter. 19

20 That this is a practice contrary to the rules of criticism will be readily allowed; but there is always an appeal open from criticism to nature. The end of writing is to instruct; the end of poetry is to instruct by pleasing. That the mingled drama may convey all the instruction of tragedy or comedy cannot be denied, because it includes both in its alternations of exhibition, and approaches nearer than either to the appearance of life, by showing how great machinations and slender designs may promote or obviate one another, and the high and the low cooperate in the general system by unavoidable concatenation.

21 It is objected, that by this change of scenes the passions are interrupted in their progression, and that the principal event, being not advanced by a due gradation of preparatory incidents, wants at last the power to move, which constitutes the perfection of dramatic poetry. This reasoning is so specious, that it is received as true even by those who in daily experience feel it to be false. The interchanges of mingled scenes seldom fail to produce the intended vicissitudes of passion. Fiction cannot move so much, but that the attention may be easily transferred; and though it must be allowed that pleasing melancholy be sometimes interrupted by unwelcome levity, yet let it be considered likewise, that melancholy is often not pleasing, and that the disturbance of one man may be the relief of another; that different auditors have different habitudes; and that, upon the whole, all pleasure consists in variety.

22 The players, who in their edition[8] divided our author's works into comedies, histories, and tragedies, seem not to have distinguished the three kinds, by any very exact or definite ideas.

23 An action which ended happily to the principal persons, however serious or distressful through its intermediate incidents, in their opinion constituted a comedy. This idea of a comedy continued long amongst us, and plays were written which, by changing the catastrophe, were tragedies today and comedies tomorrow.

24 Tragedy was not in those times a poem of more general dignity or elevation than comedy; it required only a calamitous conclusion, with which the common criticism of that age was satisfied, whatever lighter pleasure it afforded in its progress.

25 History was a series of actions, with no other than chronological succession, independent of each other, and without any

tendency to introduce or regulate the conclusion. It is not always very nicely distinguished from tragedy. There is not much nearer approach to unity of action in the tragedy of *Antony and Cleopatra*, than in the history of *Richard the Second*. But a history might be continued through many plays; as it had no plan, it had no limits.

Through all these denominations of the drama, Shakespeare's 26
mode of composition is the same: an interchange of seriousness and merriment, by which the mind is softened at one time, and exhilarated at another. But whatever be his purpose, whether to gladden or depress, or to conduct the story, without vehemence or emotion, through tracts of easy and familiar dialogue, he never fails to attain his purpose; as he commands us, we laugh or mourn, or sit silent with quiet expectation, in tranquillity without indifference.

When Shakespeare's plan is understood, most of the criticisms 27
of Rymer and Voltaire vanish away. The play of *Hamlet* is opened, without impropriety, by two sentinels; Iago bellows at Brabantio's window, without injury to the scheme of the play, though in terms which a modern audience would not easily endure; the character of Polonius is seasonable and useful; and the grave-diggers themselves may be heard with applause.[9]

Shakespeare engaged in dramatic poetry with the world open 28
before him; the rules of the ancients were yet known to few; the public judgment was unformed; he had no example of such fame as might force him upon imitation, nor critics of such authority as might restrain his extravagance. He therefore indulged his natural disposition, and his disposition, as Rymer has remarked, led him to comedy.[10] In tragedy he often writes with great appearance of toil and study, what is written at last with little felicity; but in his comic scenes, he seems to produce without labour, what no labour can improve. In tragedy he is always struggling after some occasion to be comic, but in comedy he seems to repose, or to luxuriate, as in a mode of thinking congenial to his nature. In his tragic scenes there is always something wanting, but his comedy often surpasses expectation or desire. His comedy pleases by the thoughts and the language, and his tragedy for the greater part by incident and action. His tragedy seems to be skill, his comedy to be instinct.

29 The force of his comic scenes has suffered little diminution from the changes made by a century and a half, in manners or in words. As his personages act upon principles arising from genuine passion, very little modified by particular forms, their pleasures and vexations are communicable to all times and to all places; they are natural, and therefore durable; the adventitious peculiarities of personal habits are only superficial dyes, bright and pleasing for a little while, yet soon fading to a dim tinct, without any remains of former lustre; but the discriminations of true passion are the colours of nature; they pervade the whole mass, and can only perish with the body that exhibits them. The accidental compositions of heterogeneous modes are dissolved by the chance which combined them; but the uniform simplicity of primitive qualities neither admits increase, nor suffers decay. The sand heaped by one flood is scattered by another, but the rock always continues in its place. The stream of time, which is continually washing the dissoluble fabrics of other poets, passes without injury by the adamant of Shakespeare.

30 If there be, what I believe there is, in every nation, a style which never becomes obsolete, a certain mode of phraseology so consonant and congenial to the analogy and principles of its respective language as to remain settled and unaltered; this style is probably to be sought in the common intercourse of life, among those who speak only to be understood, without ambition of elegance. The polite are always catching modish innovations, and the learned depart from established forms of speech, in hope of finding or making better; those who wish for distinction forsake the vulgar, when the vulgar is right; but there is a conversation above grossness and below refinement, where propriety resides, and where this poet seems to have gathered his comic dialogue. He is therefore more agreeable to the ears of the present age than any other author equally remote, and among his other excellencies deserves to be studied as one of the original masters of our language.

31 These observations are to be considered not as unexceptionably constant, but as containing general and predominant truth. Shakespeare's familiar dialogue is affirmed to be smooth and clear, yet not wholly without ruggedness or difficulty; as a country may be eminently fruitful, though it has spots unfit for

cultivation. His characters are praised as natural, though their sentiments are sometimes forced, and their actions improbable; as the earth upon the whole is spherical, though its surface is varied with protuberances and cavities.

Shakespeare with his excellencies has likewise faults, and faults 32
sufficient to obscure and overwhelm any other merit. I shall show them in the proportion in which they appear to me, without envious malignity or superstitious veneration. No question can be more innocently discussed than a dead poet's pretensions to renown; and little regard is due to that bigotry which sets candour higher than truth.

His first defect is that to which may be imputed most of the 33
evil in books or in men. He sacrifices virtue to convenience, and is so much more careful to please than to instruct, that he seems to write without any moral purpose. From his writings indeed a system of social duty may be selected, for he that thinks reasonably must think morally; but his precepts and axioms drop casually from him; he makes no just distribution of good or evil, nor is always careful to show in the virtuous a disapprobation of the wicked; he carries his persons indifferently through right and wrong, and at the close dismisses them without further care, and leaves their examples to operate by chance. This fault the barbarity of his age cannot extenuate; for it is always a writer's duty to make the world better, and justice is a virtue independent of time or place.

The plots are often so loosely formed, that a very slight consi- 34
deration may improve them, and so carelessly pursued, that he seems not always fully to comprehend his own design. He omits opportunities of instructing or delighting which the train of his story seems to force upon him, and apparently rejects those exhibitions which would be more affecting, for the sake of those which are more easy.

It may be observed, that in many of his plays the latter part 35
is evidently neglected. When he found himself near the end of his work, and, in view of his reward, he shortened the labour, to snatch the profit. He therefore remits his efforts where he should most vigorously exert them, and his catastrophe is improbably produced or imperfectly represented.

He had no regard to distinction of time or place, but gives to 36
one age or nation, without scruple, the customs, institutions, and

opinions of another, at the expense not only of likelihood, but of possibility. These faults Pope has endeavoured, with more zeal than judgment, to transfer to his imagined interpolators.[11] We need not wonder to find Hector quoting Aristotle,[12] when we see the loves of Theseus and Hippolyta combined with the Gothic mythology of fairies.[13] Shakespeare, indeed, was not the only violator of chronology, for in the same age Sidney, who wanted not the advantages of learning, has, in his *Arcadia*, confounded the pastoral with the feudal times, the days of innocence, quiet, and security, with those of turbulence, violence, and adventure.

37 In his comic scenes he is seldom very successful, when he engages his characters in reciprocations of smartness and contests of sarcasm; their jests are commonly gross, and their pleasantry licentious; neither his gentlemen nor his ladies have much delicacy, nor are sufficiently distinguished from his clowns by any appearance of refined manners. Whether he represented the real conversation of his time is not easy to determine; the reign of Elizabeth is commonly supposed to have been a time of stateliness, formality, and reserve, yet perhaps the relaxations of that severity were not very elegant. There must, however, have been always some modes of gaiety preferable to others, and a writer ought to choose the best.

38 In tragedy his performance seems constantly to be worse, as his labour is more. The effusions of passion which exigence forces out are for the most part striking and energetic; but whenever he solicits his invention, or strains his faculties the offspring of his throes is tumour, meanness, tediousness, and obscurity.

39 In narration he affects a disproportionate pomp of diction and a wearisome train of circumlocution, and tells the incident imperfectly in many words, which might have been more plainly delivered in few. Narration in dramatic poetry is naturally tedious, as it is unanimated and inactive, and obstructs the progress of the action; it should therefore always be rapid, and enlivened by frequent interruption. Shakespeare found it an incumbrance, and instead of lightening it by brevity, endeavoured to recommend it by dignity and splendour.

40 His declamations or set speeches are commonly cold and weak, for his power was the power of nature; when he endeavoured like other tragic writers, to catch opportunities of amplification, and instead of inquiring what the occasion demanded, to show how much his stores of knowledge could supply, he seldom escapes without the pity or resentment of his reader.

It is incident to him to be now and then entangled with an unwieldy sentiment, which he cannot well express, and will not reject; he struggles with it a while, and if it continues stubborn, comprises it in words such as occur, and leaves it to be disentangled and evolved by those who have more leisure to bestow upon it. 41

Not that always where the language is intricate the thought is subtle, or the image always great where the line is bulky; the equality of words to things is very often neglected, and trivial sentiments and vulgar ideas disappoint the attention, to which they are recommended by sonorous epithets and swelling figures. 42

But the admirers of this great poet have never less reason to indulge their hopes of supreme excellence, than when he seems fully resolved to sink them in dejection, and mollify them with tender emotions by the fall of greatness, the danger of innocence, or the crosses of love. What he does best, he soon ceases to do. He is not long soft and pathetic without some idle conceit, or contemptible equivocation. He no sooner begins to move, than he counteracts himself; and terror and pity, as they are rising in the mind, are checked and blasted by sudden frigidity. 43

A quibble is to Shakespeare, what luminous vapours are to the traveller; he follows it at all adventures, it is sure to lead him out of his way, and sure to engulf him in the mire. It has some malignant power over his mind, and its fascinations are irresistible. Whatever be the dignity or profundity of his disquisition, whether he be enlarging knowledge or exalting affection, whether he be amusing attention with incidents, or enchaining it in suspense, let but a quibble spring up before him, and he leaves his work unfinished. A quibble is the golden apple for which he will always turn aside from his career, or stoop from his elevation. A quibble poor and barren as it is, gave him such delight, that he was content to purchase it, by the sacrifice of reason, propriety and truth. A quibble was to him the fatal Cleopatra for which he lost the world, and was content to lose it. 44

45 It will be thought strange, that, in enumerating the defects of this writer, I have not yet mentioned his neglect of the unities; his violation of those laws which have been instituted and established by the joint authority of poets and of critics.

46 For his other deviations from the art of writing, I resign him to critical justice, without making any other demand in his favour, than that which must be indulged to all human excellence; that his virtues be rated with his failings. But, from the censure which this irregularity may bring upon him, I shall, with due reverence to that learning which I must oppose, adventure to try how I can defend him.

47 His histories, being neither tragedies nor comedies, are not subject to any of their laws; nothing more is necessary to all the praise which they expect, than that the changes of action be so prepared as to be understood, that the incidents be various and affecting, and the characters consistent, natural and distinct. No other unity is intended, and therefore none is to be sought.

48 In his other works he has well enough preserved the unity of action. He has not, indeed, an intrigue regularly perplexed and regularly unravelled; he does not endeavour to hide his design only to discover it, for this is seldom the order of real events, and Shakespeare is the poet of nature. But his plan has commonly, what Aristotle requires, a beginning, a middle, and an end; one event is concatenated with another, and the conclusion follows by easy consequence. There are perhaps some incidents that might be spared, as in other poets there is much talk that only fills up time upon the stage; but the general system makes gradual advances, and the end of the play is the end of expectation.

49 To the unities of time and place he has shown no regard, and perhaps a nearer view of the principles on which they stand will diminish their value, and withdraw from them the veneration which, from the time of Corneille, they have very generally received by discovering that they have given more trouble to the poet than pleasure to the auditor.

50 The necessity of observing the unities of time and place arises from the supposed necessity of making the drama credible. The critics hold it impossible, that an action of months or years can be possibly believed to pass in three hours; or that the spectator can suppose himself to sit in the theatre, while ambas-

sadors go and return between distant kings, while armies are levied and towns besieged, while an exile wanders and returns, or till he whom they saw courting his mistress, shall lament the untimely fall of his son. The mind revolts from evident falsehood, and fiction loses its force when it departs from the resemblance of reality.

From the narrow limitation of time necessarily arises the 51
contraction of place. The spectator, who knows that he saw the first act at Alexandria, cannot suppose that he sees the next at Rome, at a distance to which not the dragons of Medea could, in so short a time, have transported him; he knows with certainty that he has not changed his place; and he knows that place cannot change itself; that what was a house cannot become a plain; that what was Thebes can never be Persepolis.

Such is the triumphant language with which a critic exults 52
over the misery of an irregular poet, and exults commonly without resistance or reply. It is time therefore to tell him, by the authority of Shakespeare, that he assumes, as an unquestionable principle, a position, which, while his breath is forming it into words, his understanding pronounces to be false. It is false, that any representation is mistaken for reality; that any dramatic fable in its materiality was ever credible, or, for a single moment, was ever credited.

The objection arising from the impossibility of passing the 53
first hour at Alexandria, and the next at Rome, supposes, that when the play opens the spectator really imagines himself at Alexandria, and believes that his walk to the theatre has been a voyage to Egypt, and that he lives in the days of Antony and Cleopatra. Surely he that imagines this, may imagine more. He that can take the stage at one time for the palace of the Ptolemies, may take it in half an hour for the promontory of Actium. Delusion, if delusion be admitted, has no certain limitation; if the spectator can be once persuaded, that his old acquaintance are Alexander and Caesar, that a room illuminated with candles is the plain of Pharsalia, or the bank of Granicus, he is in a state of elevation above the reach of reason, or of truth, and from the heights of empyrean poetry, may despise the circumscriptions of terrestrial nature. There is no reason why a mind thus wandering in ecstasy should count the clock,

or why an hour should not be a century in that calenture of the brains that can make the stage a field.

54 The truth is, that the spectators are always in their senses, and know, from the first act to the last, that the stage is only a stage and that the players are only players. They come to hear a certain number of lines recited with just gesture and elegant modulation. The lines relate to some action, and an action must be in some place; but the different actions that complete a story may be in places very remote from each other; and where is the absurdity of allowing that space to represent first Athens, and then Sicily, which was always known to be neither Sicily nor Athens, but a modern theatre [?]

55 By supposition, as place is introduced, time may be extended; the time required by the fable elapses for the most part between the acts, for, of so much of the action as is represented, the real and poetical duration is the same. If, in the first act preparations for war against Mithiridates are represented to be made in Rome, the event of the war may, without absurdity, be represented, in the catastrophe, as happening in Pontus; we know that there is neither war, nor preparation for war; we know that we are neither in Rome nor Pontus; that neither Mithridates nor Lucullus are before us. The drama exhibits successive imitations of successive actions, and why may not the second imitation represent an action that happened years after the first, if it be so connected with it, that nothing but time can be supposed to intervene [?] Time is, of all modes of existence, most obsequious to the imagination; a lapse of years is as easily conceived as a passage of hours. In contemplation we easily contract the time of real actions, and therefore willingly permit it to be contracted when we only see their imitation.

56 It will be asked, how the drama moves, if it is not credited. It is credited with all the credit due to a drama. It is credited, whenever it moves, as a just picture of a real original; as representing to the auditor what he would himself feel, if he were to do or suffer what is there feigned to be suffered or to be done. The reflection that strikes the heart is not, that the evils before us are real evils but that they are evils to which we ourselves may be exposed. If there be any fallacy, it is not that we fancy the players, but that we fancy ourselves unhappy for a moment; but we rather lament the possibility than suppose the presence

of misery, as a mother weeps over her babe, when she remembers that death may take it from her. The delight of tragedy proceeds from our consciousness of fiction; if we thought murders and treasons real, they would please no more.

Imitations produce pain or pleasure, not because they are 57
mistaken for realities, but because they bring realities to mind. When the imagination is recreated by a painted landscape, the trees are not supposed capable to give us shade, or the fountains coolness; but we consider, how we should be pleased with such fountains playing beside us, and such woods waving over us. We are agitated in reading the history of *Henry the Fifth*, yet no man takes his book for the field of Agincourt. A dramatic exhibition is a book recited with concomitants that increase or diminish its effect. Familiar comedy is often more powerful on the theatre, than in the page; imperial tragedy is always less. The humour of Petruchio may be heightened by grimace; but what voice or what gesture can hope to add dignity or force to the soliloquy of Cato?[15]

A play read, affects the mind like a play acted. It is therefore 58
evident, that the action is not supposed to be real, and it follows that between the acts a longer or shorter time may be allowed to pass, and that no more account of space or duration is to be taken by the auditor of a drama, than by the reader of a narrative, before whom may pass in an hour the life of a hero, or the revolutions of an empire.

Whether Shakespeare knew the unities, and rejected them by 59
design, or deviated from them by happy ignorance, it is, I think, impossible to decide, and useless to inquire. We may reasonably suppose, that, when he rose to notice, he did not want the counsels and admonitions of scholars and critics, and that he at last deliberately persisted in a practice, which he might have begun by chance. As nothing is essential to the fable, but unity of action, and as the unities of time and place arise evidently from false assumptions, and by circumscribing the extent of the drama, lessen its variety, I cannot think it much to be lamented, that they were not known by him, or not observed; nor, if such another poet could arise, should I very vehemently reproach him, that his first act passed at Venice, and his next in Cyprus.[16] Such violations of rules merely positive, become the comprehensive genuis of Shakespeare, and such

censures are suitable to the minute and slender criticism of Voltaire:

> Non usque adeo permiscuit imis
> Longus summa dies, ut non, si voce Metelli
> Serventur leges, malint a Caesare tolli.[17]

60 Yet when I speak thus slightly of dramatic rules, I cannot but recollect how much wit and learning may be produced against me; before such authorities I am afraid to stand, not that I think the present question one of those that are to be decided by mere authority, but because it is to be suspected, that these precepts have not been so easily received but for better reasons than I have yet been able to find. The result of my inquiries, in which it would be ludicrous to boast of impartiality, is that the unities of time and place are not essential to a just drama, that, though they may sometimes conduce to pleasure, they are always to be sacrificed to the nobler beauties of variety and instruction; and that a play, written with nice observation of critical rules, is to be contemplated as an elaborate curiosity, as the product of superfluous and ostentatious art, by which is shown, rather what is possible, than what is necessary.

61 He that, without diminution of any other excellence, shall preserve all the unities unbroken deserves the like applause with the architect, who shall display all the orders of architecture in a citadel, without any deduction from its strength, but the principal beauty of a citadel is to exclude the enemy; and the greatest graces of a play, are to copy nature and instruct life.

62 Perhaps, what I have here not dogmatically but deliberately written, may recall the principles of the drama to a new examination. I am almost frighted at my own temerity; and when I estimate the fame and the strength of those that maintain the contrary opinion, am ready to sink down in reverential silence; as Aeneas withdrew from the defence of Troy, when he saw Neptune shaking the wall, and Juno heading the besiegers.[18]

63 Those whom my arguments cannot persuade to give their approbation to the judgment of Shakespeare, will easily, if they consider the condition of his life, make some allowance for his ignorance.

64 Every man's performances, to be rightly estimated, must be compared with the state of the age in which he lived, and with

his own particular opportunities; and though to the reader a book be not worse or better for the circumstances of the author, yet as there is always a silent reference of human works to human abilities, and as the inquiry, how far man may extend his designs, or how high he may rate his native force, is of far greater dignity than in what rank we shall place any particular performance, curiosity is always busy to discover the instruments, as well as to survey the workmanship, to know how much is to be ascribed to original powers, and how much to casual and adventitious help. The palaces of Peru or Mexico were certainly mean and incommodious habitations, if compared to the houses of European monarchs; yet who could forbear to view them with astonishment, who remembered that they were built without the use of iron?

The English nation, in the time of Shakespeare, was yet strug- 65
gling to emerge from barbarity. The philology of Italy had been transplanted hither in the reign of Henry the Eighth; and the learned languages had been successfully cultivated by Lily, Linacre, and More; by Pole, Cheke, and Gardiner; and afterwards by Smith, Clerk, Haddon, and Ascham.[19] Greek was now taught to boys in the principal schools; and those who united elegance with learning, read, with great diligence, the Italian and Spanish poets. But literature was yet confined to professed scholars, or to men and women of high rank. The public was gross and dark; and to be able to read and write, was an accomplishment still valued for its rarity.

Nations, like individuals, have their infancy. A people newly 66
awakened to literary curiosity, being yet unacquainted with the true state of things, knows not how to judge of that which is proposed as its resemblance. Whatever is remote from common appearances is always welcome to vulgar, as to childish, credulity; and of a country unenlightened by learning, the whole people is the vulgar. The study of those who then aspired to plebeian learning was laid out upon adventures, giants, dragons, and enchantments. *The Death of Arthur* was the favourite volume.[20]

The mind which has feasted on the luxurious wonders of fiction, 67
has no taste of the insipidity of truth. A play which imitated only the common occurrences of the world, would, upon the admirers of *Palmerin* and *Guy of Warwick*,[21] have made little impression; he that wrote for such an audience was under the necessity of looking round for strange events and fabulous trans-

actions, and that incredibility, by which maturer knowledge is offended, was the chief recommendation of writings, to unskilful curiosity.

68 Our author's plots are generally borrowed from novels, and it is reasonable to suppose, that he chose the most popular, such as were read by many, and related by more; for his audience could not have followed him through the intricacies of the drama, had they not held the thread of the story in their hands.

69 The stories, which we now find only in remoter authors, were in his time accessible and familiar. The fable of *As You Like It*, which is supposed to be copied from Chaucer's *Gamelyn*, was a little pamphlet of those times;[22] and old Mr Cibber[23] remembered the tale of *Hamlet* in plain English prose, which the critics have now to seek in Saxo Grammaticus.[24]

70 His English histories he took from English chronicles and English ballads; and as the ancient writers were made known to his countrymen by versions, they supplied him with new subjects; he dilated some of Plutarch's lives into plays, when they had been translated by North.[25]

71 His plots, whether historical or fabulous, are always crowded with incidents, by which the attention of a rude people was more easily caught than by sentiment or argumentation; and such is the power of the marvellous even over those who despise it, that every man finds his mind more strongly seized by the tragedies of Shakespeare than of any other writer, others please us by particular speeches, but he always makes us anxious for the event and has perhaps excelled all but Homer in securing the first purpose of a writer, by exciting restless and unquenchable curiosity, and compelling him that reads his work to read it through.

72 The shows and bustle with which his plays abound have the same original. As knowledge advances, pleasure passes from the eye to the ear, but returns, as it declines, from the ear to the eye. Those to whom our author's labours were exhibited had more skill in pomps or processions than in poetical language, and perhaps wanted some visible and discriminated events, as comments on the dialogue. He knew how he should most please; and whether his practice is more agreeable to nature, or whether his example has prejudiced the nation, we still find that on our stage something must be done as well as said, and inactive declama-

tion, is very coldly heard, however musical or elegant, passionate or sublime.

Voltaire expresses his wonder, that our author's extravagances are endured by a nation, which has been the tragedy of *Cato*.[26] Let him be answered, that Addison speaks the language of poets, and Shakespeare, of men. We find in *Cato* innumerable beauties which enamour us of its author, but we see nothing that acquaints us with human sentiments or human actions; we place it with the fairest and the noblest progeny which judgment propagates by conjunction with learning; but *Othello* is the vigorous and vivacious offspring of observation impregnated by genius. *Cato* affords a splendid exhibition of artificial and fictitious manners, and delivers just and noble sentiments, in diction easy, elevated, and harmonious, but its hopes and fears communicate no vibration to the heart; the composition refers us only to the writer; we pronounce the name of *Cato*, but we think on Addison. 73

The work of a correct and regular writer is a garden accurately formed and diligently planted, varied with shades, and scented with flowers; the composition of Shakespeare is a forest, in which oaks extend their branches, and pines tower in the air, interspersed sometimes with weeds and brambles, and sometimes giving shelter to myrtles and to roses; filling the eye with awful pomp, and gratifying the mind with endless diversity. Other poets display cabinets of precious rarities, minutely finished, wrought into shape, and polished unto brightness. Shakespeare opens a mine which contains gold and diamonds in unexhaustible plenty, though clouded by incrustations, debased by impurities, and mingled with a mass of meaner minerals. 74

It has been much disputed, whether Shakespeare owed his excellence to his own native force, or whether he had the common helps of scholastic education, the precepts of critical science, and the examples of ancient authors. 75

There has always prevailed a tradition, that Shakespeare wanted learning, that he had no regular education, nor much skill in the dead languages. Jonson, his friend, affirms that *he had small Latin, and no Greek*;[27] who, besides that he had no imaginable temptation to falsehood, wrote at a time when the character and acquisitions of Shakespeare were known to multitudes. His evidence ought therefore to decide the controversy, unless some testimony of equal force could be opposed. 76

77 Some have imagined, that they have discovered deep learning in many imitations of old writers; but the examples which I have known urged, were drawn from books translated in his time; or were such easy coincidences of thought, as will happen to all who consider the same subjects; or such remarks on life or axioms of morality as float in conversation, and are transmitted through the world in proverbial sentences.

78 I have found it remarked, that, in this important sentence, *Go before, I'll follow*, we read a translation of *I prae, sequar*.[28] I have been told that when Caliban, after a pleasing dream, says, *I cried to sleep again*,[29] the author imitates Anacreon, who had, like every other man, the same wish on the same occasion.

79 There are a few passages which may pass for imitations, but so few that the exception only confirms the rule; he obtained them from accidental quotations, or by oral communication, and as he used what he had, would have used more if he had obtained it.

80 The *Comedy of Errors* is confessedly taken from the *Menaechmi* of Plautus; from the only play of Plautus which was then in English. What can be more probable, than that he who copied that, would have copied more; but that those which were not translated were inaccessible?

81 Whether he knew the modern languages is uncertain. That his plays have some French scenes proves but little; he might easily procure them to be written, and probably, even though he had known the language in the common degree, he could not have written it without assistance. In the story of *Romeo and Juliet* he is observed to have followed the English translation, where it deviates from the Italian; but this on the other part proves nothing against his knowledge of the original. He was to copy, not what he knew himself, but what was known to his audience.

82 It is most likely that he had learned Latin sufficiently to make him acquainted with construction, but that he never advanced to an easy perusal of the Roman authors. Concerning his skill in modern languages, I can find no sufficient ground of determination; but as no imitations of French or Italian authors have been discovered, though the Italian poetry was then high in esteem, I am inclined to believe, that he read little more than English, and chose for his fables only such tales as he found translated.

That much knowledge is scattered over his works is very justly observed by Pope, but it is often such knowledge as books did not supply. He that will understand Shakespeare, must not be content to study him in the closet; he must look for his meaning sometimes among the sports of the field, and sometimes among the manufactures of the shop. 83

There is however proof enough that he was a very diligent reader, nor was our language then so indigent of books, but that he might very liberally indulge his curiosity without excursion into foreign literature. Many of the Roman authors were translated, and some of the Greek; the Reformation had filled the kingdom with theological learning; most of the topics of human disquisition had found English writers; and poetry had been cultivated, not only with diligence, but success. This was a stock of knowledge sufficient for a mind so capable of appropriating and improving it. 84

But the greater part of his excellence was the product of his own genius. He found the English stage in a state of the utmost rudeness; no essays either in tragedy or comedy had appeared, from which it could be discovered to what degree of delight either one or other might be carried. Neither character nor dialogue were yet understood. Shakespeare may be truly said to have introduced them both amongst us and in some of his happier scenes to have carried them both to the utmost height. 85

By what gradations of improvement he proceeded, is not easily known; for the chronology of his works is yet unsettled. Rowe is of opinion, that 'perhaps we are not to look for his beginning, like those of other writers, in his least perfect works; art had so little, and nature so large a share in what he did, that for aught I know,' says he, 'the performances of his youth, as they were the most vigorous, were the best.'[30] But the power of nature is only the power of using to any certain purpose the materials which diligence procures, or opportunity supplies. Nature gives no man knowledge, and when images are collected by study and experience, can only assist in combining or applying them. Shakespeare, however favoured by nature, could impart only what he had learned; and as he must increase his ideas, like other mortals, by gradual acquisition, he, like them, grew wiser as he grew older, could display life better, as he knew it more, and instruct with more efficacy, as he was himself more amply instructed. 86

87 There is a vigilance of observation and accuracy of distinction which books and precepts cannot confer; from this almost all original and native excellence proceeds. Shakespeare must have looked upon mankind with perspicacity, in the highest degree curious and attentive. Other writers borrow their characters from preceding writers, and diversify them only by the accidental appendages of present manners; the dress is a little varied, but the body is the same. Our author had both matter and form to provide; for except the characters of Chaucer, to whom I think he is not much indebted, there were no writers in English, and perhaps not many in other modern languages, which showed life in its native colours.

88 The contest about the original benevolence or malignity of man had not yet commenced. Speculation had not yet attempted to analyse the mind, to trace the passions to their sources, to unfold the seminal principles of vice and virtue, or sound the depths of the heart for the motives of action. All those inquiries, which from that time that human nature became the fashionable study, have been made sometimes with nice discernment, but often with idle subtilty, were yet unattempted. The tales, with which the infancy of learning was satisfied, exhibited only the superficial appearances of action, related the events but omitted the causes, and were formed for such as delighted in wonders rather than in truth. Mankind was not then to be studied in the closet; he that would know the world, was under the necessity of gleaning his own remarks, by mingling as he could in its business and amusements.

89 Boyle congratulated himself upon his high birth, because it favoured his curiosity, by facilitating his access.[31] Shakespeare had no such advantage; he came to London a needy adventurer, and lived for a time by very mean employments. Many works of genius and learning have been performed in states of life, that appear very little favourable to thought or to inquiry; so many, that he who considers them is inclined to think that he sees enterprise and perseverance predominating over all external agency, and bidding help and hindrance vanish before them. The genius of Shakespeare was not to be depressed by the weight of poverty, nor limited by the narrow conversation to which men in want are inevitably condemned; the encumbrances of his

fortune were shaken from his mind, as *dew-drops from a lion's mane.*[32]

Though he had so many difficulties to encounter, and so little assistance to surmount them, he has been able to obtain an exact knowledge of many modes of life, and many casts of native dispositions; to vary them with great multiplicity; to mark them by nice distinctions; and to show them in full view by proper combinations. In this part of his performances he had none to imitate, but has himself been imitated by all succeeding writers; and it may be doubted, whether from all his successors more maxims of theoretical knowledge, or more rules of practical prudence, can be collected, than he alone has given to his country. 90

Nor was his attention confined to the actions of men; he was an exact surveyor of the inanimate world; his descriptions have always some peculiarities gathered by contemplating things as they really exist. It may be observed that the oldest poets of many nations preserve their reputation, and that the following generations of wit, after a short celebrity, sink into oblivion. The first, whoever they be, must take their sentiments and descriptions immediately from knowledge; the resemblance is therefore just, their descriptions are verified by every eye, and their sentiments acknowledged by every breast. Those whom their fame invites to the same studies, copy partly them, and partly nature, till the books of one age gain such authority, as to stand in the place of nature to another, and imitation, always deviating a little, becomes at last capricious and casual. Shakespeare, whether life or nature be his subject, shows plainly, that he has seen with his own eyes; he gives the image which he receives, not weakened or distorted by the intervention of any other mind; the ignorant feel his representations to be just, and the learned see that they are complete. 91

Perhaps it would not be easy to find any author, except Homer, who invented so much as Shakespeare, who so much advanced the studies which he cultivated or effused so much novelty upon his age or country. The form, the characters, the language, and the shows of the English drama are his. 'He seems,' says Dennis, 'to have been the very original of our English tragical harmony, that is, the harmony of blank verse, diversified often by disyllable and trisyllable terminations. For the diversity distinguishes 92 it from heroic harmony, and by bringing it nearer to common use makes it more proper to gain attention, and more fit for action and dialogue. Such verse we make when we are writing prose; we make such verse in common conversation.'[33]

93 I know not whether this praise is rigorously just. The disyllable termination, which the critic rightly appropriates to the drama, is to be found, though, I think, not in *Gorboduc* which is confessedly before our author; yet in *Hieronimo*, of which the date is not certain, but which there is reason to believe at least as old as his earliest plays. This however is certain, that he is the first who taught either tragedy or comedy to please, there being no theatrical piece of any older writer, of which the name is known, except to antiquaries and collectors of books, which are sought because they are scarce, and would not have been scarce, had they been much esteemed.

94 To him we must ascribe the praise, unless Spenser may divide it with him, of having first discovered to how much smoothness and harmony the English language could be softened. He has speeches, perhaps sometimes scenes, which have all the delicacy of Rowe, without his effeminacy. He endeavours indeed commonly to strike by the force and vigour of his dialogue, but he never executes his purpose better, than when he tries to soothe by softness.

95 Yet it must be at last confessed, that as we owe every thing to him, he owes something to us; that, if much of his praise is paid by perception and judgment, much is likewise given by custom and veneration. We fix our eyes upon his graces, and turn them from his deformities, and endure in him what we should in another loathe or despise. If we endured without praising, respect for the father of our drama might excuse us; but I have seen, in the book of some modern critic,[34] a collection of anomalies which show that he has corrupted language by every mode of depravation, but which his admirer has accumulated as a monument of honour.

96 He has scenes of undoubted and perpetual excellence, but perhaps not one play, which, if it were now exhibited as the work of a contemporary writer, would be heard to the conclusion. I am indeed far from thinking, that his works were wrought to his own ideas of perfection; when they were such as would satisfy the audience, they satisfied the writer. It is seldom

that authors, though more studious of fame than Shakespeare, rise much above the standard of their own age; to add a little to what is best will always be sufficient for present praise, and those who find themselves exalted into fame, are willing to credit their encomiasts, and to spare the labour of contending with themselves.

97 It does not appear, that Shakespeare thought his works worthy of posterity, that he levied any ideal tribute upon future times, or had any further prospect, than of present popularity and present profit. When his plays had been acted, his hope was at an end; he solicited no addition of honour from the reader. He therefore made no scruple to repeat the same jests in many dialogues, or to entangle different plots by the same knot of perplexity, which may be at least forgiven him, by those who recollect, that of Congreve's four comedies, two are concluded by a marriage in a mask, by a deception, which perhaps never happened, and which, whether likely or not, he did not invent.

98 So careless was this great poet of future fame, that, though he retired to ease and plenty, while he was yet little *declined into the vale of years*,[35] before he could be disgusted with fatigue, or disabled by infirmity, he made no collection of his works, nor desired to rescue those that had been already published from the depravations that obscured them, or secure to the rest a better destiny, by giving them to the world in their genuine state.

99 Of the plays which bear the name of Shakespeare in the late editions, the greater part were not published till about seven years after his death; and the few which appeared in his life are apparently thrust into the world without the care of the author, and therefore probably without his knowledge.

100 Of all the publishers, clandestine or professed, their negligence and unskilfulness has by the late revisers been sufficiently shown. The faults of all are indeed numerous and gross, and have not only corrupted many passages perhaps beyond recovery, but have brought others into suspicion, which are only obscured by obsolete phraseology, or by the writer's unskilfulness and affectation. To alter is more easy than to explain, and temerity is a more common quality than diligence. Those who saw that they must employ conjecture to a certain degree, were willing to indulge it a little further. Had the author published his own

works, we should have set quietly down to disentangle his intricacies, and clear his obscurities; but now we tear what we cannot loose, and eject what we happen not to understand.

101 The faults are more than could have happened without the concurrence of many causes. The style of Shakespeare was in itself ungrammatical, perplexed and obscure; his works were transcribed for the players by those who may be supposed to have seldom understood them; they were transmitted by copiers equally unskilful, who still multiplied errors; they were perhaps sometimes mutilated by the actors, for the sake of shortening the speeches, and were at last printed without correction of the press.

102 In this state they remained, not as Dr Warburton supposes, because they were unregarded, but because the editor's art was not yet applied to modern languages, and our ancestors were accustomed to so much negligence of English printers, that they could very patiently endure it. At last an edition was undertaken by Rowe; not because a poet was to be published by a poet, for Rowe seems to have thought very little on correction or explanation; but that our author's works might appear like those of his fraternity, with the appendages of a life and recommendatory preface. Rowe has been clamorously blamed for not performing what he did not undertake, and it is time that justice be done him, by confessing, that though he seems to have had no thought of corruption beyond the printer's errors, yet he has made many emendations, if they were not made before, which his successors have received without acknowledgement, and which, if they had produced them, would have filled pages and pages with censures of the stupidity by which the faults were committed, with displays of the absurdities which they involved, with ostentatious expositions of the new reading, and self-congratulations on the happiness of discovering it.

103 Of Rowe, as of all the editors, I have preserved the preface, and have likewise retained the author's life, though not written with much elegance or spirit; it relates however what is now to be known, and therefore deserves to pass through all succeeding publications.

104 The nation had been for many years content enough with Mr. Rowe's performance, when Mr Pope made them acquainted with the true state of Shakespeare's text, showed that it was

extremely corrupt, and gave reason to hope that there were means of reforming it. He collated the old copies, which none had thought to examine before, and restored many lines to their integrity; but, by a very compendious criticism, he rejected whatever he disliked, and thought more of amputation than of cure.

I know not why he is commended by Dr Warburton for distinguishing the genuine from the spurious plays. In this choice he exerted no judgment of his own; the plays which he received, were given by Heming and Condell, the first editors; and those which he rejected, though, according to the licentiousness of the press in those times, they were printed during Shakespeare's life, with his name, had been omitted by his friends, and were never added to his works before the edition of 1664, from which they were copied by the later printers. 105

This was a work which Pope seems to have thought unworthy of his abilities, being not able to suppress his contempt of *the dull duty of an editor*. He understood but half his undertaking. The duty of a collator is indeed dull, yet, like other tedious tasks, is very necessary; but an emendatory critic would ill discharge his duty, without qualities very different from dullness. In perusing a corrupted piece, he must have before him all possibilities of meaning, with all possibilities of expression. Such must be his comprehension of thought, and such his copiousness of language. Out of many readings possible, he must be able to select that which best suits with the state, opinions, and modes of language prevailing in every age, and with his author's particular cast of thought, and turn of expression. Such must be his knowledge, and such his taste. Conjectural criticism demands more than humanity possesses, and he that exercises it with most praise has very frequent need of indulgence. Let us now be told no more of the dull duty of an editor. 106

Confidence is the common consequence of success. They whose excellence of any kind has been loudly celebrated, are ready to conclude, that their powers are universal. Pope's edition fell below his own expectations, and he was so much offended, when he was found to have left anything for others to do, that he passed the latter part of his life in a state of hostility with verbal criticism. 107

108 I have retained all his notes, that no fragment of so great a writer may be lost. His Preface, valuable alike for elegance of composition and justness of remark, and containing a general criticism on his author, so extensive that little can be added, and so exact that little can be disputed, every editor has an interest to suppress, but that every reader would demand its insertion.

109 Pope was succeeded by Theobald, a man of narrow comprehension and small acquisitions, with no native and intrinsic splendour of genius, with little of the artificial light of learning, but zealous for minute accuracy, and not negligent in pursuing it. He collated the ancient copies, and rectified many errors. A man so anxiously scrupulous might have been expected to do more, but what little he did was commonly right.

110 In his reports of copies and editions he is not to be trusted, without examination. He speaks sometime indefinitely of copies, when he has only one. In his enumeration of editions, he mentions the two first Folios as of high, and the third Folio as of middle authority; but the truth is, that the first is equivalent to all others, and that the rest only deviate from it by the printer's negligence. Whoever has any of the folios has all, excepting those diversities which mere reiteration of editions will produce. I collated them all at the beginning, but afterwards used only the first.

111 Of his notes I have generally retained those which he retained himself in his second edition, except when they were confuted by subsequent annotators, or were too minute to merit preservation. I have sometimes adopted his restoration of a comma, without inserting the panegyric in which he celebrated himself for his achievement. The exuberant excrescence of his diction I have often lopped, his triumphant exultations over Pope and Rowe I have sometimes suppressed, and his contemptible ostentation I have frequently concealed; but I have in some places shown him, as he would have shown himself, for the reader's diversion, that the inflated emptiness of some notes may justify or excuse the contraction of the rest.

112 Theobald, thus weak and ignorant, thus mean and faithless, thus petulant and ostentatious, by the good luck of having Pope for his enemy, has escaped, and escaped alone, with reputation, from this undertaking. So willingly does the world support those who solicit favour, against those who command reverence; and so easily is he praised, whom no man can envy.

Our author fell then into the hands of Sir Thomas Hanmer, the Oxford editor, a man, in my opinion, eminently qualified by nature for such studies. He had, what is the first requisite to emendatory criticism, that intuition by which the poet's intention is immediately discovered, and that dexterity of intellect which dispatches its work by the easiest means. He had undoubtedly read much; his acquaintance with customs, opinions, and traditions, seems to have been large; and he is often learned without show. He seldom passes what he does not understand, without an attempt to find or to make a meaning, and sometimes hastily makes what a little more attention would have found. He is solicitous to reduce to grammar, what he could not be sure that his author intended to be grammatical. Shakespeare regarded more the series of ideas, than of words; and his language, not being designed for the reader's desk, was all that he desired it to be, if it conveyed his meaning to the audience. 113

Hanmer's care of the metre has been too violently censured. He found the measures reformed in so many passages, by the silent labours of some editors, with the silent acquiescence of the rest, that he thought himself allowed to extend a little further the licence, which had already been carried so far without reprehension; and of his corrections in general, it must be confessed, that they are often just, and made commonly with the least possible violation of the text. 114

But, by inserting his emendations, whether invented or borrowed, into the page, without any notice of varying copies, he has appropriated the labour of his predecessors, and made his own edition of little authority. His confidence indeed, both in himself and others, was too great; he supposes all to be right that was done by Pope and Theobald; he seems not to suspect a critic of fallibility, and it was but reasonable that he should claim what he so liberally granted. 115

As he never writes without careful inquiry and diligent consideration, I have received all his notes, and believe that every reader will wish for more. 116

Of the last editor[36] it is more difficult to speak. Respect is due to high place, tenderness to living reputation, and veneration to genius and learning; but he cannot be justly offended at that liberty of which he has himself so frequently given an example, nor very solicitious what is thought of notes, which he ought 117 never to have considered as part of his serious employments, and which, I suppose, since the ardour of composition is remitted, he no longer numbers among his happy effusions.

118 The original and predominant error of his commentary, is acquiescence in his first thoughts; that precipitation which is produced by consciousness of quick discernment; and that confidence which presumes to do, by surveying the surface, what labour only can perform, by penetrating the bottom. His notes exhibit sometimes perverse interpretations, and sometimes improbable conjectures; he at one time gives the author more profundity of meaning than the sentence admits, and at another discovers absurdities, where the sense is plain to every other reader. But his emendations are likewise often happy and just; and his interpretation of obscure passages learned and sagacious.

119 Of his notes, I have commonly rejected those, against which the general voice of the public has exclaimed, or which their own incongruity immediately condemns, and which, I suppose, the author himself would desire to be forgotton. Of the rest, to part I have given the highest approbation, by inserting the offered reading in the text; part I have left to the judgment of the reader, as doubtful, though specious; and part I have censured without reserve, but I am sure without bitterness of malice, and, I hope, without wantonness of insult.

120 It is no pleasure to me, in revising my volumes, to observe how much paper is wasted in confutation. Whoever considers the revolutions of learning, and the various questions of greater or less importance, upon which wit and reason have exercised their powers, must lament the unsuccessfulness of inquiry, and the slow advances of truth, when he reflects, that great part of the labour of every writer is only the destruction of those that went before him. The first care of the builder of a new system, is to demolish the fabrics which are standing. The chief desire of him that comments an author, is to show how much other commentators have corrupted and obscured him. The opinions prevalent in one age, as truths above the reach of controversy, are confuted and rejected in another, and rise again to reception in remoter times. Thus the human mind is kept in motion without progress. Thus sometimes truth and error, and sometimes contrarieties of error, take each other's place by reciprocal invasion. The tide of seeming knowledge which is poured over one

generation, retires and leaves another naked and barren; the sudden meteors of intelligence which for a while appear to shoot their beams into the regions of obscurity, on a sudden withdraw their lustre, and leave mortals again to grope their way.

These elevations and depressions of renown, and the contra- 121
dictions to which all improvers of knowledge must for ever be exposed, since they are not escaped by the highest and brightest of mankind, may surely be endured with patience by critics and annotators, who can rank themselves but as the satellites of their authors. How canst thou beg for life, says Achilles[37] to his captive, when thou knowest that thou art now to suffer only what must another day be suffered by Achilles?

Dr Warburton had a name sufficient to confer celebrity on 122
those who could exalt themselves into antagonists, and his notes have raised a clamour too loud to be distinct. His chief assailants are the authors of *The Canons of Criticism* and of the *Revisal* of *Shakespeare's Text*;[38] of whom one ridicules his errors with airy petulance, suitable enough to the levity of the controversy; the other attacks them with gloomy malignity, as if he were dragging to justice an assassin or incendiary. The one stings like a fly, sucks a little blood, takes a gay flutter, and returns for more; the other bites like a viper, and would be glad to leave inflammations and gangrene behind him. When I think on one, with his confederates, I remember the danger of Coriolanus, who was afraid that *girls with spits, and boys with stones, should slay him in puny battle*;[39] when the other crosses my imagination, I remember the prodigy in *Macbeth*,

> A falcon towering in his pride of place,
> Was by a mousing owl hawk'd at and kill'd.[40]

Let me however do them justice. One is a wit, and one a 123
scholar. They have both shown acuteness sufficient in the discovery of faults, and have both advanced some probable interpretations of obscure passages; but when they aspire to conjecture and emendation, it appears how falsely we all estimate our own abilities, and the little which they have been able to perform might have taught them more candour to the endeavours of others.

Before Dr Warburton's edition *Critical Observations on* 124

Shakespeare had been published by Mr Upton,[41] a man skilled in languages, and acquainted with books, but who seems to have had no great vigour of genius of nicety or taste. Many of his explanations are curious and useful, but he likewise, though he professed to oppose the licentious confidence of editors, and adhere to the old copies, is unable to restrain the rage of emendation, though his ardour is ill seconded by his skill. Every cold empiric, when his heart is expanded by a successful experiment, swells into a theorist, and the laborious collator at some unlucky moment frolics in conjecture.

125 *Critical, Historical and Explanatory Notes* have been likewise published upon Shakespeare by Dr Grey,[42] whose diligent perusal of the old English writers has enabled him to make some useful observations. What he undertook he has well enough performed, but as he neither attempts judicial nor emendatory criticism, he employs rather his memory than his sagacity. It were to be wished that all would endeavour to imitate his modesty who have not been able to surpass his knowledge.

126 I can say with great sincerity of all my predecessors, what I hope will hereafter be said of me, that not one has left Shakespeare without improvement, nor is there one to whom I have not been indebted for assistance and information. Whatever I have taken from them it was my intention to refer to its original author, and it is certain, that what I have not given to another, I believed when I wrote it to be my own. In some perhaps I have been anticipated; but if I am ever found to encroach upon the remarks of any other commentator, I am willing that the honour, be it more or less, should be transferred to the first claimant, for his right, and his alone, stands above dispute; the second can prove his pretensions only to himself, nor can himself always distinguish invention, with sufficient certainty, from recollection.

127 They have all been treated by me with candour, which they have not been careful of observing to one another. It is not easy to discover from what cause the acrimony of a scholiast can naturally proceed. The subjects to be discussed by him are of very small importance; they involve neither property nor liberty; nor favour the interest of sect or party. The various readings of copies, and different interpretations of a passage, seem to be questions that might exercise the wit, without engaging

the passions. But whether it be, that *small things make mean men proud*,[43] and vanity catches small occasions; or that all contrariety of opinion, even in those that can defend it no longer, makes proud men angry; there is often found in commentaries a spontaneous strain of invective and contempt, more eager and venomous than is vented by the most furious controvertist in politics against those whom he is hired to defame.

Perhaps the lightness of the matter may conduce to the vehemence of the agency; when the truth to be investigated is so near to inexistence, as to escape attention, its bulk is to be enlarged by rage and exclamation. That to which all would be indifferent in its original state, may attract notice when the fate of a name is appended to it. A commentator has indeed great temptations to supply by turbulence what he wants of dignity, to beat his little gold to a spacious surface, to work that to foam which no art or diligence can exalt to spirit. 128

The notes which I have borrowed or written are either illustrative, by which difficulties are explained; or judicial, by which faults and beauties are remarked; or emendatory, by which depravations are corrected. 129

The explanations transcribed from others, if I do not subjoin any other interpretation, I suppose commonly to be right, at least I intend by acquiescence to confess, that I have nothing better to propose. 130

After the labours of all the editors, I found many passages which appeared to me likely to obstruct the greater number of readers, and thought it my duty to facilitate their passage. It is impossible for an expositor not to write too little for some, and too much for others. He can only judge what is necessary by his own experience; and, how long soever he may deliberate, will at last explain many lines which the learned will think impossible to be mistaken, and omit many for which the ignorant will want his help. These are censures merely relative and must be quitely endured. I have endeavoured to be neither superflously copious, nor scrupulously reserved, and hope that I have made my author's meaning accessible to many who before were frighted from perusing him, and contributed something to the public, by diffusing innocent and rational pleasure. 131

The complete explanation of an author not systematic and consequential, but desultory and vagrant, abounding in casual 132 allusions and light hints, is not to be expected from any single scholiast. All personal reflections, when names are suppressed, must be in a few years irrecoverably obliterated; and customs, too minute to attract the notice of law, such as modes of dress, formalities of conversation, rules of visits, disposition of furniture, and practices of ceremony, which naturally find places in familiar dialogue, are so fugitive and unsubstantial, that they are not easily retained or recovered. What can be known, will be collected by chance from the recesses of obscure and obsolete papers, perused commonly with some other view. Of this knowledge every man has some, and none has much; but when an author has engaged the public attention, those who can add anything to his illustration, communicate their discoveries, and time produces what had eluded diligence.

133 To time I have been obliged to resign many passages which, though I did not understand them, will perhaps hereafter be explained, having, I hope illustrated some, which others have neglected or mistaken, sometimes by short remarks, or marginal directions, such as every editor has added at his will, and often by comments more laborious than the matter will seem to deserve; but that which is most difficult is not always most important, and to an editor nothing is a trifle by which his author is obscured.

134 The poetical beauties or defects I have not been very diligent to observe. Some plays have more, and some fewer judicial observations, not in proportion to their difference of merit, but because I gave this part of my design to chance and to caprice. The reader, I believe, is seldom pleased to find his opinion anticipated; it is natural to delight more in what we find or make, than in what we receive. Judgement, like other faculties, is improved by practice, and its advancement is hindered by submission to dictatorial decisions, as the memory grows torpid by the use of a table-book. Some initiation is however necessary; of all skill, part is infused by precept, and part is obtained by habit; I have therefore shown so much as may enable the candidate of criticism to discover the rest.

135 To the end of most plays, I have added short strictures, containing a general censure of faults, or praise of excellence; in which I know not how much I have concurred with the current opinion; but I have not, by any affectation of singularity, devia-

ted from it. Nothing is minutely and particularly examined, and therefore it is to be supposed, that in the plays which are condemned there is much to be praised, and in these which are praised much to be condemned.

The part of criticism in which the whole succession of editors has laboured with the greatest diligence, which has occasioned the most arrogant ostentation, and excited the keenest acrimony, is the emendation of corrupted passages, to which the public attention having been first drawn by the violence of the contention between Pope and Theobald, has been continued by the persecution, which, with a kind of conspiracy, has been since raised against all the publishers of Shakespeare. 136

That many passages have passed in a state of depravation through all the editions is indubitably certain; of these the restoration is only to be attempted by collation of copies or sagacity of conjecture. The collator's province is safe and easy, the conjecturer's perilous and difficult. Yet as the greater part of the plays are extant only in one copy, the peril must not be avoided, nor the difficulty refused. 137

Of the readings which this emulation of emendment has hitherto produced, some from the labours of every publisher I have advanced into the text; those are to be considered as in my opinion sufficiently supported; some I have rejected without mention, as evidently erroneous; some I have left in the notes without censure or approbation, as resting in equipoise between objection and defence; and some, which seemed specious* but not right, I have inserted with a subsequent animadversion. 138

Having classed the observations of others, I was at last to try what I could substitute for their mistakes, and how I could supply their omissions. I collated such copies as I could procure, and wished for more, but have not found the collectors of these rarities very communicative. Of the editions which chance or kindness put into my hands I have given an enumeration, that I may not be blamed for neglecting what I had not the power to do. 139

By examining the old copies, I soon found that the later publishers, with all their boasts of diligence, suffered many passages to stand unauthorized, and contended themselves with 140

*attractive.

Rowe's regulation of the text, even where they knew it to be arbitrary, and with a little consideration might have found it to be wrong. Some of these alterations are only the ejection of a word for one that appeared to him more elegant or more intelligible. These corruptions I have often silently rectified; for the history of our language, and the true force of our words can only be preserved, by keeping the text of authors free from adulteration. Others, and those very frequent, smoothed the cadence, or regulated the measure; on these I have not exercised the same rigour; if only a word was transposed, or a particle inserted or omitted, I have sometimes suffered the line to stand; for the inconstancy of the copies is such, as that some liberties may be easily permitted. But this practice I have not suffered to proceed far, having restored the primitive diction wherever it could for any reason be preferred.

141 The emendations, which comparison of copies supplied, I have inserted in the text; sometimes, where the improvement was slight, without notice, and sometimes with an account of the reasons of the change.

142 Conjecture, though it be sometimes unavoidable, I have not wantonly nor licentiously indulged. It has been my settled principle, that the reading of the ancient books is probably true, and therefore is not to be disturbed for the sake of elegance, perspicuity, or mere improvement of the sense. For though much credit is not due to the fidelity, nor any to the judgment of the first publishers, yet they who had the copy before their eyes were more likely to read it right, than we who only read it by imgination. But it is evident that they have often made strange mistakes by ignorance or negligence, and that therefore something may be properly attempted by criticism, keeping the middle way between presumption and timidity.

143 Such criticism I have attempted to practise and, where any passage appeared inextricably perplexed, have endeavoured to discover how it may be recalled to sense, with least violence. But my first labour is, always to turn the old text on every side, and try if there be any interstice, through which light can find its way; nor would Huetius[44] himself condemn me, as refusing the trouble of research, for the ambition of alteration. In this modest industry I have not been unsuccessful. I have rescued many lines from the violations of temerity, and secured many scenes from

the inroads of correction. I have adopted the Roman sentiment, that it is more honourable to save a citizen, than to kill an enemy, and have been more careful to protect than to attack.

I have preserved the common distribution of the plays into 144
acts, though I believe it to be in almost all the plays void of authority. Some of those which are divided in the later editions have no division in the first Folio, and some that are divided in the Folio have no division in the preceding copies. The settled mode of the theatre requires four intervals in the play, but few, if any, of our author's compositions can be properly distributed in that manner. An act is so much of the drama as passes without intervention of time or change of place. A pause makes a new act. In every real, and therefore in every imitative action, the intervals may be more or fewer, the restriction of five acts being accidental and arbitrary. This Shakespeare knew, and this he practised; his plays were written, and at first printed in one unbroken continuity, and ought now to be exhibited with short pauses, interposed as often as the scene is changed, or any considerable time is required to pass. This method would at once quell a thousand absurdities.

In restoring the author's works to their integrity, I have con- 145
sidered the punctuation as wholly in my power; for what could be their care of colons and commas, who corrupted words and sentences. Whatever could be done by adjusting points is therefore silently performed, in some plays with much diligence, in others with less; it is hard to keep a busy eye steadily fixed upon evanescent atoms, or a discursive mind upon evanescent truth.

The same liberty has been taken with a few particles, or other 146
words of slight effect. I have sometimes inserted or omitted them without notice. I have done that sometimes, which the other editors have done always, and which indeed the state of text may sufficiently justify.

The greater part of readers, instead of blaming us for passing 147
trifles, will wonder that on mere trifles so much labour is expended, with such importance of debate, and such solemnity of diction. To these I answer with confidence, that they are judging of an art which they do not understand; yet cannot much reproach them with their ignorance, nor promise that they would become in general, by learning criticism, more useful, happier or wiser.

As I practised conjecture more, I learned to trust it less; and 148 after I had printed a few plays, resolved to insert none of my own readings in the text. Upon this caution I now congratulate myself, for every day increases my doubt of my emendations.

149 Since I have confined my imagination, it must not be considered as very reprehensible, if I have suffered it to play some freaks in its own dominion. There is no danger in conjecture, if it be proposed as conjecture; and while the text remains uninjured, those changes may be safely offered, which are not considered even by him that offers them as necessary or safe.

150 If my readings are of little value, they have not been ostentatiously displayed or importunately obtruded. I could have written longer notes, for the art of writing notes is not of difficult attainment. The work is performed, first by railing at the stupidity, negligence, ignorance, and asinine tastelessness of the former editors, and showing, from all that goes before and all that follows, the inelegance and absurdity of the old reading; then by proposing something, which to superficial readers would seem specious, but which the editor rejects with indignation; then by producing the true reading, with a long paraphrase, and concluding with loud acclamations on the discovery, and a sober wish for the advancement and prosperity of genuine criticism.

151 All this may be done, and perphaps done sometimes without impropriety. But I have always suspected that the reading is right, which requires many words to prove it wrong; and the emendation wrong, that cannot without so much labour appear to be right. The justness of a happy restoration strikes at once, and the moral precept may be well applied to criticism, *quod dubitas ne feceris*.[45]

152 To dread the shore which he sees spread with wrecks, is natural to the sailor. I had before my eye, so many critical adventures ended in miscarriage, that caution was forced upon me. I encountered in every page Wit struggling with its own sophistry, and Learning confused by the multiplicity of its views. I was forced to censure those whom I admired, and could not but reflect, while I was dispossessing their emendations, how soon the same fate might happen to my own, and how many of the readings which I have corrected may be by some other editor defended and established.

> Critics, I saw, that others' names efface,
> And fix their own, with labour, in the place;

Their own, like others, soon their place resign'd,
Or disappear'd, and left the first behind. POPE[46]

That a conjectural critic should often be mistaken, cannot be 153
wonderful either to others or himself, if it be considered, that in his art there is no system, no principal and axiomatical truth that regulates subordinate positions. His chance of error is renewed at every attempt; an oblique view of the passage, a slight misapprehension of a phrase, a casual inattention to the parts connected, is sufficient to make him not only fail, but fail ridiculously; and when he succeeds best, he produces perhaps but one reading of many probable, and he that suggests another will always be able to dispute his claims.

It is an unhappy state, in which danger is hid under pleasure. 154
The allurements of emendation are scarcely resistible. Conjecture has all the joy and all the pride of invention, and he that has once started a happy change, is too much delighted to consider what objections may rise against it.

Yet conjectural criticism has been of great use in the learned 155
world; nor is it my intention to depreciate a study, that has exercised so many mighty minds, from the revival of learning to our own age, from the bishop of Aleria[47] to English Bentley.[48] The critics on ancient authors have, in the exercise of their sagacity, many assistances, which the editor of Shakespeare is condemned to want. They are employed upon grammatical and settled languages, whose construction contributes so much to perspicuity, that Homer has fewer passages unintelligible than Chaucer. The words have not only a known regimen, but invarible quantities, which direct and confine the choice. There are commonly more manuscripts than one; and they do not often conspire in the same mistakes. Yet Scaliger could confess to Salmasius how little satisfaction his emendations gave him. *Illudunt nobis conjecturae nostrae, quarum nos pudet, posteaquam in melibres codices incidimus.*[49] And Lipsius could complain, that critics were making faults, by trying to remove them, *Ut olim vitiis, ita nunc remediis laboratur.*[50] And indeed, where mere conjecture is to be used, the emendations of Scaliger and Lipsius, notwithstanding their wonderful sagacity and erudition, are often vague and disputable, like mine or Theobald's.

Perhaps I may not be more censured for doing wrong, than 156 for doing little; for raising in the public expectations, which at last I have not answered. The expectation of ignorance is indefinite, and that of knowledge is often tyrannical. It is hard to satisfy those who know not what to demand, or those who demand by design what they think impossible to be done. I have indeed disappointed no opinion more than my own; yet I have endeavoured to perform my task with no slight solicitude. Not a single passage in the whole work has appeared to me corrupt, which I have not attempted to restore; or obscure, which I have not endeavoured to illustrate. In many I have failed, like others; and from many, after all my efforts, I have retreated, and confessed the repulse. I have not passed over, with affected superiority, what is equally difficult to the reader and to myself, but where I could not instruct him, have owned my ignorance. I might easily have accumulated a mass of seeming learning upon easy scenes; but it ought not to be imputed to negligence, that, where nothing was necessary, nothing has been done, or that, where others have said enough, I have said no more.

157 Notes are often necessary, but they are necessary evils. Let him, that is yet unacquainted with the powers of Shakespeare, and who desires to feel the highest pleasure that the drama can give, read every play from the first scene to the last, with utter negligence of all his commentators. When his fancy is once on the wing, let it not stoop at correction or explanation. When his attention is strongly engaged, let it disdain alike to turn aside to the name of Theobald and Pope. Let him read on through brightness and obscurity, through integrity and corruption; let him preserve his comprehension of the dialogue and his interest in the fable. And when the pleasures of novelty have ceased, let him attempt exactness; and read the commentators.

158 Particular passages are cleared by notes, but the general effect of the work is weakened. This mind is refrigerated by interruption; the thoughts are diverted from the principal subject; the reader is weary, he suspects not why; and at last throws away the book, which he has too diligently studied,

159 Parts are not to be examined till the whole has been surveyed; there is a kind of intellectual remoteness necessary for the comprehension of any great work in its full design and its true proportions; a close approach shows the smaller niceties, but the beauty of the whole is discerned no longer.

It is not very grateful to consider how little the succession of 160
editors has added to this author's power of pleasing. He was read, admired, studied, and imitated, while he was yet deformed with all the improprieties which ignorance and neglect could accumulate upon him; while the reading was yet not rectified, nor his allusions understood; yet then did Dryden pronounce that Shakespeare was the man, who of all modern and perhaps ancient poets, had the largest and most comprehensive soul. All the images of nature were still present to him, and he drew them not laboriously but luckily; when he describes anything, you more than see it, you feel it too. Those who accuse him to have wanted learning, give him the greater commendation; he was naturally learned; he needed not the spectacles of books to read nature; he looked inwards, and found her there. I cannot say he is everywhere alike; were he so, I should do him injury to compare him with the greatest of mankind. He is many times flat and insipid; his comic wit degenerating into clenches, his serious swelling into bombast. But he is always great, when some great occasion is presented to him: no man can say he ever had a fit subject for his wit, and did not then raise himself as high above the rest of poets,

Quantum lenta solent inter viburna cupressi.[51]

It is to be lamented, that such a writer should want a com- 161
mentary; that his language should become obsolete, or his sentiments obscure. But it is vain to carry wishes beyond the condition of human things; that which must happen to all, has happened to Shakespeare, by accident and time; and more than has been suffered by any other writer since the use of types, has been suffered by him through his own negligence of fame, or perhaps by that superiority of mind, which despised its own performances, when it compared them with its powers, and judged those works unworthy to be preserved, which the critics of following ages were to contend for the fame of restoring and explaining.

Among these candidates of inferior fame, I am now to stand 162
the judgment of the public; and wish that I could confidently produce my commentary as equal to the encouragement which I have had the honour of receiving. Every work of this kind is by its nature deficient, and I should feel little solicitude about the sentence, were it to be pronounced only by the skilful and the learned.

Notes

from Johnson's edition of the Plays of William Shakespeare (1765)

THE TEMPEST

1.2.250 PROSPERO *Dost thou Forget/From what a torment I did free thee*?] That the character and conduct of Prospero may be understood, something must be known of the system of enchantment which supplied all the marvellous found in the romances of the Middle Ages. This system seems to be founded on the opinion that the fallen spirits, having different degrees of guilt, had different habitations allotted them at their expulsion, some being confined in hell, *some* (as Hooker, who delivers the opinion of our poet's age, expresses it) *dispersed in air, some on earth some in water, others in caves, dens, or minerals under the earth.* Of these, some were more malignant and mischievous than others. The earthy spirits seem to have been thought the most depraved, and the aerial the least vitiated. Thus Prospero observes of Ariel:

> Thou wast a spirit too delicate
> To act her *earthy* and abhorr'd commands.

Over these spirits a power might be obtained by certain rites performed or charms learned. This power was called *The Black Art* or *Knowledge of Enchantment*. The enchanter being, as King James observes in his *Demonology*, one *who commands the devil, whereas the witch serves him.* Those who thought best of this art, the existence of which was, I am afraid, believed very seriously, held that certain sounds and characters had a physical power over spirits and compelled their agency; others who condemned the practice, which in reality was surely never practised, were of opinion, with more reason, that the power of charms arose *only* from compact and was no more than the spirits voluntar[il]y allowed them for the seduction of man. The art was held by all, though not equally criminal, yet unlawful, and therefore Causabon, speaking of one who had commerce with spirits, blames him, though he imagines him *one of the best kind who dealt with them by way of command.* Thus Prospero repents of his art in the last scene. The spirits were always considered as in some measure enslaved to the enchanter, at least for a time, and as serving with unwillingness; therefore Ariel so often begs for liberty; and Caliban observes that the spirits serve Prospero with no good will but *hate him rootedly.*—Of these trifles enough.

1.2.321 CALIBAN *As wicked dew, as e'er mother brush'd/With raven's feather from unwholesome fen/Drop on you both!*] Whence these critics [Bentley and others] derived the notion of a new language appropriated to Caliban, I cannot find; they certainly mistook brutality of sentiment for uncouthness of words. Caliban had learned to speak of Prospero and his daughter, he had no names for the sun and the moon before their arrival, and could not have invented a language of his own without more understanding than Shakespeare has thought it proper to bestow upon him. His diction is indeed somewhat clouded by the gloominess of his temper and the malignity of his purposes; but let any other being entertain the same thoughts, and he will find them easily issue in the same expressions.

General Observation. It is observed of *The Tempest* that its plan is regular; this the author of the *Revisal* thinks, what I think too, an accidental effect of the story, not intended or regarded by our author. But whatever Shakespeare's intention in forming or adopting the plot, he has made it instrumental to the production of many characters, diversified with boundless invention, and preserved with profound skill in nature, extensive knowledge of opinions, and accurate observation of life. In a single drama are here exhibited princes, courtiers, and sailors, all speaking in their real characters. There is the agency of airy spirits and of an earthly goblin. The operation of magic, the tumults of a storm, the adventures of a desert island, the native effusion of untaught affection, the punishment of guilt, and the final happiness of the pair for whom our passions and reason are equally interested.

A MIDSUMMER NIGHT'S DREAM

1.2 *Enter Quince the carpenter, Snug the joiner, Bottom the weaver, Flute the bellows-mender, Snout the tinker, and Starveling the tailor.*] In this scene Shakespeare takes advantage of his knowledge of the theatre to ridicule the prejudices and competitions of the players. Bottom, who is generally acknowledged the principal actor, declares his inclination to be for a tyrant, for a part of fury, tumult, and noise, such as every young man pants to perform when he first steps upon the stage. The same Bottom, who seems bred in a tiring room, has another histrionical passion. He is for engrossing every part and would exclude his inferiors from all possibility of distinction. He is therefore desirous to play Pyramus, Thisbe, and the Lion at the same time.

1.2.49 FLUTE *Nay, faith, let not me play a woman—I have a beard coming.* QUINCE *That's all one: you shall play it in a mask, and you may speak as small as you will.*] This passage shows how the want of women on the old stage was supplied. If they had not a young man who could perform the part with a face that might pass for feminine, the character was acted in a mask, which was at that time a part of a lady's dress so much in use that it did not give any unusual appearance to the scene; and he that could modulate his voice in a female tone might play the woman very successfully. It is observed in Downes's *Memoirs of the Playhouse* that one of these counterfeit heroines moved the passions more strongly than the women that have since been brought upon the stage. Some of the catastrophes of the old comedies, which make lovers marry the wrong women, are, by recollection of the common use of masks, brought nearer to probability.

3.1 In the time of Shakespeare, there were many companies of players, sometimes five at the same time, contending for the favour of the public. Of these some were undoubtedly very unskilful and very poor, and it is probable that the design of this scene was to ridicule their ignorance and the odd expedients to which they might be driven by the want of proper decorations. Bottom was perhaps the head of a rival house and is therefore honoured with an ass's head.

3.1.173 TITANIA *the fiery glow-warm's eyes.* I know not how Shakespeare, who commonly derived his knowledge of nature from his own observation, happened to place the glow-worm's light in his eyes, which is only in his tail.

4.1.108 I know not why Shakespeare calls this play *A Midsummer Night's Dream*, when he so carefully informs us that it happened on the night preceding *May* day. [See 1.1.167]

General Observation. Of this play there are two editions in Quarto, one printed for Thomas Fisher, the other for James Roberts, both in 1600. I have used the copy of Roberts, very carefully collated, as it seems, with that of Fisher. Neither of the editions approach to exactness. Fisher is sometimes preferable, but Roberts was followed, though not without some variations, by Heming and Condell, and they by all the folios that succeeded them.

Wild and fantastical as this play is, all the parts in their various modes are well written and give the kind of pleasure which the author designed. Fairies in his time were much in fashion; common tradition had made them familiar, and Spenser's poem had made them great.

MEASURE FOR MEASURE

There is perhaps not one of Shakespeare's plays more darkened than this by the peculiarities of its author and the unskilfulness of its editors, by distortions of phrase or negligence of transcription.

1.1.52 DUKE *We have with a* leaven'd *and prepared choice*.] [*Leaven'd* has no sense in this place: we should read LEVEL'D *choice*. The allusion is to archery, when a man has fixed upon his object, after taking good aim.—WARBURTON.] No emendation is necessary. Leaven'd choice is one of Shakespeare's harsh metaphors. His train of ideas seems to be this. *I have proceeded to you with choice* mature, concocted, fermented, *leavened*. When Bread is *leavened*, it is left to ferment; a *leavened* choice is therefore a choice not hasty, but considerate, not declared as soon as it fell into the imagination, but suffered to work long in the mind. Thus explained it suits better with *prepared* than *levelled*.

2.2.142 ANGELO *That my sense breeds with it*. Thus all the folios. Some later Editor has changed *breeds* to *bleeds*, and Dr. Warburton blames poor Mr. Theobald for recalling the old word, which yet is certainly right. *My sense* breeds *with her sense*, that is, new thoughts are stirring in my mind, new conceptions are *hatched* in my imagination. So we say to *brood* over thought.

2.3.11 PROVOST *Who falling in the flaws of her own youth,/Hath* blister'd *her report*. [Who doth not see that the integrity of the metaphor requires we should read FLAMES of *her own youth.*—WARBURTON.] Who does not see that upon such principles there is no end of correction.

3.1.16 DUKE *The soft and tender fork/of a poor worm. Worm* is put for any creeping thing or *serpent*. Shakespeare supposes falsely, but according to the vulgar notion, that a serpent wounds with his tongue, and that his tongue is *forked*. He confounds reality and fiction, a serpent's tongue is *soft* but not *forked* nor hurtful. If it could hurt, it could not be soft. In *Midsummer Night's Dream* he has the same notion:—*With* doubler *tongue/ Than thine, O serpent, never adder* stung.

3.1.17 DUKE *Thy best of rest is sleep,/And that thou oft provok'st; yet grossly fear'st/Thy death, which is no more*.] Here Dr. Warburton might have found a sentiment worthy of his animadversion. I cannot without indignation find Shakespeare saying that *death is only sleep*, lengthening out his exhortation by a sentence which in the friar is impious, in the reasoner is foolish, and in the poet trite and vulgar.

3.1.32 DUKE *Thou hast nor youth nor age; / But, as it were, an after-dinner's sleep, / Dreaming on both*.] This is exquisitely imagined. When we are young, we busy ourselves in forming schemes for succeeding time and miss the gratifications that are before us; when we are old, we amuse the languor of age with the recollection of youthful pleasures or performances; so that our life, of which no part is filled with the business of the present time, resembles our dreams after dinner, when the events of the morning are mingled with the designs of the evening.

3.1.113 CLAUDIO *If it were damnable, he being so wise, / Why would he for the momentary trick / Be perdurably fin'd?*] Shakespeare shows his knowledge of human nature in the conduct of

Claudio. When Isabella first tells him of Angelo's proposal, he answers, with honest indignation, agreeably to his settled principles.

> Thou shalt not do't.

But the love of life, being permitted to operate, soon furnishes him with sophistical arguments; he believes it cannot be very dangerous to the soul, since Angelo, who is so wise, will venture it.

3.1.139 ISABELLA *Is't not a kind of incest, to take life / From thine own sister's shame?*] In Isabella's declamation there is something forced and far-fetched. But her indignation cannot be thought violent when we consider her not only as a virgin but as a nun.

4.5.1 DUKE *These letters at fit time deliver me.*] Peter never delivers the letters, but tells his story without any credentials. The poet forgot the plot which he had formed.

5.1.452 ISABELLA *Till he did look on me*] The duke has justly observed that Isabel is *importuned against all sense* to solicit for Angelo, yet here *against all sense* she solicits for him. Her argument is extraordinary.

> A due sincerity govern'd his deeds,
> Till he did look on me: since it is so,
> Let him not die.

That Angelo had committed all the crimes charged against him, as far as he could commit them, is evident. The only *intent* which *his* act did not overtake was the defilement of Isabel. Of this Angelo was only intentionally guilty.

Angelo's crimes were such as must sufficiently justify punishment, whether its end be to secure the innocent from wrong or to deter guilt by example; and I believe every reader feels some indignation when he finds him spared. From what extenuation of his crime can Isabel, who yet supposes her brother dead, form any plea in his favour. *Since he was good, till he looked on me, let him not die*. I am afraid our varlet poet intended to inculcate that women think ill of nothing that raises the credit of their beauty and are ready, however virtuous, to pardon any act which they think incited by their own charms.

5.1.499 DUKE *By this, Lord Angelo perceives he's safe.*] It is somewhat strange that Isabel is not made to express either gratitude, wonder, or joy at the sight of her brother.

5.1.504 DUKE *And yet here's one in place I cannot pardon.* After the pardon of two murderers, Lucio might be treated by the good Duke with less harshness; but perhaps the poet intended to show, what is too often seen, *that men easily forgive wrongs which are not committed against themselves.*

General Observation. Of this play the light or comic part is very natural and pleasing, but the grave scenes, if a few passages be excepted, have more labour than elegance. The plot is rather intricate than artful The time of the action is indefinite; some time, we know not how much, must have elapsed between the recess of the Duke and the imprisonment of Claudio; for he must have learned the story of Mariana in his disguise, or he delegated his power to a man already known to be corrupted. The unities of action and place are sufficiently preserved.

The Merchant of Venice

2.1.7 MOROCCO *To prove whose blood is reddest, his or mine.* To understand how the tawney Prince, whose savage dignity is very well supported, means to recommend himself by his challenge, it must be remembered that *red* blood is a traditionary sign of courage: Thus Macbeth calls one of his frighted soldiers, a *lily liver'd* Lown; again in this play, Cowards are said to *have livers white as milk*; and an effeminate and timorous man is termed a *milksop.*

2.1.25 MOROCCO *That slew the Sophy and a Persian Prine.* Shakespeare seldom escapes well when he is entangled with Geography. The Prince of *Morocco* must have travelled far to kill the *Sophy* of *Persia.*

2.7. end *A gentle riddance—draw the curtains; go—Let all of his complexion chuse me so.*] The old quarto Edition of 1600 has no distribution of acts, but proceed from the beginning to the end in an unbroken tenour. This play therefore having been probably divided without authority by the publishers of the first folio, lies open to a new regulation, if any more commodious division can be proposed. The story is itself so wildly incredible, and the changes of the scene so frequent and capricious, that the probability of action does not deserve much care; yet it may be proper to observe, that, by concluding the second act here, time is given for Bassanio's passage to Belmont.

5.1.33 STEPHANO *None, but a holy hermit, and her maid.*] I do not perceive the use of this hermit, of whom nothing is seen or heard afterwards. The poet had first planned his fable some other way, and inadvertently, when he changed his scheme, retained something of the original design.

5.1.129 PORTIA *Let me give light, but let me not be light;*] There is scarcely any word with which Shakespeare so much delights to trifle as with light, in its various significations.

General Observation. Of THE MERCHANT OF VENICE the stile is even and easy, with few peculiarities of diction, or anomalies of construction. The comic part raises laughter, and the serious fixes expectation. The probability of either one or the other story cannot be maintained. The union of two actions in one event is in this drama eminently happy. Dryden was much pleased with his own address in connecting the two plots of his *Spanish Friar*, which yet, I believe, the critic will find excelled by this play.

AS YOU LIKE IT

1.1.59 ORLANDO *I am no villain*] The word *villain* is used by the elder brother, in its present meaning, for a *wicked*, or *bloody man*; by Orlando in its original signification, for a *fellow of base extraction*.

1.3.30 CELIA *... you should love his son dearly? By this kind of chase, I should hate him, for my father hated his father dearly.*] That is, by this way of *following* the argument. *Dear* is used by Shakespeare in a double sense, for *beloved*, and for *hurtful, hated baleful*. Both senses are authorized, and both drawn from etymology, but properly *beloved* is *dear*, and *hateful* is *dere*. Rosalind uses *dearly* in the good, and Celia in the bad sense.

2.1.13 DUKE *Which like the toad, ugly and venomous, / Wears yet a precious jewel in his head*] It was the current opinion in Shakespeare's time that in the head of an old toad was to be found a stone, or pearl, to which great virtues were ascribed. This stone has been often sought, but nothing has been found more than accidental or perhaps morbid indurations of the skull.

2.7.94 ORLANDO *The thorny point / Of sharp distress has* ta'en *from me the shew / Of smooth civility.*] We might read *torn* with more elegance, but elegance alone will not justify alteration.

3.2.155 CELIA Atalanta's *better part*] I know not well what could be the better part of *Atalanta* here ascribed to Rosalind. Of the *Atalanta* most celebrated, and who therefore must be intended here where she has no epithet of discrimination, the *better part* seems to have been her heels, and the worse part was so bad that Rosalind would not thank her lover for the comparison. There is a more obscure *Atalanta,* a Huntress and a Heroine, but of her nothing bad is recorded, and therefore I know not which was the better part. Shakespeare was no despicable mythologist, yet he seems here to have mistaken some other character for that of *Atalanta.*

3.2.186 ROSALIND *I was never so be-rhymed since* Pythagoras *time, that I was an* Irish *rat*]. Rosalind is a very learned lady. She alludes to the Pythagorean doctrine which teaches that souls transmigrate from one animal to another, and relates that in his time she was an *Irish rat,* and by some metrical charm was rhymed to death. The power of killing rats with rhymes Donne mentions in his satires, and Temple in his treatises. Dr. Gray has produced a similar passage from Randolph.

My Poets
Shall with a saytire steeped in vinegar
Rhyme them to death, as they do rats in Ireland.

3.4.9 ROSALIND *I' faith, his hair is of a good colour.*] There is much of nature in this petty perverseness of Rosalind; she finds faults in her lover, in hope to be contradicted, and when Celia in sportive malice too readily seconds her accusations, she contradicts herself rather than suffer her favourite to want a vindication.

4.1.33 ROSALIND ... *swam in a gondola*] That is, *been at* Venice, the seat at that time of all licentiousness, where the young English gentlemen wasted their fortunes, debased their morals, and sometimes lost their religion.

The fashion of travelling, which prevailed very much in our author's time, was considered by the wiser men as one of the principal causes of corrupt manners. It was therefore gravely censured by Ascham in his *Schoolmaster* and by Bishop Hall in his *Quo vadis*; and is here, and in other passages, ridiculed by Shakespeare.

General Observation. Of this play the fable is wild and pleasing. I know not how the ladies will approve the facility with which both Rosalind and Celia give away their hearts. To Celia much may be forgiven for the heroism of her friendship. The character of Jaques is natural and well preserved. The comic dialogue is very sprightly, with less mixture of low buffoonery than in some other plays; and the graver part is elegant and harmonious. By hastening to the end of his work, Shakespeare suppressed the dialogue between the usurper and the hermit and lost an opportunity of exhibiting a moral lesson in which he might have found matter worthy of his highest powers.

LOVE'S LABOUR'S LOST

1.1.150 BEROWNE *Necessity will make us all forsworn.*] Biron amidst his extravagancies, speaks with great justness against the folly of vows. They are made without sufficient regard to the variations of life, and are therefore broken by some unforeseen necessity. They proceed commonly from a presumptuous confidence, and a false estimate of human power.

4.2 *Enter Holofernes, Sir Nathaniel, and Dull*]. I am not of the learned commentator's [Warburton's] opinion that the satire of Shakespeare is so seldom personal. It is of the nature of personal invectives to be soon unintelligible; and the author that gratifies private malice *animam in vulnere ponit*, destroys the future efficacy of his own writings and sacrifices the esteem of succeeding times to the laughter of a day. It is no wonder, therefore, that the sarcasms which, perhaps in the author's time, set the playhouse in a roar, are now lost among general reflections. Yet whether the character of Holofernes was pointed at any particular man, I am, notwithstanding the plausibility of Dr Warburton's conjecture, inclined to doubt. Every man adheres as long as he can to his own preconceptions. Before I read this note I considered the character of Holofernes as borrowed from the Rhombus of Sir Philip Sidney, who, in a kind of pastoral entertainment exhibited to Queen Elizabeth, has introduced a schoolmaster so called, speaking *a leash of languages at once* and puzzling himself and his auditors with a jargon like that of Holofernes in the present play. Sidney himself might bring the character from Italy; for, as Pescham observes, the schoolmaster has long been one of the ridiculous personages in the farces of that country.

5.2.69 PRINCESS *None are so surely caught, when they are catch'd, As wit turn'd fool: folly, in wisdom hatch'd / Hath wisdom's warrant, and the help of school; / And wit's own grace to grace a learned fool.*] These are observations worthy of a man who has surveyed human nature with the closest attention.

5.2.205 KING *Vouchsafe, bright moon, and these thy stars, to shine.*] When Queen Elizabeth asked an ambassador how he liked her Ladies. *It is hard*, said he, *to judge of stars in the presence of the sun.*

General Observation. In this play, which all the editors have concurred to censure and some have rejected as unworthy of our poet, it must be confessed that there are many passages mean, childish, and vulgar; and some which ought not to have been exhibited, as we are told they were, to a maiden queen. But there are scattered through the whole many sparks of genius; nor is there any play that has more evident marks of the hand of Shakespeare.

THE WINTER'S TALE

1.2.260 CAMILLO *Whereof the execution did cry out / Against the non-performance.*] This is one of the expressions by which Shakespeare too frequently clouds his meaning. This sounding phrase means, I think, no more than *a thing necessary to be done.*

3.1.2 CLEOMENES *Fertile the isle*] [Warburton had argued that 'isle' is incorrect geographically and had suggested 'soil'.] Shakespeare is little careful of geography. There is no need of this emendation in a play of which the whole plot depends upon a geographical error, by which Bohemia is supposed to be a maritime country.

3.2.55 LEONTES *I ne'er heard yet, / That any of those bolder vices* wanted / Less *impudence to gainsay what they did, / Than to perform it first.*] It is apparent that according to the proper, at least according to the present, use of words, *less* should be *more,* or *wanted* should be *had.* But Shakespeare is very uncertain in his use of negatives. It may be necessary once to observe, that in our language two negatives did not originally affirm, but strengthen the negation. This mode of speech was in time changed, but as the change was made in opposition to long custom, it proceeded gradually, and uniformity was not obtained but through an intermediate confusion.

3.2.152 LEONTES *I have too much believed mine own suspicion.*] This vehement retractation of *Leontes,* accompanied with the confession of more crimes than he was suspected of, is agreeable to our daily experience of the vicissitudes of violent tempers, and the eruptions of minds oppressed with guilt.

4.4.21 PERDITA *How would he look, to see his works, so noble, Vilely bound up*!] It is impossible for any man to rid his mind of his profession. The authorship of Shakespeare has supplied him with a metaphor, which rather than he would lose it, he has put with no great propriety into the mouth of a country maid. Thinking of his own works his mind passed naturally to the Binder. I am glad that he has no hint at an Editor.

5.2.45 GENTLEMAN *Did you see the meeting of the two Kings*?] It was, I suppose only to spare his own labour that the poet put this whole scene into narrative, for though part of the transaction was already known to the audience, and therefore could not properly be shewn again, yet the two kings might have met upon the stage, and after the examination of the old shepherd, the young Lady might have been recognized in sight of the spectators.

General Observation. Of this play no edition is known published before the Folio of 1623.

The story is taken from the novel of *Dorastus and Faunia,* which may be read in *Shakespeare Illustrated.*

This play, as Dr Warburton justly observes, is with all its absurdities, very entertaining. The character of Autolycus is very naturally conceived and strongly represented.

TWELFTH NIGHT

1.1.21 ORSINO *That instant I was turn'd into a hart.*] This image evidently alludes to the story of Acteon, by which Shakespeare seems to think men cautioned against too great familiarity with forbidden beauty. Acteon, who saw Diana naked, and was torn in pieces by his hounds, represents a man, who indulging his eyes, or his imagination, with the view of a woman that he cannot gain, has his heart torn with incessant longing. An interpretation far more elegant and natural than that of Sir Francis Bacon, who, in his *Wisdom of the Ancients* supposes this story to warn us against enquiring into the secrets of princes, by showing, that those who know that which for reasons of state is to be concealed, will be detected and destroyed by their own servants.

1.2.41 VIOLA *O' that I serv'd that lady.*] Viola seems to have formed a very deep design with very little premeditation; she is thrown by shipwreck on an unknown coast, hears that the prince is a bachelor; and resolves to supplant the lady whom he courts.

1.2.55 VIOLA *I'll serve this Duke.*] Viola is an excellent schemer, never at a loss; if she cannot serve the lady, she will serve the Duke.

2.3.81 SIR TOBY *Malvolio's a Peg-a-Ramsey . . . . Tilly valley, Lady!*] *Peg-a-Ramsey* I do not understand. *Tilly valley* was an interjection of contempt, which Sir Thomas More's lady is recorded to have had very often in her mouth.

2.5.66 MALVOLIO *wind up my watch.*] In our author's time watches were very uncommon. When Guy Faux was taken, it was urged as a circumstance of suspicion that a watch was found upon him.

3.4.183 SIR TOBY *Fare thee well, and God have mercy upon one of our souls; he may have mercy upon mine, but my hope is better.*] It were much to be wished, that Shakespeare in this and some other passages, had not ventured so near profaneness.

3.4.257 SIR TOBY *He is Knight, dubb'd with unhack'd rapier and on carpet consideration;*] That is, he is no soldier by profession, not a Knight Banneret, dubbed in the field of battle, but, *on carpet consideration*, at a festivity, or on some peaceable occasion, when knights receive their dignity kneeling not on the ground, as in war, but on a *carpet*. This is, I believe, the original of the contemptuous term a *carpet knight*, who was naturally held in scorn by the men of war.

4.2.123 CLOWN . . . . *like to the old Vice*] *Vice* was the fool of the old moralities. Some traces of this character are still preserved in puppet shows and by country mummers.

General Observation. This play is in the graver part elegant and easy, and in some of the lighter scenes exquisitely humorous. Aguecheek is drawn with great propriety, but his character is, in a great measure, that of natural fatuity and is therefore not the proper prey of a satirist. The soliloquy of Malvolio is truly comic; he is betrayed to ridicule merely by his pride. The marriage of Olivia and the succeeding perplexity, though well enough contrived to divert on the stage, wants credibility and fails to produce the proper instruction required in the drama, as it exhibits no just picture of life.

The Merry Wives of Windsor

3.5.156 FORD *I'll be horn-mad.*] There is no image which our author appears so fond of as that of a cuckold's horns. Scarcely a light character is introduced that does not endeavour to produce merriment by some allusion to horned husbands. As he wrote his plays for the stage rather that the press, he perhaps reviewed them seldom, and did not observe this repetition, or finding the jest, however frequent: still successful, did not think correction necessary.

4.2.204 EVANS *I spy a great peard under her muffler.*] As the second stratagem, by which Falstaff escapes, is much the grosser of the two, I wish it had been practised first. It is very unlikely that Ford having been so deceived before, and knowing that he had been deceived, would suffer him to escape in so slight a disguise.

4.3.13 BARDOLPH *They must* come *off*.] *To come off*, signifies in our author, sometimes *to be uttered with spirit and volubility*. In this place it seems to mean what is in our time expressed by *to come down*, to pay liberally and readily. These accidental and colloquial senses are the disgrace of language and the plague of commentators.

4.5.128 QUICKLY *Good hearts.*] The great fault of this play is the frequency of expressions so profane, that no necessity of preserving character can justify them. There are laws of higher authority than those of criticism,

General Observation. Of this play there is a tradition preserved by Mr Rowe that it was written at the command of Queen Elizabeth, who was so delighted with the character of Falstaff that she wished it to be diffused through more plays; but, suspecting that it might pall by continued uniformity, directed the poet to diversify his manner, by showing him in love. No task is harder than that of writing to the ideas of another. Shakespeare knew what the queen, if the story be true, seems not to have known, that by any real passion of tenderness, the selfish craft, the careless jollity, and the lazy luxury of Falstaff must have suffered so much abatement that little of his former cast would have remained. Falstaff could not love but by ceasing to be Falstaff. He could only counterfeit love, and his professions could be prompted, not by the hope of pleasure, but of money. Thus the poet approached as near as he could to the work enjoined him; yet, having perhaps in the former plays completed his own idea, seems not to have been able to give Falstaff all his former power of entertainment.

This comedy is remarkable for the variety and number of the personages, who exhibit more characters appropriated and discriminated than perhaps can be found in any other play.

Whether Shakespeare was the first that produced upon the English stage the effect of language distorted and depraved by provincial or foreign pronunciations, I cannot certainly decide.

This mode of forming ridiculous characters can confer praise only on him who originally discovered it, for it requires not much of either wit or judgment; its success must be derived almost wholly from the player, but its power in a skilful mouth even he that despises it is unable to resist.

The conduct of this drama is deficient; the action begins and ends often before the conclusion, and the different parts might change places without inconvenience; but its general power, that power by which all works of genius shall finally be tried, is such that perhaps it never yet had reader or spectator who did not think it too soon at an end.

Much Ado About Nothing

1.1.66 BEATRICE *Four of his five wits.*] In our author's time wit was the general term for intellectual powers. So Davies on the Soul,

> *Wit, seeking truth from cause to cause ascends,*
> *And never rests till it the first attain;*
> *Will, seeking good, finds many middle ends,*
> *But never stays till it the last do gain.*

And in another part,

> *But if a phrenzy do possess the brain,*
> *It so disturbs and blots the form of things,*
> *As fantasy proves altogether vain,*
> *And to the wit no true relation brings.*
> *Then doth the wit, admitting all for true,*
> *Build fond conclusions on those idle grounds;—*

The *wits* seem to have reckoned five, by analogy to the five senses, or the five inlets of ideas.

1.1.243 BENEDICK *A recheate winded in my forehead.*] That is, *I will wear a horn on my forehead which the huntsman may blow. A recheate* is the sound by which dogs are called back. Shakespeare had no mercy upon the poor cuckold, his horn is an inexhaustible subject of merriment.

1.3.14 DON JOHN *I cannot hide what I am.*] This is one of our author's natural touches. An envious and unsocial mind, too proud to give pleasure, and too sullen to receive it, always endeavours to hide its malignity from the world and from itself, under the plainness of simple honesty, or the dignity of haughty independence.

2.1.330 BEATRICE *Thus goes every one to the world but I, and I am sunburnt.*] What is it, *to go to the world?* perhaps, to enter by marriage into a settled state; but why is the unmarried Lady *sunburnt*? I believe we should read, *thus goes every one to the* wood *but I, and I am sunburnt*. Thus does every one but I find a shelter, and I am left exposed to wind and *sun. The nearest way to the* wood, is a phrase for the readiest means to any end. It is said of a woman, who accepts a worse match than those which she had refused, that she has passed through the *wood*, and at last taken a crooked stick. But conjectural criticism has always something to abate its confidence. Shakespeare, in *All's Well That Ends Well*, uses the phrase, *to go to the world*, for *marriage*. So that my emendation depends only on the opposition of *wood* to *sun-burnt*.

3.3.43 DOGBERRY, *Have a care that your bills be not stolen.*] A *bill* is still carried by the watchmen at Lichfield. It was the old weapon of the English infantry, which, says Temple, gave the most ghastly and deplorable wounds.

4.1 251 LEONATO *Being that I flow in grief. / The smallest twine may lead me*. This is one of our author's observations upon life. Men overpowered with distress eagerly listen to the first offers of relief, close with every scheme, and believe every promise. He that has no longer any confidence in himself, is glad to repose his trust in any other that will undertake to guide him.

The Taming of the Shrew

General Observation. Of this play the two plots are so well united that they can hardly be called two without injury to the art with which they are interwoven. The attention is entertained with all the variety of a double plot, yet is not distracted by connected incidents.

The part between Katharina and Petruchio is eminently spritely and diverting. At the marriage of Bianca the arrival of the real father perhaps produces more perplexity than pleasure. The whole play is very popular and diverting.

All's Well That Ends Well

1.3 *Enter Countess, Steward, and Clown.*] A *Clown* in Shakespeare is commonly taken for a *licensed jester* or domestic *fool*.

We are not to wonder that we find this character often in his plays, since fools were at that time maintained in all great families, to keep up merriment in the house. In the picture of Sir Thomas More's family, by Hans Holbein, the only servant represented is Paterson the *fool*. This is a proof of the familiarity to which they were admitted, not by the great only but the wise.

In some plays, a servant or rustic of remarkable petulance and freedom of speech is likewise called a clown.

4.2.73 DIANA *Since Frenchmen are so braid, / Marry that will, I'll live and die a maid.*] . . . Nothing is more common than for girls, on such occasions, to say in a pet what they do not think or to think for a time what they do not finally resolve.

4.3.280 PAROLLES *He will steal, Sir, an egg out of a cloister.*] I know not that *cloister*, though it may etymologically signify *any thing shut* is used by our author, otherwise than for a *monastery*, and therefore I cannot guess whence this hyberbole could take its original: perhaps it means only this: *He will steal any thing, however trifling, from any place, however holy.*

4.3.317 2. LORD *Why does he ask him of me?*] This is nature. Every man is on such occasions more willing to hear his neighbour's character than his own.

5.2.50 LAFEU . . . *though you are a fool and a knave, you shall eat.*] Parolles has many of the lineaments of Falstaff and seems to be the character which Shakespeare delighted to draw, a fellow that had more wit than virtue. Though justice required that he should be detected and exposed, yet his *vices sit so fit in him* that he is not at last suffered to starve.

5.3.21 KING . . . *the first view shall kill / All repetition.*] *The first interview shall put an end to all recollection of the past.* Shakespeare is now hastening to the end of the play, finds his matter sufficient to fill up his remaining scenes, and therefore, as on other such occasions, contracts his dialogue and precipitates his action. Decency required that Bertram's double crime of cruelty and disobedience, joined likewise with some hypocrisy, should raise more resentment; and that though his mother might easily forgive him, his king should more pertinaciously vindicate his own authority and Helen's merit. Of all this Shakespeare could not be ignorant, but Shakespeare wanted to conclude his play.

5.3.101 KING *Plutus himself, / That knows the tinct and multiplying medicine*] Plutus the grand alchemist, who knows the *tincture* which confers the properties of gold upon base metals, and the *matter* by which *gold* is *multiplied*, by which a small quantity of gold is made to communicate its qualities to a large mass of metal.

In the reign of Henry the Fourth a law was made to forbid *all men thence-forth to* multiply *gold, or use any craft of multiplication.* Of which law Mr Boyle, when he was warm with the hope of transmutation, procured a repeal.

5.3.231. This dialogue is too long, since the audience already knew the whole transaction; nor is there any reason for puzzling the king and playing with his passions; but it was much easier than to make a pathetical interview between Helen and her husband, her mother, and the king.

General Observation. This play has many delightful scenes, though not sufficiently probable, and some happy characters, though not new, nor produced by any deep knowledge of human nature. Parolles is a boaster and a coward, such as has always been the sport of the stage, but perhaps never raised more laughter or contempt than in the hands of Shakespeare.

I cannot reconcile my heart to Bertram; a man noble without generosity, and young without truth; who marries Helen as a coward and leaves her as a profligate; when she is dead by his unkindness, sneaks home to a second marriage, is accused by a woman whom he has wronged, defends himself by falsehood, and is dismissed to happiness

The story of Bertram and Diana had been told before of Mariana and Angelo, and, to confess the truth, scarcely merited to be heard a second time. The story is copied from a novel of Boccaccio, which may be read in *Shakespeare Illustrated*, with remarks not more favourable to Bertram than my own.

KING JOHN

1.1.24 K. JOHN *Be thou as lightning in the eyes of* France, / *For ere thou canst report I will be there, / The thunder of my cannon shall be heard.*] The simile does not suit well: the lightning indeed appears before the thunder is heard, but the lightning is destructive, and the thunder innocent.

1.1.27 K. JOHN *Be thou the trumpet of our wrath, / And sullen presage of your own decay.*] By the epithet *sullen*, which cannot be applied to a trumpet, it is plain, that our author's imagination had now suggested a new idea. It is as if he had said, be a *trumpet* to alarm with our invasion, be a *bird* of *ill* omen to croak out the prognostic of your own ruin.

2.1.300 FRENCH HERALD *Ye men of* Angiers.] This speech is very poetical and smooth, and except the conceit of the *widow's husband* embracing *the earth*, is just and beautiful.

2.1.477 ELINOR *Lest zeal now melted by the windy breath / Of soft petitions pity and remorse, / Cool and congeal again to what it was.*] We have here a very unsual, and, I think, not very just image of *zeal*, which in its highest degree is represented by others as a flame, but by Shakespeare as a frost. To *repress zeal*, in the language of others, is to *cool*, in Shakespeare's to *melt* it; when it exerts its utmost power it is commonly said to *flame*, but by Shakespeare to be *congealed*.

3.1.70 CONSTANCE *To me and to the state of my great grief / Let kings assemble.*] In *Much Ado About Nothing*, the father of Hero, depressed by her disgrace, declares himself so subdued by grief that a *thread may lead him*. How is it that grief in Leonato and Lady Constance produces effects directly opposite, and yet both agreeable to nature? Sorrow softens the mind while it is yet warmed by hope, but hardens it when it is congealed by despair. Distress, while there remains any prospect of relief, is weak and flexible, but when no succour remains, is fearless and stubborn; angry alike at those that injure and at those that do not help; careless to please where nothing can be gained and fearless to offend when there is nothing further to be dreaded. Such was this writer's knowledge of the passions.

3.1.147 KING JOHN *Thou canst not, Cardinal, devise a name / So slight, unworthy, and ridiculous, / To charge me to an answer, as the Pope.*] This must have been at the time when it was written, in our struggles with popery, a very captivating scene.

So many passages remain in which Shakespeare evidently takes his advantage of the facts then recent, and of the passions then in motion, that I cannot but suspect that time has obscured much of his art, and that many allusions yet remain undiscovered which perhaps may be gradually retrieved by succeeding commentators.

3.2.1 BASTARD *Now, by my life, this day grows wond'rous hot; / Some airy devil hovers in the sky, / And pours down mischief.*] [We must read, *Some fiery devil*, if we will have the *cause* equal to the *eflect*.—WARBURTON.] There is no end of such alterations; every page of a vehement and negligent writer will afford opportunities for changes of terms, if mere propriety will justify them. Not that of this change the propriety is out of controversy. Dr. Warburton will have the devil *fiery*, because he makes the day *hot*; the author makes him *airy*, because *he hovers in the sky*, and the *heat* and *mischief* are natural consequences of his malignity.

3.4.61 KING PHILIP *Bind up those tresses.*] It was necessary that Constance should be interrupted, because a passion so violent cannot be borne long. I wish the following speeches had been equally happy; but they only serve to shew, how difficult it is to maintain the pathetick long.

3.4.99 CONSTANCE *Had you such a loss as I, / I could give better comfort.*] This is a sentiment which great sorrow always dictates. Whoever cannot help himself casts his eyes on others for assistance, and often mistakes their inability for coldness.

3.4.107 LEWIS *There's nothing in this world can make me joy.*] The young Prince feels his defeat with more sensibility than his father. Shame operates most strongly in the earlier years, and when can disgrace be less welcomed than when a man is going to his bride?

4.1.101 ARTHUR *Or, Hubert, if you will, cut out my tongue, / So I may keep mine eyes.*] This is according to nature. We imagine no evil so great as that which is near us.

4.2.197 HUBERT—*slippers' which his nimble haste / Had falsely thrust upon contrary feet.*] I know not how the commentators understand this important passage, which, in Dr. Warburton's edition, is marked as eminently beautiful, and, in the whole, not without justice. But Shakespeare seems to have confounded a man's shoes with his gloves. He that is frighted or hurried may put his hand into the wrong glove, but either shoe will equally admit either foot. The author seems to be disturbed by the disorder which he describes.

4.2.231 KING JOHN *Hadst thou but shook thy head.*] There are many touches of nature in this conference of John with Hubert. A man engaged in wickedness would keep the profit to himself and transfer the guilt to his accomplice. These reproaches vented against Hubert are not the words of art or policy, but the eruptions of mind swelling with consciousness of a crime and desirous of discharging its misery on another.

This account of the timidity of guilt is drawn *ab ipsis recessibus mentis*, from an intimate knowledge of mankind, particularly that line in which he says that *to have bid him tell his tale* in *express* words would have *struck him dumb*; nothing is more certain than that bad men use all the arts of fallacy upon themselves, palliate their actions to their own minds by gentle terms, and hide themselves from their own detection in ambiguities and subterfuges.

General Observation. The tragedy of *King John*; though not written with the utmost power of Shakespeare, is varied with a very pleasing interchange of incidents and characters. The lady's grief is very affecting, and the character of the Bastard contains that mixture of greatness and levity which this author delighted to exhibit.

There is extant another play of *King John* published with Shakespeare's name, so different from this, and I think from all his other works, that there is reason to think his name was prefixed only to recommend it to sale. No man writes upon the same subject twice without concurring in many places with himself.

RICHARD II

1.3.277 GAUNT *Shorten my days thou canst with sullen sorrow, / And pluck nights from me, but not lend a morrow*;] / It is matter of very melancholy consideration, that all human advantages confer more power of doing evil than good.

2.1.21 YORK *Report of fashions in proud Italy.*] Our author, who gives to all nations the customs of England, and to all ages the manners of his own; has charged the times of Richard with a folly not perhaps known then, but very frequent in

Shakespeare's time, and much lamented by the wisest and best of our ancestors.

3.2.56 KING RICHARD *The breath of worldly men cannot depose / The Deputy elected by the Lord.*] Here is the doctrine of indefeasible right expressed in the strongest terms, but our poet did not learn it in the reign of King James, to which it is now the practice of all writers, whose opinions are regulated by fashion or interset, to impute the original of every tenet which they have been taught to think false or foolish.

3.2.93 KING RICHARD *Mine ear is open and my heart prepar'd.*] It seems to be the design of the poet to raise Richard to esteem in his fall and consequently to interest the reader in his favour. He gives him only passive fortitude, the virtue of a confessor rather than of a king. In his prosperity we saw him imperious and oppressive; but in his distress he is wise, patient, and pious.

3.2.153 KING RICHARD *And that small model of the barren earth, / Which serves as paste and cover to our bones.*] A metaphor, not of the most sublime kind, taken from a *pie*.

3.2.207 KING RICHARD *I'll hate him everlastingly / That bids me be of comfort any more.*] This sentiment is drawn from nature. Nothing is more offensive to a mind convinced that his distress is without a remedy, and preparing to submit quietly to irresistible calamity, than these petty and conjectured comforts which unskilful officiousness thinks it virtue to administer.

3.3.156 KING RICHARD. . . *where subjects' feet/May hourly trample on their sovereign's head.*] Shakespeare is very apt to deviate from the pathetic to the ridiculous. Had the speech of Richard ended at this line, it had exhibited the natural language of submissive misery, conforming its intention to the present fortune and calmly ending its purposes in death.

4.1.40 FITZWATER *My rapier's point.*] Shakespeare deserts the manners of the age in which his drama is placed very often, without necessity or advantage. The edge of a sword had served his purpose as well as the *point of a rapier*, and he had then escaped the impropriety of giving the English nobles a weapon which was not seen in England till two centuries afterwards.

4.1.125 CARLISLE *And shall the figure of God's Majesty, / His Captain, Steward, Deputy elect.*] Here is another proof that our author did not learn in King James's court his elevated notions of the right of kings. I know not any flatterer of the Stuarts who has expressed this doctrine in much stronger terms. It must be observed that the poet intends from the beginning to the end to exhibit this bishop as brave, pious, and venerable.

4.1.322 CARLISLE *The children yet unborn, / Shall feel this day as sharp to them as thorn.*] This pathetic denunciation shows that Shakespeare intended to impress his auditors with dislike of the deposal of Richard.

5.1.46 KING RICHARD *For why? the senseless brands will sympathize.*] The poet should have ended this speech with the foregoing line, and have spread his childish prattle about the fire.

5.3.5 BOLINGBROKE *Inquire at London 'mongst the taverns there,/ For there, they say, he daily doth frequent, / With unrestrained loose companions.*] This is a very proper introduction to the future character of Henry the fifth, to his debaucheries in his youth and his greatness in his manhood.

General Observation. This play is extracted from the *Chronicle of Holinshed*, in which many passages may be found which Shakespeare has, with very little alteration, transplanted into his scenes; particularly a speech of the bishop of Carlisle in defence of King Richard's unalienable right and immunity from human jurisdiction.

Jonson, who in his *Catiline* and *Sejanus* has inserted many speeches from the Roman historians, was perhaps induced to that practice by the example of Shakespeare, who had condescended sometimes to copy more ignoble writers. But Shakespeare had more of his own than Jonson and, if he sometimes was willing to spare his labour, showed by what he performed at other times that his extracts were made by choice or idleness rather than necessity.

This play is one of those which Shakespeare has apparently revised; but as success in works of invention is not always proportionate to labour, it is not finished at last with the happy force of some other of his tragedies nor can be said much to affect the passions or enlarge the understanding.

The First Part of King Henry IV

Shakspeare has apparently designed a regular connection of these dramatic histories from *Richard the Second* to *Henry the Fifth.* King Henry, at the end of *Richard the Second,* declares his purpose to visit the Holy Land, which he resumes in this speech. The complaint made by King Henry in the last act of *Richard the Second,* of the wildness of his son, prepares the reader for the frolics which are here to be recounted, and the characters which are now to be exhibited.

1.1.4-5 KING HENRY *To be commenc'd in strands afar remote, / No more the thirsty entrance of this soil.*] We may suppose a verse or two lost between these two lines. This is a cheap way of palliating an editor's inability; but I believe such omissions are more frequent in Shakespeare than is commonly imagined.

1.1.19 KING HENRY *As far as to the sepulchre of Christ.*] The lawfulness and justice of the holy wars have been much disputed; but perhaps there is a principle on which the question may be easily determined. If it be part of the religion of the Mahometans, to extirpate by the sword all other religions, it is, by the law of self defence, lawful for men of every other religion, and for Christians among others, to make war upon Mahometans, simply as Mahometans, as men obliged by their own principles to make war upon Christians, and only lying in wait till opportunity shall promise them success.

1.2.217 PRINCE HENRY *I know you all and will a while uphold / The unyok'd humour of your idleness.*] This speech is very artfully introduced to keep the Prince from appearing vile in the opinion of the audience; it prepares them for his future reformation, and, what is yet more valuable, exhibits a natural picture of a great mind offering excuses to itself, and palliating those follies which it can neither justify nor forsake.

1.3.201 HOTSPUR *By heav'n, methinks, it were an easy leap, / To pluck bright honour from the pale fac'd Moon.*] [So that we see, tho' the expression be sublime and daring, yet the thought is the natural movement of an heroic mind. Euripides at least thought so, when he put the very same sentiment, in the same words, into the mouth of Eleocles—*I will not, madam, disguise my thoughts; I could scale heaven I could descend to the very entrails of the earth, if so be that by that price I could obtain a kingdom.*—WARBURTON.] Though I am very far from condemning this speech, with Gildon and Theobald, as absolute madness, yet I cannot find in it that profundity of reflection and beauty of allegory which the learned commentator [Warburton] has endeavoured to display. This sally of Hotspur may be, I think, soberly and rationally vindicated as the violent eruption of a mind inflated with ambition and fired with resentment; as the boastful clamour of a man able to do much and eager to do more; as the hasty motion of turbulent desire; as the dark expression of indetermined thoughts. The passage from Euripides [which Warburton adduces] is surely not allegorical, yet it is produced, and properly, as parallel.

2.1.96 GADSHILL *We have the receipt of Fern-seed, we walk invisible.*] *Fern* is one of those plants which have their seed on the back of the leaf so small as to escape the sight. Those who perceived that *fern* was propagated by semination and yet could never see the seed, were much at a loss for a solution of the difficulty; and as wonder always endeavours to augment itself, they ascribed to *Fern-seed* many strange properties, some of which the rustic virgins have not yet forgotten or exploded.

2.4.41 *Enter Francis the drawer.*] This scene, helped by the distraction of the drawer, and grimaces of the prince, may entertain upon the stage, but affords not much delight to the reader. The author has judiciously made it short.

2.4.395 FALSTAFF *You may buy land now as cheap as stinking mackerel.*] In former times the prosperity of the nation was known by the value of land as now by the price of stocks. Before Henry the seventh made it safe to serve the king regnant, it was the practice at every revolution for the conqueror to confiscate the estates of those that opposed, and perhaps of those who did not assist him. Those, therefore, that foresaw a change of government, and thought their estates in danger, were desirous to sell them in haste for something that might be carried away.

2.4.442 FALSTAFF *Though the camomile, the more it is trodden on, the faster it grows.*] This whole speech is supremely comic. The simile of camomile used to illustrate a contrary effect, brings to my remembrance an observation of a later writer of some merit, whom the desire of being witty has betrayed into a like thought. Meaning to enforce with great vehemence the mad temerity of young soldiers, he remarks, that *though* Bedlam *be in the road to* Hogsden, *it is out of the way to promotion.*

2.4.549 PRINCE HENRY *Go, hide thee behind the arras.*] The bulk of Falstaff made him not the fittest to be concealed behind the hangings, but every poet sacrifices something to the scenery; if Falstaff had not been hidden he could not have been found asleep, nor had his pockets searched.

3.1.27 HOTSPUR *Diseased Nature oftentimes breaks forth / In strange eruptions.*] The poet has here taken, from the perverseness and contrariousness of Hotspur's temper, an opportunity of raising his character, by a very rational and philosophical confutation of superstitious error.

3.1.96 HOTSPUR *Methinks, my moiety, north from Burton here./ In quantity equals not one of yours.*] Hotspur is here just such a divider as the Irishman who made *three halves*; Therefore, for the honour of Shakespeare, I will suppose, with the Oxford Editor, that he wrote *portion.*—WARBURTON.] I will not suppose it.

3.3.30 FALSTAFF *Thou art the Knight of the burning lamp.*] This is a natural picture. Every man who feels in himself the pain of deformity, however, like this merry knight, he may affect to make sport with it among those whom it is his interest to please, is ready to revenge any hint of contempt upon one whom he can use with freedom.

4.1.97 VERNON *All furnisht, all in arms, / All plum'd like Estridges, that with the wind / Baited like Eagles.*] I read,

All furnish'd' all in arms,
All plum'd like Estridges that wing *the wind*
Baited like Eagles.

This gives a strong image. They were not only plum'd like Estridges, but their plumes fluttered like those of an Estridge on the wing mounting against the wind. A more lively representation of young men ardent for enterprize perhaps no writer has ever given.

4.2.31 FALSTAFF *Younger sons to younger brothers.*] Raleigh, in his discourse on *war*, uses this very expression for men of desperate fortune and wild adventure. Which borrowed it from the other I know not, but I think the play was printed before the discourse.

5.3.59 FALSTAFF *If Percy be alive, I'll pierce him;*] To *pierce* a *vessel* is to *tap* it. Falstaff takes up his bottle which the Prince had tossed at his head, and being about to animate himself with a draught, cries if *Percy be alive I'll pierce him*, and so draws the cork. I do not propose this with much confidence.

THE SECOND PART OF KING HENRY IV

Induction

This speech of Rumour is not inelegant or unpoetical, but is wholly useless, since we are told nothing which the scene does not clearly and naturally discover. The only end of such prologues is to inform the audience of some facts previous to the action, of which they can have no knowledge from the persons of the drama.

1.1.159 NORTHUMBERLAND *The rude scene may end, / And darkness be the burier of the dead*] The conclusion of this noble speech is extremely striking. There is no need to suppose it exactly philosophical, *darkness* in poetry may be absence of eyes as well as privation of light. Yet we may remark, that by an ancient opinion it has been held, that if the human race, for whom the world was made, were extirpated, the whole system of sublunary nature would cease.

1.2.166 FALSTAFF *The young Prince hath mis-led me. I am the fellow with the great belly, and he my dog.*] I do not understand this joke. Dogs lead the blind, but why does a dog lead the fat?

1.2.206 CHIEF JUSTICE *Is not your voice broken? your wind short? your chin double? your wit single?*] We call a man *single-witted* who attains but one species of knowledge. This sense I know not how to apply to Falstaff, and rather think that the Chief Justice hints at a calamity always incident to a gray-haired wit, whose misfortune is, that his merriment is unfashionable. His allusions are to forgotten facts; his illustrations are drawn from notions obscured by time; his *wit* is therefore *single*, such as none has any part in but himself.

2.2.189 POINS *Put on two leather jerkins and aprons, and wait upon him at his table, as drawers.*] This was a plot very unlikely to succeed where the Prince and the drawers were all known, but it produces merriment, which our author found more useful than probability.

4.2.122 PRINCE JOHN OF LANCASTER *Guard these traitors to the block of death.*] It cannot but raise some indignation to find this horrible violation of faith passed over thus slightly by the poet, without any note of censure or detestation.

4.3.93 FALSTAFF *This same sober-blooded boy doth not love me, nor a man cannot make him laugh.*] Falstaff speaks; here like a veteran in life. The young prince did not love him, and he despaired to gain his affection, for he could not make him laugh. Men only become friends by community of pleasures. He who cannot be softened into gayety cannot easily be melted into kindness.

4.5.129 KING HENRY England *shall double gild his treble Guilt.*] [Evidently the nonsense of some foolish Player . . . . —WARBURTON.] I know not why this commentator should speak with so much confidence what he cannot know, or determine so positively what so capricious a writer as our poet might either deliberately or wantonly produce. This line is indeed such as disgraces a few that precede and follow it, but it suits well enough with the *daggers hid in thought' and whetted on the flinty hearts* [11. 107-108] and the answer which the prince makes, and which is applauded for wisdom, is not of a strain much higher than this ejected line.

4.5.211 KING HENRY *To lead out many to the Holy Land.*] This journey to the Holy Land, of which the king very frequently revives the mention, had two motives, religion and policy. He durst not wear the ill-gotten crown without expiation, but in the act of expiation he contrives to make his wickedness successful.

4.5.219 KING HENRY *How I came by the Crown, O God, forgive!/ And grant it may with thee in true peace live.*] This is a true picture of a mind divided between heaven and earth. He prays for the prosperity of guilt while he deprecates its punisment.

5.1.90 FALSTAFF *Four terms or two actions.*] There is something humorous in making a spendthrift compute time by the operation of an action for debt.

5.5.66 KING HENRY *Not to come near our person by ten mile*] Mr Rowe observes that many readers lament to see Falstaff so hardly used by his old friend. But if it be considered that the fat knight has never uttered one sentiment of generosity, and with all his power of exciting mirth has nothing in him that can be esteemed, no great pain will be suffered from the reflection that he is compelled to live honestly, and maintained by the king, with a promise of advancement when he shall deserve it.

I think the poet more blamable for Poins, who is always represented as joining some virtues with his vices and is therefore treated by the prince with apparent distinction, yet he does nothing in the time of action and, though after the bustle is over he is again a favourite, at last vanishes without notice. Shakespeare certainly lost him by heedlessness, in the multiplicity of his characters, the variety of his action, and his eagerness to end the play.

5.5.97 CHIEF JUSTICE *Go, carry Sir John Falstaff to the Fleet.*] I do not see why Falstaff is carried to the Fleet. We have never lost sight of him since his dismission from the king; he has committed no new fault, and therefore incurred no punishment; but the different agitations of fear, anger, and surprise in him and his company, make a good scene to the eye; and our author, who wanted them no longer on the stage, was glad to find this method of sweeping them away.

General Observation. I fancy every reader, when he ends this play, cries out with Desdemona, *O most lame and impotent conclusion*! As this play was not, to our knowledge, divided into acts by the author, I could be content to conclude it with the death of Henry the fourth.

In thal Jerusalem shall Harry dye.

These scenes which now make the fifth act of *Henry the Fourth*, might then be the first of *Henry the Fifth*; but the truth is, that they do unite very commodiously to either play. When these plays were represented, I believe they ended as they are now ended in the books; but Shakespeare seems to have designed that the whole series of action from the beginning of *Richard the Second*, to the end of *Henry the Fifth*, should be considered by the reader as one work, upon one plan, only broken into parts by the necessity of exhibition.

None of Shakespeare's plays are more read than the first and second parts of *Henry the Fourth*. Perhaps no author has ever in two plays afforded so much delight. The great events are interesting, for the fate of kingdoms depends upon them; the slighter occurrences are diverting and, except one or two, sufficiently probable; the incidents are multiplied with wonderful fertility of invention, and the characters diversified with the utmost nicety of discernment and the profoundest skill in the nature of man.

The prince, who is the hero both of the comic and tragic part, is a young man of great abilities and violent passions, whose sentiments are right, though his actions are wrong; whose virtues are obscured by negligence, and whose understanding is dissipated by levity. In his idle hours he is rather loose than wicked; and when the occasion forces out his latent qualities, he is great without effort and brave without tumult. The trifler is roused into a hero, and the hero again reposes in the trifler. This character is great, original, and just.

Percy is a rugged soldier, choleric, and quarrelsome, and has only the soldier's virtues, generosity and courage.

But Falstaff, unimitated, unimitable Falstaff, how shall I describe thee? Thou compound of sense and vice; of sense which may be admired but not esteemed, of vice which may be despised but hardly detested, Falstaff is a character loaded with faults, and with those faults which naturally produce contempt. He is a thief and a glutton, a coward and a boaster, always ready to cheat the weak and prey upon the poor; to terrify the timorous and insult the defenceless. At once obsequious and malignant, he satirizes in their absence those whom he lives by flattering. He is familiar with the prince only as an agent of vice, but of this familiarity he is so proud as not only to be supercilious and haughty with common men but to think his interest of importance to the Duke of Lancaster. Yet the man thus corrupt, thus despicable, makes himself necessary to the prince that despises him, by the most pleasing of all qualities, perpetual gaiety, by an unfailing power of exciting laughter, which is the more freely indulged as his wit is not of the splendid or ambitious kind but consists in easy escapes and sallies of levity, which make sport but raise no envy. It must be observed that he is stained with no enormous or sanguinary crimes, so that his licentiousness is not so offensive but that it may be borne for his mirth.

The moral to be drawn from this representation is that no man is more dangerous than he that, with a will to corrupt, hath the power to please; and that neither wit nor honesty ought to think themselves safe with such a companion when they see Henry seduced by Falstaff.

Henry V

Prologue. 13 CHORUS *Within this wooden O*] Nothing shows more evidently the power of custom over language than that the frequent use of calling a circle an O could so much hide the meanness of the metaphor from Shakespeare that he has used it many times where he makes his most eager attempts at dignity of style.

Prologue. 18 CHORUS *Imaginary forces.*] *Imaginary for imaginative*, or your powers of fancy. Active and passive words are by this author frequently confounded.

Prologue. 25 CHORUS *And make imaginary puissance*]. This passage shows that Shakespeare was fully sensible of the absurdity of showing battles on the theatre, which indeed is never done but tragedy becomes farce. Nothing can be represented to the eye but by something like it, and *within a wooden* O nothing very like a battle can be exhibited.

1.1.38 ARCHBISHOP OF CANTERBURY *Hear him but reason in divinity.*] Why these lines should be divided [by Warburton] from the rest of the speech and applied to King James, I am not able to conceive; nor why an opportunity should be so eagerly snatched to treat with contempt that part of his character which was least contemptible. King James's theological knowledge was not inconsiderable. To preside at disputations is not very suitable to a king, but to understand the questions is surely laudable. The poet, if he had James in his thoughts, was no skilful encomiast; for the mention of Harry's skill in war, forced upon the remembrance of his audience the great deficiency of their present king; who yet with all his faults, and many faults he had, was such that Sir Robert Cotton says, *he would be content that* England *should never have a better, provided that it should never have a worse.*

1.1.47 ARCHBISHOP OF CANTERBURY *When he speaks, / The air, a charter'd libertine, is still.*] This line is exquisitely beautiful.

2.2.126 KING HENRY *Oh, how hast thou with jealousy infected / The sweetness of affiance*?] Shakespeare urges this aggravation of the guilt of treachery with great judgment. One of the worst consequences of breach of trust is the dimunition of that confidence which makes the happiness of life, and the dissemination of suspicion, which is the poison of society.

2.3.25 HOSTESS . . . *cold as any stone.*] Such is the end of Falstaff from whom Shakespeare had promised us in his epilogue to *Henry IV* that we should receive more entertainment. It happened to Shakespeare, as to other writers, to have his imagination crowded with a tumultuary confusion of images which, while they were yet unsorted and unexamined, seemed sufficient to furnish a long train of incidents and a new variety of merriment; but which, when he was to produce them to view, shrunk suddenly from him or could not be accommodated to his general design. That he once designed to have brought Falstaff on the scene again, we know from himself; but whether he could contrive no train of adventures suitable to his character, or could match him with no companions likely to quicken his humour, or could open no new vein of pleasantry, and was afraid to continue the same strain lest it should not find the same reception, he has here for ever discarded him, and made haste to dispatch him, perhaps for the same reason for which Addison killed Sir Roger, that no other hand might attempt to exhibit him.

Let meaner authors learn from this example that it is dangerous to sell the bear which is yet not hunted; to promise to the public what they have not written.

This disappointment probably inclined Queen Elizabeth to command the poet to produce him once again and to show him in love or courtship. This was indeed a new source of humour and produced a new play from the former characters.

I forgot to note in the proper place, and therefore note here, that Falstaff's courtship, or *The Merry Wives of Windsor*, should be read between *Henry IV* and *Henry V*.

2.3.33-44 It were to be wished that the poor merriment of this dialogue had not been purchased with so much profaneness.

3.4 *Enter Katharine, and an old gentlewoman.*] ['I have left this ridiculous scene as I found it; and am sorry to have no colour left, from any of the editions, to imagine it interpolated.' Warburton.] Sir T. Hanmer has rejected it. The scene is indeed mean enough when it is read, but the grimaces of two French women and the odd accent with which they uttered the English made it divert upon the stage. It may be observed that there is in it not only the French language but the French spirit. Alice compliments the princess upon her knowledge of four words and tells her that she pronounces like the English themselves. The princess suspects no deficiency in her instructress, nor the instructress in herself. Throughout the whole scene there may be found French servility and French vanity.

3.5.50 FRENCH KING *Rush on his host, as doth the melted snow / Upon the vallies; whose low vassal seat / The Alps doth spit and void his rheum upon.* The poet has here defeated himself by passing too soon from one image to another. To bid the *French* rush upon the *English* as the torrents formed from melted snow stream from the *Alps*, was at once vehement and proper, but its force is destroyed by the grossness of the thought in the next line.

3.6.102 FLUELLEN . . . *his fire's out*]. This is the last time that any sport can be made with the red face of Bardolph, which to confess the truth, seems to have taken more hold on Shakespeare's imagination than on any other. The conception is very cold to the solitary reader, though it may be somewhat invigorated by the exhibition on the stage. This poet is always more careful about the present than the future, about his audience than his readers.

3.6.131 MONTJOY *Now speak we on our cue.*] In our turn. This phrase the author learned among players, and has imparted it to kings.

4. Prologue. 2 CHORUS *The poring dark / Fills the wide vessel of the universe.*] . . . we are not to think Shakespeare so ignorant as to imagine it was night over the whole globe at once.—WARBURTON.] There is a better proof that Shakespeare knew the order of night and day in *Macbeth.*

Now o'er one half the *world*
Nature seems dead.

But there was no great need of any justification. The *universe*, in its original sense, no more means this globe singly than the circuit of the horizon; but, however large in its philosophical sense, it may be poetically used for as much of the world as falls under observation. Let me remark further; that ignorance cannot be certainly inferred from inaccuracy. Knowledge is not always present.

4.1.247 KING HENRY *Upon the King!*] There is something very striking and solemn in this soliloquy, into which the king breaks immediately as soon as he is left alone. Something like this, on less occasions, every breast has felt. Reflection and seriousness rush upon the mind upon the separation of a gay company, and especially after forced and unwilling merriment.

4.3.24 KING HENRY *By Jove, I am not covetous of gold.*] The king prays like a christian, and swears like a heathen.

4.3.50 KING HENRY *He'll remember, with advantages, / What feats they did that day.*] Old men, not withstanding the natural foregetfulness of age, shall remember *their feats of this day*, and remember to tell them *with advantage.* Age is commonly boastful, and inclined to magnify past acts and past times.

4.3.57 KING HENRY *Crispin Crispian shall ne'er go by, / From this day to the ending of the world, / But we in it shall be remembered.*] It may be observed that we are apt to promise to ourselves a more lasting memory than the changing state of human things admits. This prediction is not verified; the feast of *Crispin* passes by without any mention of *Agincourt*. Late events obliterate the former; the civil wars have left in this nation scarcely any tradition of more ancient history.

4.7.50 FLUELLEN *The fat Knight with the great belly-doublet.*] This is the last time that Falstaff can make sport. The poet was loath to part with him, and has continued his memory as long as he could.

5.1.83 PISTOL *To England will I steal, and there I'll steal : / And patches will I get into these cudgell'd scars, / And swear I got them in the Gallia wars.*] The comic scenes of *The History of Henry the Fourth* and *Fifth* are now at an end, and all the comic personages are now dismissed. Falstaff and Mrs. Quickly are dead; Nym and Bardolph are hanged; Gadshill was lost immediately after the robbery; Poins and Petro have vanished since, one knows not how; and Pistol is now beaten into obscurity. I believe every reader regrets their departure.

5.2.124 KING HENRY. . .*thou wouldst find me such a plain king*] I know not why Shakespeare now gives the king nearly such a character as he made him formerly ridicule in Percy. This military grossness and unskilfulness in all the softer arts does not suit very well with the gaieties of his youth, with the general knowledge ascribed to him at his accession, or with the contemptuous message sent him by the Dauphin, who represents him as fitter for the ballroom than the field and tells him that he is not *to reveal into duchies* or win provinces *with a nimble galliard*. The truth is that the poet's matter failed him in the fifth act, and he was glad to fill it up with whatever he could get; and not even Shakespeare can write well without a proper subject. It is a vain endeavour for the most skilful hand to cultivate barrenness or to paint upon vacuity.

5.2.307 We have here but a mean dialogue for princes; the merriment is very gross, and the sentiments are very worthless.

General Observation. This play has many scenes of high dignity and many of easy merriment. The character of the King is well supported, except in his courtship, where he has neither the vivacity of Hal nor the grandeur of Henry. The humour of Pistol is very happily continued; his character has perhaps been the model of all the bullies that have yet appeared on the English stage.

The lines given to the Chorus have many admirers; but the truth is that in them a little may be praised and much must be forgiven; nor can it be easily discovered why the intelligence given by the Chorus is more necessary in this play than in many others where it is omitted. The great defect of this play is the emptiness and narrowness of the last act, which a very little dilligence might have easily avoided.

[At Versailles the people showed us the theatre. As we stood on the stage looking at some machinery for play-house purposes; 'Now we are here, what shall we act, Mr Johnson. The Englishman at Paris?' 'No no' replied he, 'we will try to act Harry the

Fifth.' Hester Lynch Thrale Piozzi, *Anecdotes*, in *Johnsonian Miscellanies*, ed. G.B. Hill, Oxford, 1907, I, 216].

HENRY VI, PARTS I, II AND III

General Observation. The three parts of *Henry VI* are suspected, by Mr. Theobald, of being suppositious, and are declared, by Dr. Warburton, to be *certainly not Shakespeare's*. Mr. Theobald's suspicion arises from some obsolete words; but the phraseology is like the rest of our author's style, and single words, of which however I do not observe more than two, can conclude little.

Dr. Warburton gives no reason, but I suppose him to judge upon deeper principles and more comprehensive views, and to draw his opinion from the general effect and spirit of the composition, which he thinks inferior to the other historical plays.

From mere inferiority nothing can be inferred; in the productions of wit there will be inequality. Sometimes judgement will err, and sometimes the matter itself will defeat the artist. Of every author's works one will be the best, and one will be the worst. The colours are not equally pleasing, nor the attitudes equally graceful, in all the pictures of Titian or Reynolds.

Dissimilitude of stile and heterogeneousness of sentiment, may sufficiently show that a work does not really belong to the reputed author. But in these plays no such marks of spuriousness are found. The diction, the versification, and the figures, are Shakespeare's. These plays, considered, without regard to characters and incidents, merely as narratives in verse, are more happily conceived and more accurately finished than those of *King John*, *Richard II*, or the tragic scenes of *Henry IV* and *V*. If we take these plays from Shakespeare, to whom shall they be given? What author of that age had the same easiness of expression and fluency of numbers?

Having considered the evidence given by the plays themselves, and found it in their favour, let us now enquire what corroboration can be gained from other testimony. They are ascribed to Shakespeare by the first editors, whose attestation may be received in questions of fact, however unskilfully they superintended their edition. They seem to be declared genuine by the voice of Shakespeare himself, who refers to the second plays in his epilogue to *Henry V*, and apparently connects the first act of *Richard III* with the last of the third part of *Henry VI*. If it be objected that the plays were popular, and therefore he alluded to them as well known; it may be answered, with equal probability, that the natural passions of a poet would have disposed him to separate his own works from those of an inferior hand. And indeed if an author's own testimony is to be overthrown by speculative criticism, no man can be any longer secured of literary reputation.

Of these three plays I think the second the best. The truth is, that they have not sufficient variety of action, for the incidents are too often of the same kind; yet many of the characters are well discriminated. King Henry, and his queen, king Edward, the duke of Gloucester, and the earl of Warwick, are very strongly and distinctly painted.

The old copies of the two latter parts of *Henry VI* and *Henry V* are so apparently imperfect and mutilated, that there is no reason for supposing them the first draughts of Shakespeare. I am inclined to believe them copies taken by some auditor who wrote down, during the representation, what the time would permit, then perhaps filled up some of his omissions at a second or third hearing, and when he had by this method formed something like a play, sent it to the printer.

RICHARD III

1.1.28 RICHARD *And therefore, since I cannot prove a lover.*] Shakespeare very diligently inculcates, that the wickedness of Richard proceeded from his deformity, from the envy that rose at the comparison of his own person with others, and which incited him to disturb the pleasures that he could not partake.

1.2.180 RICHARD *I did kill King Henry; / But 'twas thy beauty that provoked me.*] Shakespeare countenances the observation, that no woman can ever be offended with the mention of her beauty.

2.1.102 KING EDWARD *Have I a tongue to doom my brother's death.*] This lamentation is very tender and pathetic. The recollection of the good qualities of the dead is very natural, and no less naturally does the king endeavour to communicate the crime to others.

5.3.177 KING RICHARD *Give me another horse.*] There is in this, as in many of our author's speeches of passion, something very trifling, and something very striking. Richard's debate, whether he should quarrel with himself, is too long continued, but the subsequent exaggeration of his crimes is truly tragical.

General Observation. This is one of the most elaborated of our author's performances; yet I know not whether it has not happened to him, as to others, to be praised most when praise is not most deserved. That this play has scenes noble in themselves and very well contrived to strike in the exhibition, cannot be denied. But some parts are trifling, others shocking, and some improbable.

HENRY VIII

4.2 *Enter Katharine Dowager, sick : led between Griffith her gentleman-usher and Patience her woman.*] This scene is above any other part of Shakespeare's tragedies, and perhaps above any scene of any other poet, tender and pathetic, without gods, or furies, or poisons, or precipices, without the help of romantic circumstances, without improbable sallies of poetical lamentation, and without any throes of tumultuous misery.

5.3.10 LORD CHANCELLOR *we are all men / In our own natures frail, and capable / Of frailty,——*] This sentence I think needed no commentary. The meaning, and the plain meaning, is, *we are men frail by nature, and therefore liable to acts of frailty*, to deviations from the right. I wish every commentator, before he suffers his confidence to kindle, would repeat.

—We are all men
In our own natures frail, and capable
Of frailty; few are angels.

General Observation. The play of *Henry the Eighth* is one of those which still keeps possession of the stage by the splendour of its pageantry. The coronation about forty years ago drew the people together in multitudes for a great part of the winter. Yet pomp is not the only merit of this play. The meek sorrows and virtuous distress of Katharine have furnished some scenes which may be justly numbered among the greatest efforts of tragedy. But the genius of Shakespeare comes in and goes out with Katharine. Every other part may be easily conceived and easily written.

Though it is very difficult to decide whether short pieces be genuine or spurious, yet I connot restrain myself from expressing my suspicion that neither the prologue nor epilogue to this play is the work of Shakespeare; *non vultus, non color*. It appears to me very likely that they were supplied by the friendship or officiousness of Jonson, whose manner they will be perhaps found exactly to resemble. There is yet another supposition possible: the prologue and epilogue may have been written after Shakespeare's departure from the stage, upon some accidental revisal of the play, and there will then be reason for imagining that the writer, whoever he was, intended no great kindness to him, this play being recommended by a subtle and covert censure of his other works. . . . All this, however, must be received as very dubious, since we know not the exact date of this or the other plays, and cannot tell how our author might have changed his practice or opinions.

The historical dramas are now concluded, of which the two parts of *Henry the Fourth* and *Henry the Fifth* are among the happiest of our author's compositions; and *King John*, *Richard the Third*, and *Henry the Eighth* deservedly stand in the second class. Those whose curiosity would refer the historical scenes to their original may consult Holinshed and sometimes Hall; from Holinshed Shakespeare has often inserted whole speeches with no more alteration than was necessary to the numbers of his verse. To transcribe them into the margin was unnecessary, because the original is easily examined, and they are seldom less perspicuous in the poet than in the historian.

To play histories, or to exhibit a succession of events by action and dialogue, was a common entertainment among our rude ancestors upon great festivities. The parish clerks once performed at Clerkenwell a play which lasted three days, containing *The History of the World*.

KING LEAR

1.1.149 KENT *Think'st thou, that duty shall have dread to speak.*] I have given this passage according to the old folio, from which the modern editions have silently departed, for the sake of better numbers, with a degree of insincerity, which, if not sometimes detected and censured, must impair the credit of ancient books, One of the editors, and perhaps only one, knew how much mischief may be done by such clandestine alterations.

The quarto agrees with the folio, except for that *reserve thy state*, it gives, *reverse thy doom*, and has *stoops* instead of *falls to folly*.

The meaning of *answer my life my judgment* is, *Let my life be answerable for my judgment*, or *I will stake my life on my opinion*.

The reading which, without any right, has possessed all the modern copies is this,

> *—to plainness Hononr*
> *Is bound, when Majesty to folly falls.*
> *Reserve thy state; with better judgment check*
> *This hideous rashness*; *with my life I answer,*
> *Thy youngest daughter*, *&c.*

I am inclined to think that *reverse thy doom* was Shakespeare's first reading, as more apposite to the present occasion, and that he changed it afterwards to *reserve thy state*, which conduces more to the progress of the action.

1.1.174 KING LEAR *Which nor our nature, nor our place can bear,/Our potency made good.*] Lear, who is characterized as hot, heady and violent, is, with very just observation of life, made to entangle himself with vows, upon any sudden provocation to vow revenge, and then to plead the obligation of a vow in defence of implacability.

1.2.128 EDMUND *This is the excellent foppery of the world.*] In Shakespeare's best plays, besides the vices that arise from the subject, there is generally some peculiar prevailing folly, principally ridiculed, that runs through the whole piece. Thus in *The Tempest*, the lying disposition of travellers, and in *As You Like It*, the fantastic humour of courtiers, is exposed and satirised with infinite pleasantry. In like manner, in his play of *Lear*, the dotages of judicial astrology are severely ridiculed . . . .

But to return to Shakespeare. So blasphemous a delusion, therefore, it became the honesty of our poet to expose. But it was a tender point, and required managing. For this impious juggle had in his time a kind of religious reverence paid to it. It was therefore to be done obliquely; and the circumstances of the scene furnished him with as good an opportunity as he could wish. The persons in the drama are all pagans, so that as, in compliance to custom, his good characters were not to speak ill of judicial Astrology, they could on account of their religion give no reputation to it. But in order to expose it the more, he, with great judgment, makes these pagans Fatalists; as appears by these words of *Lear*.

By all the operations of the orbs.
From whom we do exist and cease to be,

For the doctrine of fate is the true foundation of judicial Astrology. Having thus discredited it by the very commendations given to it, he was in no danger of having his direct satire against it mistaken, by its being put (as he was obliged, both in paying regard to custom, and in following nature) into the mouth of the villain and atheist, especially when he has added such force of reason to his ridicule, in the words referred to in the beginning of the note.

4.1.70 GLOUCESTER *Let the superfluous and lust-dieted man, / That slaves your ordinance.*] The language of *Shakespeare* is very licentious, and his words have often meanings remote from the proper and original use. To *slave* or *beslave* another is to *treat* him *with terms of indignity;* in a kindred sense, to *slave the ordinance* may be, *to* slight *or* ridicule *it.*

4.5.22 REGAN *Let me unseal the letter.*] I know not well why Shakespeare gives the Steward, who is a mere factor of wickedness, so much fidelity. He now refuses the letter, and afterwards, when he is dying, thinks only how it may be safely delivered.

4.6.11 EDGAR *How fearful/And dizzy 'tis to cast one's eyes so low!*] This description has been much admired since the time of Addison, who has remarked, with a poor attempt at pleasantry, that 'he who can read it without being giddy has a very good head or a very bad one'. The description is certainly not mean, but I am far from thinking it wrought to the utmost excellence of poetry. He that looks from a precipice finds himself assailed by one great and dreadful image of irresistible destruction. But this overwhelming idea is dissipated and enfeebled from the instant that the mind can restore itself to the observation of particulars and diffuse its attention to distinct objects. The enumeration of the choughs and crows, the samphireman, and the fishers, counteracts the great effect of the prospect, as it peoples the desert of intermediate vacuity and stops the mind in the rapidity of its descent through emptiness and horror.

[Boswell reports an extended conversation on the same passage in *King Lear*, between Johnson and several theatrical friends, under the date of 16 October 1769. In the following excerpt illustrative quotations from Congreve's *The Mourning Bride* and *King Lear* are inserted within double brackets.

Johnson said that the description of the temple in *The Mourning Bride* was the finest poetical passage he had ever read; he recollected none in Shakespeare equal to it.

[[ALMERIA

It was a fancied noise; for all is hushed.

LEONORA

It bore the accent of a human voice.

ALMERIA

It was thy fear; or else some transient wind
Whistling through hollows of this vaulted aisle,
We'll listen.

LEONORA

Hark!

ALMERIA

No, all is hushed and still as Death—'Tis dreadful!
How reverend is the face of this tall pile,
Whose ancient pillars rear their marble heads,
To bear aloft its arched and ponderous roof
By its own weight, made steadfast and immovable,
Looking tranquillity. It strikes an awe

And terror on my aching sight; the tombs
And monumental caves of death look cold
And shoot a chillness to my trembling heart.
Give my thy hand and speak to me, nay, speak,
And let me hear thy voice;
My own affrights me with its echoes.
—William Congreve, *The Mourning Bride*, 1697, II, 1]]

'But', said Garrick, all alarmed for 'the god of his idolatry', 'we know not the extent and variety of his powers. We are to suppose there are such passages in his works. Shakespeare must not suffer from the badness of our memories.' Johnson, diverted by this enthusiastic jealousy, went on with great ardour; 'No, Sir, Congreve has *nature*'. Smiling on the tragic eagerness of Garrick, but composing himself, he added, 'Sir, this is not comparing Congreve on the whole with Shakespeare on the whole; but only maintaining that Congreve has one finer passage than any that can be found in Shakespeare. Sir, a man may have no more than ten guineas in the world, but he may have those ten guineas in one piece; and so may have a finer piece than a man who has ten thousand pounds; but then he has only one ten-guinea piece. What I mean is that you can show me no passage where there is simply a description of material objects, without any intermixture of moral notions, which produces such an effect.' Mr Murphy mentioned Shakespeare's description of the night before the battle of Agincourt; but it was observed it had *men* in it. Mr Davies suggested the speech of Juliet, in which she figures herself awakening in the tomb of her ancestors. Someone mentioned the description of Dover Cliff.

[[How fearful
And dizzy 'tis to cast one's eyes so low!
The crows and choughs that wing the midway air
Show scarce so gross as beetles; half way down
Hangs one that gathers samphire—dreadful trade!
Methinks he seems no bigger than his head.
The fishermen that walk upon the beach
Appear like mice; and yond tall anchoring bark
Diminish'd to her cock; her cock, a buoy
Almost too small for sight. The murmuring surge,

That on the unnumber'd idle pebbles chafes,
Cannot be heard so high. I'll look no more,
Lest my brain turn, and the deficient sight
Topple down headlong.

—*King Lear*, IV. 6.II-24]].

JOHNSON 'No, Sir, it should be all precipice—all vacuum. The crows impede your fall. The diminished appearance of the boats and other circumstances are all very good description; but do not impress the mind at once with the horrible idea of immense height. The impression is divided; you pass on by computation, from one stage of the tremendous space to another. Had the girl in *The Mourning Bride* said she could not cast her shoe to the top of one of the pillars in the temple, it would not have aided the idea, but weakened it.'

General Observation. The tragedy of *Lear* is deservedly celebrated among the dramas of Shakespeare. There is perhaps no play which keeps the attention so strongly, fixed; which so much agitates our passions and interests our curiosity. The artful involutions of distinct interests, the striking opposition of contrary characters, the sudden changes of fortune, and the quick succession of events, fill the mind with a perpetual tumult of indignation, pity, and hope. There is no scene which does not contribute to the aggravation of the distress or conduct of the action, and scarce a line which does not conduce to the progrsss of the scene. So powerful is the current of the poet's imagination that the mind which once ventures within it is hurried irresistibly along.

On the seeming improbability of Lear's conduct it may be observed that he is represented according to the histories at that time vulgarly received as true. And perhaps if we turn our thoughts upon the barbarity and ignorance of the age to which this story is referred, it will appear not so unlikely as while we estimate Lear's manners by our own. Such preference of one daughter to another, or resignation of dominion on such conditions, would be yet credible if told of a petty prince of Guinea or Madagascar. Shakespeare, indeed, by the mention of his earls and dukes, has given us the idea of times more civilized and of life regulated by softer manners; and the truth is that though he so nicely discriminates and so minutely describes the characters of men, he commonly neglects and confounds the characters of ages, by mingling customs ancient and modern, English and foreign.

My learned friend Mr Warton, who has in the *Adventurer* very minutely criticized this play, remarks that the instances of cruelty are too savage and shocking, and that the intervention of Edmund destroys the simplicity of the story. These objections may, I think, be answered by repeating that the cruelty of the daughters is an historical fact, to which the poet has added little, having only drawn it into a series by dialogue and action. But I am not able to apologize with equal plausibility for the extrusion of Gloucester's eyes, which seems an act too horrid to be endured in dramatic exhibition, and such as must always compel the mind to relieve its distress by incredulity. Yet let it be remembered that our author well knew what would please the audience for which he wrote.

The injury done by Edmund to the simplicity of the action is abundantly recompensated by the addition of variety, by the art with which he is made to cooperate with the chief design, and the opportunity which he gives the poet of combining perfidy with perfidy and connecting the wicked son with the wicked daughters, to impress this important moral, that villainy is never at a stop, that crimes lead to crimes and at last terminate in ruin.

But though this moral be incidentally enforced, Shakespeare has suffered the virtue of Cordelia to perish in a just cause, contrary to the natural ideas of justice, to the hope of the reader, and, what is yet more strange, to the faith of chronicles. Yet this conduct is justified by the spectator, who blames Tate for giving Cordelia success and happiness in his alteration and declares that, in his opinion, *the tragedy has lost half its beauty.* Dennis has remarked, whether justly or not, that to secure the favourable reception of *Cato, the town was poisoned with much false and abominable criticism*, and that endeavours had been used to discredit and decry poetical justice. A play in which the wicked prosper and the virtuous miscarry may doubtless be good, because it is a just representation of the common events of human life; but since all reasonable beings naturally love justice, I cannot easily be persuaded that the observation of justice makes a play worse; or that, if other excellencies are equal, the audience will not always rise better pleased from the final triumph of persecuted virtue.

In the present case the public has decided. Cordelia, from the time of Tate, has always retired with victory and felicity. And, if my sensations could add anything to the general suffrage, I might relate that I was many years ago so shocked by Cordelia's death that I know not whether I ever endured to read again the last scenes of the play till I undertook to revise them as an editor.

There is another controversy among the critics concerning this play. It is disputed whether the predominant image in Lear's disordered mind be the loss of his kingdom or the cruelty of his daughters. Mr Murphy, a very judicious critic, has evinced by induction of particular passages that the cruelty of his daughters is the primary source of his distress and that the loss of royalty affects him only as a secondary and subordinate evil. He observes with great justness that Lear would move our compassion but little, did we not rather consider the injured father than the degraded king.

The story of this play, except the episode of Edmund, which is derived I think, from Sidney, is taken originally from Geoffery of Monmouth, whom Holinshed generally copied; but perhaps immediately from an old historical ballad. ... My reason for believing that the play was posterior to the balled, rather than the ballad to the play, is that the ballad has nothing of Shakespeare's nocturnal tempest, which is too striking to have been omitted, and that it follows the chronicle; it has the rudiments of the play but none of its amplifications; it first hinted Lear's madness but did not array it in circumstances. The writer of the balled added something to the history, which is a proof that he would have added more if more had occurred to his mind, and more must have occurred if he had seen Shakespeare.

TIMON OF ATHENS

4.2 *Enter Flavius.*] Nothing contributes more to the exaltation of Timon's character than the zeal and fidelity of his servants. Nothing but real virtue can be honoured by domestics; nothing but impartial kindness can gain affection from dependants.

4.3.252 TIMON *Hadst thou, like us.*] There is in this speech a sullen haughtiness, and malignant dignity, suitable at once to the lord and the manhater. The impatience with which he bears to have his luxury reproached by one that never had luxury within his reach, is natural and graceful . . . .

4.3.275 TIMON *If thou hadst not been born the worst of men, Thou hadst been knave and flatterer.*] Dryden has quoted two verses of Virgil to shew how well he could have written satires. Shakespeare has here given a specimen of the same power by a line bitter beyond all bitterness, in which Timon tells Apemantus, that he had not virtue enough for the vices which he condemns.

4.3.478 TIMON . . . *all / I keep were knaves, to serve in meat to villains,*] *Knave* is here in the compounded sense of a *servant* and a *rascal.*

General Observation. The play of *Timon* is a domestic tragedy and therefore strongly fastens on the attention of the reader. In the plan there is not much art, but the incidents are natural, and the characters various and exact. The catastrophe affords a very powerful warning against that ostentatious liberality which scatters bounty but confers no benefits, and buys flattery but not friendship.

In this tragedy are many passages perplexed, obscure, and probably corrupt, which I have endeavoured to rectify or explain, with due diligence; but, having only one copy, cannot promise myself that my endeavours will be much applauded.

TITUS ANDRONICUS

General Observation. All the editors and critics agree with Mr. Theobald in supposing this play spurious. I see no reason for differing from them; for the colour of the style is wholly different from that of the other plays, and there is an attempt at regular versification, and artificial closes, not always inelegant, yet seldom pleasing. The barbarity of the spectacles, and the general massacre which are here exhibited, can scarcely be conceived tolerable to any audience yet we are told by Jonson, that they were not only born but praised. That Shakespeare wrote any part, though Theobald declares it *incontestable*, I see no reason for believing.

The chronology of this play does not prove it not to be Shakespeare's. If it had been written twenty-five years, in 1614, it might have been written when Shakespeare was twenty-five years old. When he left Warwickshire I know not, but at the age of twenty-five it was rather too late to fly for deerstealing.

Ravenscroft, who, in the reign of Charles II revised this play, and restored it to the stage, tells us in his preface, from a theatrical tradition I suppose, which in his time might be of sufficient authority, that this play was touched in different parts by Shakespeare, but written by some other poet. I do not find Shakespeare's touches very discernible.

MACBETH

Most of the notes which the present editor [Johnson] has subjoined to this play were published by him in a small pamphlet in 1745.

1.1 *Enter three Witches.*] In order to make a true estimate of the abilities and merit of a writer, it is always necessary to examine the genius of his age and the opinions of his contemporaries. A poet who should now make the whole action of his tragedy depend upon enchantment and produce the chief events by the assistance of supernatural agents, would be censured as transgressing the bounds of probability, be banished from the theatre to the nursery, and condemned to write fairy tales instead of tragedies; but a survey of the notions that prevailed at the time when this play was written will prove that Shakespeare was in no danger of such censures, since he only turned the system that was then universally admitted to his advantage and was far from overburdening the credulity of his audience.

The reality of witchcraft or enchantment, which, though not strictly the same, are confounded in this play, has in all ages and countries been credited by the common people, and in most, by the learned themselves. These phantoms have indeed appeared more frequently in proportion as the darkness of ignorance has been more gross; but it cannot be shown that the brightest gleams of knowledge have at any time been sufficient to drive them out of the world . . .

The Reformation did not immediately arrive at its meridian,

and though day was gradually increasing upon us, the goblins of witchcraft still continued to hover in the twilight. In the time of Queen Elizabeth was the remarkable trial of the witches of Warbois, whose conviction is still commemorated in an annual sermon at Huntingdon. But in the reign of King James, in which this tragedy was written, many circumstances concurred to propagate and confirm this opinion. The king, who was much celebrated for his knowledge, had, before his arrival in England, not only examined in person a woman accused of witchcraft but had given a very formal account of the practices and illusions of evil spirits, the compacts of witches, the ceremonies used by them, the manner of detecting them, and the justice of punishing them, in his dialogues of *Demonology*, written in the Scottish dialect, and published at Edinburgh. This book was, soon after his accession, reprinted at London and as the ready way to gain King James's favour was to flatter his speculations, the system of *Demonology* was immediately adopted by all who desired either to gain preferment or not to lose it. Thus the doctrine of witchcraft was very powerfully inculcated; and as the greatest part of mankind have no other reason for their opinions than that they are in fashion, it cannot be doubted but this persuasion made a rapid progress, since vanity and credulity cooperated in its favour. The infection soon reached the Parliament, who, in the first year of King James, made a law, by which it was enacted, Chapter xii: That 'if any person shall use any invocation or conjuration of any evil or wicked spirit; 2. or shall consult, covenant with, entertain, employ, feed or reward any evil or cursed spirit to or for any intent or purpose; 3. or take up any dead man, woman or child out of the grave, —or the skin, bone, or any part of the dead person, to be employed or used in any manner of witchcraft, sorcery, charm, or enchantment; 4. or shall use, practice, or exercise any sort of witchcraft, corcery, charm, or enchantment; 5. whereby any person shall be destroyed, killed, wasted, consumed, pined, or lame in any part of the body; 6. that every such person being convicted shall suffer death.' This law was repealed in our own time.

Thus, in the time of Shakespeare, was the doctrine of witchcraft at once established by law and by the fashion, and it became not only unpolite, but criminal, to doubt it; and as prodigies are always seen in proportion as they are expected, witches were every day discovered and multiplied so fast in some places that Bishop Hall mentions a village in Lancashire where their number was greater than that of the houses. The Jesuits and sectaries took advantage of this universal error and endeavoured to promote the interest of their parties by pretended cures of persons afflicted by evil spirits; but they were detected and exposed by the clergy of the Established Church.

Upon this general infatuation Shakespeare might be easily allowed to found a play, especially since he has followed with great exactness such histories as were then thought true; nor can it be doubted that the scenes of enchantment, however they may now be ridiculed, were both by himself and his audience thought awful and affecting.

1.7.28 *Enter Lady Macbeth.*] The arguments by which Lady Macbeth persuades her husband to commit the murder afford a proof of Shakespeare's knowledge of human nature. She urges the excellence and dignity of courage, a glittering idea which has dazzled mankind from age to age and animated sometimes the house breaker and sometimes the conqueror; but this sophism Macbeth has for ever destroyed, by distinguishing true from false fortitude, in a line and a half; of which it may almost be said that they ought to bestow immortality on the author, though all his other productions had been lost;

> I dare do all that may become a man,
> Who dares do more, is none.

This topic, which has been always employed with too much success, is used in this scene with peculiar propriety to a soldier by a woman. Courage is the distinguishing virtue of a soldier, and the reproach of cowardice cannot be borne by any man from a woman, without great impatience.

She then urges the oaths by which he had bound himself to murder Duncan, another art of sophistry by which men have sometimes deluded their consciences and persuaded themselves that what would be criminal in others is virtuous in them; this argument Shakespeare, whose plan obliged him to make Macbeth yield, has not confuted, though he might easily have shown that a former obligation could not be vacated by a latter; that obligations laid on us by a higher power could not be overruled by obligations which we lay upon ourselves.

2.1.49 MACBETH *Now o'er the one half world/Nature seems dead.*] That is, *over our hemisphere all action and motion seem to have ceased.* This image, which is perhaps the most striking that poetry can produce, has been adopted by Dryden in his *Conquest of Mexico*:

> All things are hush'd as Nature's self lay dead,
> The mountains seem to nod their drowsy head;
> The little birds in dreams their songs repeat,
> And sleeping flow'rs beneath the night dews sweat.
> Even lust and envy sleep!

These lines, though so well known, I have transcribed, that the contrast between them and this passage of Shakespeare may be more accurately observed.

Night is described by two great poets, but one describes a night of quiet, the other of perturbation. In the night of Dryden, all the disturbers of the world are laid asleep; in that of Shakespeare, nothing but sorcery, lust, and murder is awake. He that reads Dryden finds himself lulled with serenity and disposed to solitude and contemplation. He that peruses Shakespeare looks round alarmed and starts to find himself alone. One is night of a lover, the other, of a murderer.

2.2.56 LADYMACBETH ... *gild the faces of the grooms withal; / For it must seem their guilt*] Could Shakespeare possibly mean to play upon the similitude of *gild* and *guilt*?

2.3.108 MACBETH *Here lay Duncan, / His silver skin lac'd with his golden blood.*] Mr Pope has endeavoured to improve one of these lines by substituting *gory blood* for *golden blood*; but it may easily be admitted that he who could on such occasion talk of *lacing the silver skin* would *lace it* with *golden blood.* No amendment can be made to this line, of which every word is equally faulty, but by a general blot.

It is not improbable that Shakespeare put these forced and unnatural metaphors into the mouth of Macbeth as a mark of artifice and dissimulation, to show the difference between the studied language of hypocrisy and the natural outcries of sudden passion. This whole speech so considered is a remarkable instance of judgment, as it consists entirely of antithesis and metaphor.

3.1.55 MACBETH ... *as it is said, / Mark Antony's was by Caesar*]. Though I would not often assume the critic's privilege of being confident where certainty cannot be obtained, nor indulge myself too far in departing from the established reading, yet I cannot but propose the rejection of this passage, which I believe was an insertion of some player, that, having so much learning as to discover to what Shakespeare alluded, was not willing that his audience should be less knowing than himself and has therefore weakened the author's sense by the intrusion of a remote and useless image into a speech bursting from a man wholly possessed with his own present condition and therefore not at leisure to explain his own allusions to himself. If these words are taken away, by which not only the thought but the numbers are injured, the lines of Shakespeare close together without any traces of a breach.

My genius is rebuk'd. He chid the sisters.

This note was written before I was fully acquainted with Shakespeare's manner, and I do not now think it of much weight; for though the words, which I was once willing to eject, seem interpolated, I believe they may still be genuine, and added by the author in his revision. The author of the *Revisal* cannot admit the measure to be faulty. There is only one foot, he says, put for another. This is one of the effects of literature in minds not naturally perspicacious. Every boy or girl finds the metre imperfect, but the pedant comes to its defence with a tribrachys or an anapest and sets it right at once by applying to one language the rules of another. If we may be allowed to change feet, like the old comic writers, it will not be easy to write a line not metrical. To hint this once is sufficient.

3.1.68 MACBETH ... *mine eternal jewel / Giv'n to the common enemy of man*] It is always an entertainment to an inquisitive reader, to trace a sentiment to its original source, and therefore though the term *enemy of man*, applied to the devil, is in itself natural and obvious, yet some may be pleased with being informed, that Shakespeare probably borrowed it from the first lines of the destruction of Troy, a book which he is known to have read...

4.1 As this is the chief scene of inchantment in the play, it is proper in this place to observe, with how much judgment Shakespeare has selected all the circumstances of his infernal ceremonies, and how exactly he has conformed to common opinions and traditions.

Thrice the brinded cat hath mew'd.

The usual form in which familiar spirits are reported to converse with witches, is that of a cat. A witch, who was tried about half a century before the time of Shakespeare, had a cat named Rutterkin, as the spirit of one of those witches was Grimalkin; and when any mischief was to be done she used to bid Rutterkin go and fly, but once when she would have sent Rutterkin to torment a daughter of the countess of Rutland, instead of going or flying, he only cried *mew*, from whence she discovered that the lady was out of his power, the power of witches not being universal, but limited, as Shakespeare has taken care to inculcate.

> *Though his bark cannot be lost,*
> *Yet it shall be tempest tost.*

The common afflictions which the malice of witches produced were melancholy, fits, and loss of flesh, which are threatened by one of Shakespeare's witches.

> *Weary sev'n-nights, nine times nine,*
> *Shall he dwindle, peak and pine.*

It was likewise their practice to aestroy the cattle of their neighbours, and the farmers have to this day many ceremonies to secure their cows and other cattle from witchcraft; but they seem to have been most suspected of malice against swine. Shakespeare has accordingly made one of his witches declare that she has been *killing swine*, and Dr. Harsenet observes, that about that time, a *sow could not be ill of the measles, nor a girl of the sullens, but some old woman was charged with witchcraft.*

> *Toad, that under the cold stone,*
> *Days and nights has, thirty-one.*
> *Swelter'd venom sleeping got;*
> *Boil thou first i'th' charmed pot.*

Toads have likewise long lain under the reproach of being by some means accessary to witchcraft, for which reason Shakespeare, in the first scene of this play, calls one of the spirits *Padocke* or *Toad*, and now takes care to put a toad first into the pot. When Vaninus was seized at Tholouse, there was found at his lodgings *ingens Bufo vitro inclusus a great Toad shut in a Vial*, upon which those that prosecuted him *Veneficium ex probrabant, charged him*, I suppose, with witchcraft.

Fillet of a fenny snake,
In the cauldron boil and bake;
Eye of newt, and toe of frog;—
For a charm, & c.

The propriety of these ingredients may be known by consulting the books *de Viribus Animalium* and *de Mirabilibus Mundi* ascribed to Albert Magnus, in which the reader, who has time and credulity, may discover wonderful secrets.

Finger of birth-strangled babe,
Ditch-delivere'd by a drab;—

It has been already mentioned in the law against witches, that they are supposed to take up dead bodies to use in enchantments, which was confessed by the woman whom King James examined, and who had of a dead body that was divided in one of their assemblies, two fingers for her share. It is observable that Shakespeare, on this great occasion, which involves the fate of a king, multiplies all the circumstances of horror. The babe, whose finger is used, must be strangled in its birth; the grease must not only be human, but must have dropped from a gibbet, the gibbet of a murderer; and even the sow, whose blood is used, must have offended nature by devouring her own farrow. These are touches of judgment and genius.

And now about the cauldron sing—
Black spirits and white,
Blue spirits and grey,
Mingle, mingle, mingle,
You that mingle may.

And in a former part,

——weyward sisters, hand in hand,——
Thus do go about, about,
Thrice to thine, and thrice to mine,
And thrice again to make up nine!

These two passages I have brought together, because they both seem subject to the objection of too much levity for the solemnity of enchantment, and may both be shown, by one quotation from Camden's account of Ireland, to be founded upon a practice really observed by the uncivilised natives of that country. "When any one gets a fall, says the informer of Camden, he starts up, and *turning three times to the right* digs a hole in the earth; for they imagine that there is a spirit in the ground, and if he falls sick in two or three days, they send one of their women that is skilled in that way to the place, where she says, I call thee from the east, west, north and south, from the groves, the woods, the rivers, and the fens, from the *fairies red, black, white*." There was likewise a book written before the time of Shakespeare, describing, amongst other properties, the *colours* of spirits.

Many other circumstances might be particularised, in which Shakespeare has shown his judgment and his knowledge.

General Observation. This play is deservedly celebrated for the propriety of its fictions, and solemnity, grandeur, and variety of its action; but it has no nice discriminations of character, the events are too great to admit the influence of particular dispositions, and the course of the action necessarily determines the conduct of the agents.

The danger of ambition is well described; and I know not whether it may not be said in defence of some parts which now seem improbable, that, in Shakespeare's time, it was necessary to warn credulity against vain and illusive predictions.

The passions are directed to their true end. Lady Macbeth is merely detested; and though the courage of Macbeth preserves some esteem, yet every reader rejoices at his fall.

CORIOLANUS

General Observation. The tragedy of *Coriolanus* is one of the most amusing of our author's performances. The old man's merriment in Menenius; the lofty lady's dignity in Volumnia; the bridal modesty in Virgilia; the patrician and military haughtiness in Coriolanus; the plebeian malignity and tribunitian insolence in Brutus and Sicinius, make a very pleasing and interesting variety; and the various revolutions of the hero's fortune fill the mind with anxious curiosity. There is, perhaps, too much bustle in the first act and too little in the last.

Julius Caesar

General Observation. Of this tragedy many particular passages deserve regard, and the contention and reconcilement of Brutus and Cassius is universally celebrated; but I have never been strongly agitated in perusing it and think it somewhat cold and unaffecting compared with some other of Shakespeare's plays; his adherence to the real story and to Roman manners seems to have impeded the natural vigour of his genius.

Antony and Cleopatra

1.1.10 PHILO . . . *gypsy's lust*] *Gypsy* is here used both in the original meaning for an *Egyptian* and in its accidental sense for a *bad woman.*

3.13.127 ANTONY . . . *O that I were / Upon the hill of* Basan, *to out-roar / The horned herd.*] It is not without pity and indignation that the reader of this great Poet meets so often with this low jest, which is too much a favourite to be left out of either mirth or fury.

4.9.15 ENOBARBUS . . . *Throw my heart / Against the flint and hardness of my fault, / Which, being dried with grief, will break to powder, / And finish all foul thoughts.*] The pathetic of Shakespeare too often ends in the ridiculous. It is painful to find the gloomy dignity of this noble scene destroyed by the intrusion of a conceit so far-fetched and unaffecting.

5.2.4 CLEOPATRA . . . *it is great/To do that thing that ends all other deeds, / Which shackles accidents, and bolts up change, /Which sleeps, and never palates more the dung, / The beggar's nurse and Caesar's.*] [Warburton had added a line and changed 'dung' to 'dug'.] I cannot perceive the loss of a line or the need of an emendation. The commentator seems to have entangled his own ideas; his supposition that *suicide* is called *the beggar's nurse and Caesar's,* and his concession that the position is *intelligible,* show, I think, a mind not intent on the business before it. The difficulty of the passage, if any difficulty there be, arises only from this, that the act of suicide and the state which is the effect of suicide are confounded. Voluntary death, says she, is an act *which bolts up change*; it produces a state.

Which sleeps, and never palates more the dung,
The beggar's nurse, and Caesar's.

Which has no longer need of the gross and terrene sustenance, in the use of which Caesar and the beggar are on a level.

The speech is abrupt, but perturbation in such a state is surely natural. [The first Folio reads 'dung'. Modern editors incline to accept Warburton's emendation.]

General Observation. This play keeps curiosity always busy and the passions always interested. The continual hurry of the action, the variety of incidents, and the quick succession of one personage to another, call the mind forward without intermission from the first act to the last. But the power of delighting is derived principally from the frequent changes of the scene; for except the feminine arts, some of which are too low, which distinguish Cleopatra, no character is very strongly discriminated. Upton, who did not easily miss what he desired to find, has discovered that the language of Antony is, with great skill and learning, made pompous and superb, according to this real practice. But I think his diction not distinguishable from that of others; the most tumid speech in the play is that which Caesar makes to Octavia.

The events, of which the principal are described according to history, are produced without any art of connexion or care of disposition.

CYMBELINE

2.3.118 CLOTEN *The contract you pretend with that base wretch.*] Here Shakespeare has not preserved, with his common nicety, the uniformity of character. The speech of Cloten is rough and harsh, but certainly not the talk of one.

Who can't take two from twenty, for his heart,
And leave eighteen.

His argument is just and well enforced, and its prevalence is allowed throughout all civil nations: As for rudeness, he seems not to be much undermatched.

3.3.35 ARVIRAGUS *What should we speak of / When we are old as you?*] This dread of an old age unsupplied with matter for discourse and mediation, is a sentiment natural and noble. No state can be more destitute than that of him who, when the delights of sense forsake him, has no pleasures of the mind.

3.5.72 CLOTEN *And that she hath all courtly parts more exquisite/ Than lady, ladies, woman; from every one / The best she hath*] '[The second line is intolerable nonsense. It should be read and pointed thus, "Than lady ladies; *winning* from each one." Warburton.]

I cannot perceive the second line to be intolerable, or to be nonsense. The speaker only rises in his ideas. *She has all courtly parts*, says he, *more exquisite than* any *lady*, than all *ladies*, than all *womankind*. Is this nonsense?

4.2.105 BELARIUS *the snatches in his voice, / and burst of speaking', were as his; I'm absolute / 'Twas very Cloten.*] This is one of our author's strokes of observation. An abrupt and tumultuous utterance very frequently accompanies a confused and cloudy understanding.

5.1.1-33 POSTHUMUS *Yea, bloody cloth, I'll keep thee.*] This is a soliloquy of nature, uttered when the effervescence of a mind agitated and perturbed spontaneously and inadvertently discharges itself in words. The speech, throughout all its tenor, if the last conceit be excepted, seems to issue warm from the heart. He first condemns his own violence; then tries to disburden himself by impuring part of the crime to Pisanio; he next soothes his mind to an artificial and momentary tranquility by trying to think that he has been only an instrument of the gods for the happiness of Imogen. He is now grown reasonable enough to determine that having done so much evil he will do no more; that he will not fight against the country which he has already injured; but as life is not longer supportable, he will die in a just cause and die with the obscurity of a man who does not think himself worthy to be remembered.

General Observation. This play has many just sentiments, some natural dialogues, and some pleasing scenes, but they are obtained at the expense of much incongruity.

To remark the folly of the fiction, the absurdity of the conduct, the confusion of the names and manners of different times, and the impossibility of the events in any system of life, were to waste criticism upon unresisting imbecility, upon faults too evident for detection, and too gross for aggravation.

TROILUS AND CRESSIDA

General Observation. This play is more correctly written than most of Shakespeare's compositions, but it is not one of those in which either the extent of his views or elevation of his fancy is fully displayed. As the story abounded with materials, he has exerted little invention; but he has diversified his characters with great variety and preserved them with great exactness. His vicious characters sometimes disgust but cannot corrupt, for both Cresside and Pandarus are detected and condemned. The comic characters seem to have been the favourites of the writer; they are of the superficial kind and exhibit more of manners than nature; but they are copiously filled and powerfully impressed.

Shakespeare has in his story followed, for the greater part, the old book of Caxton, which was then very popular; but the character of Thersites, of which it makes no mention, is a proof that this play was written after Chapman had published his version of *Homer*.

ROMEO AND JULIET

1.2.25 CAPULET *Earth-treading stars that made dark* HEAVEN'S *light*. [This nonsense should be reformed thus, *Earth-treading stars that make dark* EVEN *light*. . . WARBURTON] But why nonsense? Is anything more commonly said, than that beauties eclipse the sun. Has not Pope the thought and the word?

Sol through white curtains shot a tim'r ous ray.
And ope'd those eyes that must eclipse the day.

Both the old and the new reading are philosophical nonsense, but they are both, and both equally poetical sense.

2.4.129 MERCUTIO *No hare, sir*] Mercutio having roared out, *So ho*!, the cry of the sportsmen when they start a hare, Romeo asks *what he has found*. And Mercutio answers, *No hare*, etc. The rest is a series of quibbles unworthy of explanation, which he who does not understand needs not lament his ignorance.

3.5.85 JULIET *Ay, madam, from the reach of these my hands./ Would none but I might venge my cousin's death*!] Juliet's equivocations are rather too artful for a mind disturbed by the loss of a new lover.

4.3.2 JULIET... *leave me to myself to-night;/ For I have need of many Orisons.*] Juliet plays most of her pranks under the appearance of religion: perhaps Shakespeare meant to punish her hypocrisy.

5.1.3 ROMEO *My bosom's Lord sits lightly on his throne.*] These three lines are very gay and pleasing. But why does Shakespeare give Romeo this involuntary cheerfulness just before the extremity of unhappiness? Perhaps to shew the vanity of trusting to those uncertain and casual exaltations or depressions, which many consider as certain foretokens of good and evil.

5.3.229 FRIAR LAURENCE *I will be brief.*] It is much to be lamented that the Poet did not conclude the dialogue with the action, and avoid a narrative of events which the audience already knew.

General Observation. This play is one of the most pleasing of our author's performances. The scenes are busy and various, the incidents numerous and important, the catastrophe irresistibly affecting, and the process of the action carried on with such probability, at least with such congruity to popular opinions, as tragedy requires.

Here is one of the few attempts of Shakespeare to exhibit the conversation of gentlemen, to represent the airy sprightliness of juvenile elegance. Mr. Dryden mentions a tradition, which might easily reach his time, of a declaration made by Shakespeare, that *he was obliged to kill Mercutio in the third act, lest he should have been killed by him.* Yet he thinks him *no such formidable person but that he might have lived through the play and died in his bed*, without danger to a poet . Dryden well knew, had he been in quest of truth, that in a pointed sentence more regard is commonly had to the words than the thought, and that it is very seldom to be rigorously understood. Mercutio's wit, gaiety, and courage will always procure his friends that wish him a longer life; but his death is not precipitated, he has lived out the time allotted him in the construction of the play; nor do I doubt the ability of Shakespeare to have continued his existence, though some of his sallies were perhaps out of the reach of Dryden, whose genius was not very fertile of merriment nor ductile to humour, but acute, argumentative, comprehensive, and sublime.

The nurse is one of the characters in which the author delighted; he has, with great subtlety of distinction, drawn her at once loquacious and secret, obsequious and insolent, trusty and dishonest.

His comic scenes are happily wrought, but his pathetic strains are always polluted with some unexpected depravations. His persons, however distressed, *have a conceit left them in their misery, a miserably conceit.*

HAMLET

2.2.86-166 POLONIUS *My liege, and madam, to expostulate*] [Warburton believed that Polonius should be interpreted as a 'weak, pedant, minister of state', a satire on Elizabethan courtly rhetoric and stock moralizing.] This account of the character of Polonius, though it sufficiently reconciles the seeming inconsistency of so much wisdom with so much folly, does not perhaps correspond exactly to the ideas of our author. The commentator makes the character of Polonius a character only of manners, discriminated by properties superficial, accidental, and acquired. The poet intended a nobler delineation of a mixed character of manners and of nature. Polonius is a man bred in courts, exercised in business, stored with observation, confident of his knowledge, proud of his eloquence, and declining into dotage. His mode of oratory is truly represented as designed to ridicule the practice of those times, of prefaces that made no introduction, and of method that embarrassed rather than explained. This part of his character is accidental, the rest is natural. Such a man is positive and confident, because he knows that his mind was once strong and knows not that it is become weak. Such a man excels in general principles but fails in the particular application. He is knowing in retrospect and ignorant in foresight. While he depends upon his memory and can draw from his repositories of knowledge, he utters weighty sentences and gives useful counsel; but as the mind in its enfeebled state cannot be kept long busy and intent, the old man is subject to sudden dereliction of his faculties, he loses the order of his ideas and entangles himself in his own thoughts, till he recovers the leading principle and falls again into his former train. This idea of dotage encroaching upon wisdom will solve all the phenomena of the character of Polonius.

3.1.56 HAMLET *To be or not to be*?] Of this celebrated soliloquy, which bursting from a man distracted with contrariety of desires, and overwhelmed with the magnitude of his own purposes, is connected rather in the speaker's mind, than on his tongue, I shall endeavour to discover the train, and to shew how one sentiment produces another.

Hamlet, knowing himself injured in the most enormous and atrocious degree, and seeing no means of redress, but such as must expose him to the extremity of hazard, meditates on his situation in this manner; *Before I can form any rational scheme of action under this pressure of distress*, it is necessary to decide, whether, *after our present state, we are* to be or not to be. That is the question, which, as it shall be answered will determine, *whether 'tis nobler*, and more suitable to the dignity of reason, to *suffer the outrages of fortune* patiently, or to take arms against *them*, and by opposing end them, *though perhaps* with the loss of life. If *to die, were to sleep, no more, and by a sleep to end* the miseries of our nature, such a sleep were *devoutly to be wished*; but if *to sleep* in death, be *to dream*, to retain our powers of sensibility, we must *pause* to consider, *in that sleep of death what dreams may come.* This consideration *makes calamity* so long endured; for *who would bear* the vexations of life, which might be ended *by a bare bodkin*, but that he is afraid of something in unknown futurity? This fear it is that gives efficacy to conscience, which, by turning the mind upon *this regard*, chills the ardour of *resolution*, checks the vigour of *enterprise*, and makes the *current* of desire stagnate in inactivity.

We may suppose that he would have applied these general observations to his own case, but that he discovered Ophelia.

3.1.59 HAMLET *Or to take arms against a sea of troubles*] [For 'against a sea' Warburton had suggested 'against assail'.] Mr Pope proposed *siege*. I know not why there should be so much solicitude about this metaphor. Shakespeare breaks his metaphors often, and in this desultory speech there was less need of preserving them.

3.1.77 HAMLET *To groan and sweat*.] All the old copies have, to *grunt and sweat*. It is undoubtedly the true reading, but can scarcely be borne by modern ears.

3.1.89 HAMLET *Nymph, in thy orisons.*] This is a touch of nature. Hamlet, at the sight of Ophelia, does not immediately recollect, that he is to personate madness, but makes her an address grave and solemn, such as the foregoing, meditation excited in his thoughts.

3.2.124 HAMLET *Nay. then, let the devil wear black, for I'll have a suit of sables.*] I know not why our editors should, with such implacable anger, persecute our predecessors .... The dead, it is true, can make no resistance, they may be attacked with great security; but since they can neither feel nor mend, the safety of mauling them seems greater than the pleasure; nor perhaps would it much misbeseem us to remember, amidst our triumphs over the *non-sensical* and the *senseless*, that we likewise are men; that *debemur morti*, and, as Swift observed to Burnet, shall soon be among the dead ourselves.

I cannot find how the common reading is nonsense, nor why Hamlet, when he laid aside his dress of mourning, in a country where it was *bitter cold* and the air was *nipping and eager*, should not have a *suit of sables*. I suppose it is well enough known that the fur of sables is not black.

3.3.94 HAMLET .... *his soul may be as damn'd and black / As hell, whereto it goes.*] This speech, in which Hamlet, represented as a virtuous character, is not content with taking blood for blood, but contrives damnation for the man that he would punish, is too horrible to be read or to be uttered.

4.5.81 KING *In hugger mugger to inter him.*] All the modern editions that I have consulted give it.

In private to inter him.

That the words now replaced are better, I do not undertake to prove; it is sufficient that they are Shakespeare's. If phraseology is to be changed as words grow uncouth by disuse or gross by vulgarity, the history of every language will be lost; we shall no longer have the words of any author; and as these alterations will be often unskilfully made, we shall in time have very little of his meaning.

4.7.20 KING *Would, like the spring that turneth wood to stone, / Convert his gyves to graces.*] This simile is neither very seasonable in the deep interest of this conversation, nor very accurately applied. If the *spring* had changed base metals to gold, the thought had been more proper.

5.1.85 HAMLET *This might be the pate of a politician, which this ass o'er-offices.*] In the quarto, for *over-offices* is, *over-reaches*, which agrees better with the sentence; I believe both the words were Shakespeare's. An author in revising his work, when his original ideas have faded from his mind, and new observations have produced new sentiments, easily introduces images which have been more newly impressed upon him, without observing their want of congruity to the general texture of his original design.

5.2.6 HAMLET ... *Rashly, / And prais'd be rashness for it.*] Hamlet, delivering an account of his escape, begins with saying that he *rashly*—and then is carried into a reflection upon the weakness of human wisdom. I rashly—praised be rashness for it—*Let us* not think these events causal, but *let us know*, that is, *take notice and remember*, that we sometimes succeed by *indiscretion*, when we *fail* by *deep plots*, and infer the perpetual superintendence and *agency* of the *Divinity*. The observation is just, and will be allowed by every human being who shall reflect on the course of his own life.

5.2.41 HAMLET *As Peace should still her wheaten garland wear, And stand a* COMMA *'tween their amities*;] The expression of our author is, like many of his phrases, sufficiently constrained and affected, but it is not incapable of explanation. The *Comma* is the note of *connection* and continuity of sentences; the *Period* is the note of *abruption* and disjunction. Shakespeare had it perhaps in his mind to write, That unless *England* complied with the mandate, *war should put* a period *to their amity*; he altered his mode of diction, and thought that, in an opposite sense, he might put. That *Peace should stand* a Comma *between their amities*. This is not an easy style; but is it not the style of Shakespeare?

5.2.237 HAMLET *Give me your pardon*; *Sir*. *I've done you wrong*;] I wish Hamlet had made some other defence; it is unsuitable to the character of a good or a brave man, to shelter himself in falsehood.

General Observation. If the dramas of Shakespeare were to be characterised each by the particular excellence which distinguishes it from the rest, we must allow to the tragedy of *Hamlet* the praise of variety. The incidents are so numerous that the argument of the play would make a long tale. The scenes are interchangeably diversified with merriment and solemnity; with merriment that includes judicious and instructive observations, and solemnity not strained by poetical violence above the natural sentiments of man. New characters appear from time to time in continual succession, exhibiting various forms of life and particular modes of conversation. The pretended madness of Hamlet causes much mirth, the mournful distraction of Ophelia fills the heart with tenderness, and every personage produces the effect intended, from the apparition that in the first act chills the blood with horror to the fop in the last that exposes affectation to just contempt.

The conduct is perhaps not wholly secure against objections. The action is indeed for the most part in continual progression, but there are some scenes which neither forward nor retard it. Of the feigned madness of Hamlet there appears no adequate cause, for he does nothing which he might not have done with the reputation of sanity. He plays the madman most when he treats Ophelia with so much rudeness, which seems to be useless and wanton cruelty.

Hamlet is, through the whole play, rather an instrument than an agent. After he has, by the stratagem of the play, convicted the king, he makes no attempt to punish him, and his death is at last effected by an incident which Hamlet has no part in producing.

The catastrophe is not very happily produced; the exchange of weapons is rather an expedient of necessity than a stroke of art. A scheme might easily have been formed, to kill Hamlet with the dagger, and Laertes with the bowl.

The poet is accused of having shown little regard to poetical justice and may be charged with equal neglect of poetical probability. The apparition left the regions of the dead to little purpose; the revenge which he demands is not obtained but by the death of him that was required to take it; and the gratification which would arise from the destruction of an usurper and a murderer, is abated by the untimely death of Ophelia, the young, the beautiful, the harmless, and the pious.

OTHELLO

1.3.139-69 OTHELLO *Wherein of antres vast and deserts idle*] Whoever ridicules this account of the progress of love shows his ignorance, not only of history, but of nature and manners. It is no wonder that, in any age, or in any nation, a lady, recluse, timorous, and delicate, should desire to hear of events and scenes which she could never see, and should admire the man who had endured dangers and performed actions which, however great, were yet magnified by her timidity. [For 'deserts idle' Pope had suggested 'deserts wild'.] Every mind is liable to absence and inadvertency, else Pope could never have rejected a word so poetically beautiful.

2.1.305 IAGO . . . *The thought where of / Doth, like a poisonous mineral, gnaw my innards.*] This is philosophical. Mineral poisons kill by corrosion.

3.3.90 OTHELLO *Excellent wretch! Perdition catch my soul / But I do love thee!*] The meaning of the word *wretch* is not generally understood. It is now, in some parts of England, a term of the softest and fondest tendernesses. It express the utmost degree of amiableness, joined with an idea, which perhaps all tenderness includes, of feebleness, softness, and want of protection. Othello, considering Desdemona as excelling in beauty and virtue, soft and timorous by her sex, and by her situation absolutely in *his* power, calls her *excellent wretch!* It may be expressed, *Dear, harmless, helpless excellence.*

3.3.206 IAGO *She did deceive her father, marrying you.*] This and the following argument of Iago ought to be deeply impressed on every reader. Deceit and falsehood, whatever conveniences they may for a time promise or produce, are, in the sum of life, obstacles to happiness. Those who profit by the cheat, distrust the deceiver, and the act by which kindness was sought, puts an end to confidence.

The same objection may be made with a lower degree of strength against the imprudent generosity of disproportionate marriages. When the first heat of passion is over, it is easily succeeded by suspicion, that the same violence of inclination which caused one irregularity, may stimulate to another; and those who have shewn, that their passions are too powerful for their prudence, will, with very slight appearances against them, be censured, as not very likely to restain them by their virtue.

3.4.99 EMILIA *'Tis not a year or two shows us a man*]. From this line it may be conjectured that the author intended the action of this play to be considered as longer than is marked by any note of time. Since their arrival at Cyprus, to which they were hurried on their wedding night, the fable seems to have been in one continual progress, nor can I see any vacuity into which a *year or two*, or even a month or two, could be put. On the night of Othello's arrival, a feast was proclaimed; at that feast Cassio was degraded; and immediately applies to Desdemona to get him restored. Iago indeed advises Othello to hold him off a while, but there is no reason to think that he has been held off long. A little longer interval would increase the probability of the story, though it might violate the rules of the drama.

4.1.40 OTHELLO *Nature would not invest herself in such shadowing passion without some instruction.*] There has always prevailed in the world an opinion, that when any great calamity happens at a distance, notice is given of it to the sufferer by some dejection or perturbation of mind, of which he discovers no external cause. This is ascribed to that general communication of one part of the universe with another, which is called sympathy and antipathy; or to the secret monition, instruction, and influence of a superior Being, which superintends the order of Nature and of life. Othello says *Nature could not invest herself in such shadowing passion without instruction. It is not words that shakes me thus. This passion which spreads its clouds over me is the effect of some agency more than the operation of Words; it is one of those notices which men have of unseen calamities.*

5.2.20 OTHELLO *I must weep, / But they are cruel tears. This sorrow's heavenly; It strikes where it doth live. She wakes.*] This tenderness, with which I lament the punishment which justice compels me to inflict, is a holy passion.

I wish these two lines could be honestly ejected. It is the fate of Shakespeare to counteract his own pathos.

5.2.63 OTHELLO *Oh perjur'd woman! thou dost stone my heart, / And mak'st me call, what I intend to do, / A murder, which I thought a sacrifice.*] This line is difficult. *Thou hast hardened my heart, and makest me* kill thee with the rage of a *murderer*, when

I thought to have sacrificed thee to justice with the calmness of a priest striking a victim . . . .

I am glad that I have ended my revisal of this dreadful scene. It is not to be endured.

General Observation. The beauties of this play impress themselves so strongly upon the attention of the reader that they can draw no aid from critical illustration. The fiery openness of Othello, magnanimous, artless and credulous, boundless in his confidence, ardent in his affection, inflexible in his resolution, and obdurate in his revenge; the cool malignity of Iago, silent in his resentment, subtle in his designs, and studious at once of his interest and his vengeance; the soft simplicity of Desdemona, confident of merit and conscious of innocence, her artless perseverance in her suit, and her slowness to suspect that she can be suspected, are such proofs of Shakespeare's skill in human nature as, I suppose, it is vain to seek in any modern writer. The gradual progress which Iago makes in the Moor's coviction and the circumstances which he employs to inflame him are so artfully natural that, though it will perhaps not be said of him, as he says of himself, that he is *a man not easily jealous*, yet we cannot but pity him when at last we find him *perplexed in the extreme*.

There is always danger lest wickedness; conjoined with abilities, should steal upon esteem, though it misses of approbation; but the character of Iago is so conducted that he is from the first scene to the last hated and despised.

Even the inferior characters of this play would be very conspicuous in any other piece, not only for their justness but their strength. Cassio is brave, benevolent, and honest, ruined only by his want of stubbornness to resist an insidious invitation. Roderigo's suspicious credulity and impatient submission to the cheats which he sees practised upon him, and which by persuasion he suffers to be repeated, exhibit a strong picture of a weak mind betrayed by unlawful desires, to a false friend; and the virtue of Emilia is such as we often find, worn loosely but not cast off, easy to commit small crimes, but quickened and alarmed at atrocious villainies.

The scenes from the beginning to the end are busy, varied by happy interchanges, and regularly promoting the progression of the story; and the narrative in the end, though it tells but what is known already, yet is necessary to produce the death of Othello.

Had the scene opened in Cyprus, and the preceding incidents been occasionally related, there had been little wanting to a drama of the most exact and scrupulous regularity.

[Boswell reports the following under the date of 12 April 1776: I observed the great defect of the tragedy of *Othello* was that it had not a moral; for that no man could resist the circumstances of suspicion which were artfully suggested to Othello's mind. JOHNSON. 'In the first place, Sir, we learn from *Othello* this very useful moral, not to make an unequal match; in the second place, we learn not to yield too readily to suspicion. The handkerchief is merely a trick, though a very pretty trick; but there are no other circumstances of reasonable suspicion, except what is related by Iago of Cassio's warm expressions concerning Desdemona in his sleep; and that depended entirely upon the assertion of one man. No, Sir, I think *Othello* has more moral than almost any play.']

ENDNOTES

Editor's Notes and Bibliography

INTRODUCTION

1. Samuel Johnson, *Rasselas and Essays*, ed. Charles Peake (London: Routledge and Kegan Paul, 1967), p. 65, chapter 31.
2. Samuel Johnson, *The Complete English Poems*, ed. J.D. Fleeman (Harmondsworth: Penguin, 1971), p. 140.
3. Dr. Levet was a physician who had for many years occupied an apartment in Dr. Johnson's house. He died in his seventy-seventh year. Though "an obscure practiser in physick," as Boswell describes him, Levet was held in high esteem by Johnson who was heard to say that he "should not be satisfied, though attended by all the College of Physicians, unless he had Mr. Levet with him". James Boswell, *Life of Johnson*, ed. R.W. Chapman (London : OUP, 1970], p. 172 [1752]; hereafter cited as *Life*.
4. W.B. Yeats, *Essays and Introductions* (London : Macmillan, 1961), p. 333.
5. Page 83, above.
6. Joseph Wood Krutch, *Samuel Johnson* (New York : Harcourt, Brace, 1944), p. 285.
7. James L. Clifford, *Young Samuel Johnson* (London: Heinemann, 1962), p. 270.
8. The book was by Arthur Symons, Yeat's friend, and was dedicated to Yeats. It was published in 1899.
9. *Johnson's Journey to the Western Islands of Scotland and Boswell's Journal of a Tour to the Hebrides With Samuel Johnson, LL.D.*, ed. R.W. Chapman (London : Oxford University Press, 1965), pp. 62 and 232.
10. From *Private Papers of James Boswell from Malahide Castle in the Collection of Lieutenant-Colonel Ralph Heyward Isham*, IX, ed.. Frederick A. Pottle (1930), pp 265.
11. *Rasselas*, chapter 10.
12. Sarup Singh, *The Theory of Drama in the Restoration Period* (New Delhi : Orient Longman, 1963). pp. 17, 18, 19.
13. *Samuel Johnson's Literary Criticism* (Chicago : The University of Chicago Press, 1967), pp. 56-75.
14. Johnson's wholehearted approval of Shakespeare's tragicomedy in the *Preface* represents a shift in attitude. Fourteen years earlier, in

Rambler No. 156 dated 14 September 1751, he had praised Shakespeare's tragicomedy, but had gone on to add that Shakespeare's work might have been yet greater had he kept tragedy and comedy apart:

"I do not, however, think it safe to judge of works of genius merely by the event. These resistless vicissitudes of the heart, this alternate prevalence of merriment and solemnity, may sometimes be more properly ascribed to the vigour of the writer than the justness of the design; and instead of vindicating tragicomedy by the success of Shakespeare, we ought perhaps to pay new honours to that transcendent and unbounded genius that could preside over the passions in sport; who, to actuate the affections, needed not the slow gradation of common means, but could fill the heart with instantaneous jollity or sorrow and vary our disposition as he changed his scenes. Perhaps the effects even of Shakespeare's poetry might have been yet greater had he not counteracted himself; and we might have been more interested in the distresses of his heroes had we not been so frequently diverted by the jokes of his buffoons."

15. In *Oxford Lectures on Poetry* (1904, rpt. London : Macmillan, 1950), pp. 247-73.
16. See e.g. Hagstrum, pp. 72-73 (op. cit. n 13 above).
17. See e.g. Robert Rogers, "Endopsychic Drama in *Othello*", *Shakespeare Quarterly*, 20 (Spring, 1969), 205-15; Marvin Rosenberg, "In Defense of Iago," *Shakespeare Quarterly*, 6 (Spring, 1955), 145-48.
18. Johnson uses this phrase in a letter to Bennet Langton. In the paragraph in which it occurs, Johnson has been speaking of his own growing fame—"Burke is a great man by nature, and is expected soon to attain civil greatness. I am grown greater too, for I have maintained the newspapers these many weeks". It is likely that Johnson is here referring to the controversy over his edition of *Shakespeare* that went on for some time after it had appeared, and that kept the newspapers active (see *Life*, p. 351, [Oct, 1765]).
19. *Rasselas,* chapter 46.
20. Krutch, p. 156.
21. *The Literary Critics* (Harmondsworth : Penguin, 1964), p. 103.
22. Samuel Johnson, *Lives of the Poets*, introduction Arthur Waugh (London : OUP, 1968), Vol. 1, pp. 321-22.

PROLOGUE (1747)

1. Boswell's record of the event is as follows; "This year his old pupil and friend, David Garrick, having become joint patentee and manager of Drury-lane theatre, Johnson honoured his opening of it with a Prologue, which for just and manly dramatick criticism, on the whole range of the English stage, as well as for poetical excellence, is unrivalled" (*Life*, p. 131 [Antumn, 1747]).

2. A reference, not to Marlowe's Faustus but to a series of farcical pieces in which 'Harlequin Doctor Faustus' was the hero. "Great" here is ironic.
3. Aphra Behn (1640-89), author of several coarse comedies based on London life.
4. Tom Durfey (1653-1723), poetaster and the butt of wits during the time of Dryden and Pope.
5. Edward Hunt, a boxer who often appeared on the contemporary stage.
6. Mahomet, a Turkish rope-dancer, popular on the contemporary stage.

RAMBLER No. 168 (1751)

1. The words are spoken by Lady Macbeth.

PREFACE (1765)

1. A reference to Pythagoras's discovery that the basic musical harmonies depend on very simple numerical ratios between the lengths of the instruments (strings or pipes) producing them.
2. The schools of rhetoric at Athens and Rome.
3. ". . . had all the speeches been printed without the very names of the persons, I believe one might have applied them with certainty to every speaker" (Pope, *Preface*, 1725, fourth paragraph).
4. See John Dennis, *An Essay on the Genius and Writings of Shakespeare*, 1712; Thomas Rymer, *A Short View of Tragedy: Its Original Excellency and Corruption, with Some Reflections on Shakespeare and Other Practitioners for the Stage*, 1693. The *Critical Works of* John Dennis have been edited by E.N. Hooker, 2 vols, Baltimore, 1939-43 (for the present reference see II.5-6), and the *Critical Works of Rymer*, by Curt A. Zimansky, New Haven, 1956 (see pp. 164-9).
5. *Essay on the Genius and Writings of Shakespeare*, in *Critical Works*, ed Hooker, 11.5.
6. Voltaire pronounces a general censure on the conversation of Shakespeare's 'princes' in L'*Appel a toutes les nations d' Europe*, 1761 (*Oeuvres*' ed. Moland, xxiv. 203). In this *Dissertation sur la tragedie ancienne et moderne*, 1749, he notices a number of *grossieretes* in *Hamlet*. Such a work seems to him 'the fruit of the imagination of a drunken savage' (*Oeuvres*' ed. Moland, iv. 502). The word 'perhaps' in Johnson's phrase about the Danish drunkard may indicate a degree of extrapolation.
7. "In his Preface to *Shakespeare*, Johnson treated Voltaire very contemptuously, observing, upon some of his remarks, 'These are the petty criticisms of petty wits'. Voltaire, in revenge, made an attack upon Johnson, in one of his numerous literary sallies. . . . Voltaire was an

antagonist with whom I thought Johnson should not disdain to contend. I pressed him to answer. He said, he perhaps might; but he never did" (*Life*, pp. 351-52 [Oct. 1765]).

8. John Heming and Henry Condell, friends of Shakespeare and fellow actors, issued the first Folio in 1623.
9. The censures of *Hamlet* and *Othello* which Johnson answers in this paragraph are to be found in Voltaire, *L' Appel a toutes les nations d' Europe*. (*Oeuvres* ed. Moland, xxiv. 193, 196, 198, 204, 208), and in Rymer, *A Short View of Tragedy* (*Critical Works*, ed. Zimansky, pp. 131-64).
10. *A Short View of Tragedy* (*Critical Works*, ed. Zimansky, p. 169).
11. Pope's *Preface*, twenty-second and following paragraphs.
12. *Troilus and Cressida*, II.2.166-7.
13. *A Midsummer Night's Dream*, throughout.
14. Pierre Cornielle (1606-84), French dramatist.
15. Addison's *Cato*, *V*, i.
16. *Othello*, Acts I and II.
17. Lucan, *Pharsalia*, III.138-40: 'The course of time has not wrought such confusion that the laws would not rather be trampled on by Caesar than saved by Metellus' (trans. J.D. Duff); i.e. the laws would rather be violated by Caesar than be saved by Metellus. For "Caesar" substitute "Shakespeare," and for "Mettelus" "Voltaire". Voltaire's anger towards Johnson, mentioned by Boswell, is understandable. *Life*, p. 351.
18. *Aeneid*, II, 610-14.
19. A roster of Tudor humanists and scholars; William Lily wrote a Latin grammar which was used by Shakespeare. Thomas Linacre and Sir John Cheke were teachers of Greek, at Oxford and Cambridge respectively. Stephen Gardiner and Reginald Pole were churchmen and chancellors of Cambridge University. Sir Thomas More, Henry VIII's Chancellor, is best known to the woild of letters as the author of the sophisticated Latin work *Utopia*. Sir Thomas Smith and Walter Haddon were Regius Professors of civil law and Vice-Chancellors of Cambridge University. John Clerk was Bishop of Bath and Wells. Roger Ascham was Latin secretary to Queen Mary, private tutor to Queen Elizabeth, and author of *Toxophilus* and *The Schoolmaster*.
20. Sir Thomas Malory, *Morte d' Arthur*, published by Caxton in 1485.
21. *Palmerin d'Oliva* and *Palmerin of England* were Spanish prose romances translated into English by Anthony Munday in 1588 and 1596. Johnson read an Italian version of the latter in 1776 but 'did not like it much'. *Guy of Warwick* was an English verse romance written about 1308 and published by Pynson early in the sixteenth century.
22. The *Tale of Gamelyn* was rejected from the Chaucer canon by Tyrwhitt in 1775. It was a predecessor of Thomas Lodge's *Rosalynde* (1590), which was the immediate source of Shakespeare's *As You Like It*. D.N. Smith, 1928, p. 51, suggests that Johnson withheld the name of the 'pamphlet' in order not to take credit from the actual discoverer, his

friend Richard Farmer of Cambridge, who in 1767 was to publish his *Essay on the Learning of Shakespeare*.

23. Colley Cibber, actor and dramatist, Poet Laureate in 1730.
24. Danish historian (*c.* 1150-1206), author of *Gesta Danorum* or *Historia Danica*, printed at Paris in 1514, translated from the Latin into Danish in 1575.
25. Sir Thomas North published the first edition of his translation of Plutarch's *Lives of the Noble Grecians and Romans*, from the French of Amyot, in 1579.
26. See n. 15 above.
27. Ben Jonson, "To the Memory of My Beloved ... Mr. William Shakespeare," prefixed to the First Folio.
28. Zachary Grey, *Critical, Historical, and Explanatory Notes on Shakespeare*, 1754. Grey compared *Richard III*, I, i, 144 to Terence, *Andria*, 1. 17.
29. *The Tempest*, III, ii, 144; "I cried to dream again."
30. Nicholas Rowe, *Some Account of the Life of Mr. William Shakespeare*, prefixed to his edition of 1709.
31. Thomas Birch, *Life of the Hon. Robert Boyle* (1744).
32. *Troilus and Cressida*, III, iii, 224.
33. John Dennis, *An Essay on the Genius and Writings of Shakespeare*, 1712.
34. John Upton, *Critical Observations on Shakespeare*, 1746.
35. *Othello*, III, iii, 262.
36. Warburton, 1747.
37. *Iliad*, XXI, 99 ff.
38. Thomas Edward, *The Canons of Criticism*, and Benjamin Heath, *Revisal of Shakespeare's Text*. The first edition has *Review of Shakespeare's Text* which is an error. In the second edition the error was corrected.
39. *Coriolanus*, IV, iv, 5.
40. *Macbeth*, II, iv, 12-13. The first edition has "eagle" instead of "falcon". The error was corrected in the second edition.
41. See n. 34 above.
42. See n. 28 above.
43. 2 *Henry VI*, IV, i, 106.
44. Pierre Huet (1630-1721). French scholar whose *De interpretatione* was published in 1661.
45. "When in doubt, don't do it."
46. *Temple of Fame*, 11. 37-40.
47. Joannes Andreas (1417*c.*-1480), librarian to Pope Sixtus IV.
48. Richard Bentley (1662-1742), Keeper of the King's Libraries, Master of Trinity College, Cambridge, famous for his emendations of the texts of Horace and Manilius.
49. 'Our conjectures make us look silly; we are ashamed of them after we have come upon better manuscripts'. Joseph Justus Scaliger (1540-1609), French philologist, was the 'founder of historical criticism'. The quotation is from a letter of July 1608 to Claude de Saumaise (1583-

1653), to be found In Scaliger's *Opuscula varia antehac non edita* (Paris: 1610), p. 469.

50 The Latin is paraphrased in the preceding words of Johnson. Justus Lipsius (1547-1606), Flemish humanist, professor at Jena and later at Leyden, was succeded at Leyden by Scaliger.

51. Dryden, *An Essay of Dramatic Poesy*, 1668 "Quantum. . . Cupressi": "As cypresses do among the bending osiers" (*Virgil*, *Eclogues*, I.25).

A READING LIST FOR JOHNSON ON SHAKESPEARE

ADLER, JACOB H. "Johnson's 'He That Imagines This'," *Shakespeare Quarterly*, 11 (Spring, 1960), 225-28.

BATE, WALTER JACKSON, *The Achievement ot Samuel Johnson* (New York: Oxford University Press, 1970). See particularly chapter I, "A Life of Allegory", and chapter V. 'Johnson as a Critic'.

———, *Samuel Johnson* (London: Chatto & Windus, 1978). See particularly chapter 22, "Shakespeare".

BOSKER, A. *Literary Criticism in the Age of Johnson* (Groningen, Netherlands: J.B. Wolters, 1954). See particularly chapter IX. "Samuel Johnson'.

BOSWELL, JAMES, *Life of Johnson*, ed. R.W. Chapman, corrected by J.D. Fleeman (London: Oxford University Press, 1970).

EASTMAN, ARTHUR M. *A Short History of Shakespearean Criticism* (New York: Random House, 1968). See particularly chapter II, "Johnson".

ELIOT, T.S. "Johnson as Critic and Poet" in *On Poetry and Poets* (London: Faber and Faber, 1957).

HAGSTRUM, J.H. *Samuel Johnson's Literary Criticism* (Chicago: The University of Chicago Press, 1967).

Krutch, Joseph Wood, *Samuel Johnson* (New York: Harcourt, Brace, 1944). See particularly chapter IX, "Shakespeare".

RALEIGH, WALTER, *Johnson on Shakespeare* (Oxford, 1925).

SCHOLES, ROBERT E. "Dr. Johnson and the Bibliographical Criticism of Shakespeare" *Shakespeare Quarterly*, 11 (Spring, 1960), 163-71.

SHERBO, ARTHUR, "Johnson as Editor of Shakespeare: The Notes," in *Samuel Johnson : A Collection of Critical Essays*, ed. Donald J. Greene (Englewood Cliffs, New Jersey : Prentice-Hall, Twentieth-Century Views, 1965), pp. 124-37.

WATSON, GEORGE, *The Literary Critics* (Harmondsworth : Penguin, 1964). See Particularly chapter IV, "Samuel Johnson".

WIMSATT, W.K. ed. "Introduction" to *Dr. Johnson on Shakespeare* (Harmondsworth : Penguin, 1969).